ISBN 978-1-332-03666-0
PIBN 10273622

This book is a reproduction of an important historical work. Forgotten Books uses
state-of-the-art technology to digitally reconstruct the work, preserving the original format
whilst repairing imperfections present in the aged copy. In rare cases, an imperfection in
the original, such as a blemish or missing page, may be replicated in our edition. We do,
however, repair the vast majority of imperfections successfully; any imperfections that
remain are intentionally left to preserve the state of such historical works.

For support please visit www.forgottenbooks.com

1 MONTH OF
FREE
READING

at

www.ForgottenBooks.com

By purchasing this book you are eligible for one month membership to ForgottenBooks.com, giving you unlimited access to our entire collection of over 700,000 titles via our web site and mobile apps.

To claim your free month visit:

www.forgottenbooks.com/free273622

Similar Books Are Available from
www.forgottenbooks.com

THROUGH NORWAY WITH

A KNAPSACK.

THROUGH NORWAY WITH A KNAPSACK.

A NEW AND IMPROVED EDITION.

WITH NOTES ON RECENT CHANGES SUGGESTED BY A
RECENT REVISIT.

By W. MATTIEU WILLIAMS, F.R.A.S., F.C.S.,
AUTHOR OF 'THE FUEL OF THE SUN,' ETC ETC.

THE RINGEDALS FOSS. *page* 245.

LONDON:
EDWARD STANFORD, 55, CHARING CROSS, S.W.

1876.

LONDON: PRINTED BY EDWARD STANFORD, 55, CHARING CROSS, S.W.

PREFACE.

———◆◇◆———

I HAVE been frequently urged by friends and Norwegian tourists to prepare a new edition of this book which has been out of print for some years, but have postponed doing so until I could revisit the country and supplement the account of my first journey with such information as is necessary to fairly represent the changes that have been wrought in Norway and Norwegian travelling since 1856.

An excellent opportunity of doing this was lately afforded. Some young ladies to whom I had been lecturing on Physical Geography desired to extend their studies by taking—in company with their governess—a holiday object-lesson on Arctic and Scandinavian phenomena. They invited me to continue my teaching in this pleasant form by becoming their pilot through the country I had previously visited and described.

I accepted this grave responsibility, and thus travelled again "through Norway," but this time with six ladies and more than one knapsack.

My original intention was to incorporate in one

book an account of both journeys, but acting upon the advice of the publishers and of several friends, I have now separated the two narratives and publish them as literary twins, each complete in itself, but presenting opposite sides of Norwegian travel, the rough and the smooth.

I may as well confess that I have had some commercial difficulty in the republication of this volume. Books of travel having lately become a sort of literary millinery, the latest, the newest, rather than the best, being the chief objects of demand, the booksellers naturally affirm that they must supply the market accordingly, with novelties for each season, and let the old books drop into oblivion.

With all due deference to commercial experience, for which I have great respect, I believe that on this point it has been rather delusive. Admitting the existing demand for such literary frippery as mere "books for the season," and that they are quite good enough for the idle people who "look at" books merely that they may chatter about them, I maintain that there still exists, even in these galloping days, a respectable public of intelligent people who remain addicted to the old-fashioned practice of reading books attentively from beginning to end, and that some of these will thus read plain unpretending narratives of travelling experience that are carefully and honestly written for the purpose of supplying sound information, and not merely to satisfy the vanity of the writer.

Many old and excellent works of this class that have been cruelly neglected by the trade—cast aside and replaced by inferior novelties,—might be profitably republished if suitably revised, annotated to present date, and "pushed" as vigorously as the new millinery.

These convictions and a natural affection for my literary first-born have induced me to face the risk of being accused of unwarrantable presumption in re-offering 'Through Norway with a Knapsack,' as one of these endurable books, and doing this with the frankly avowed expectation that it will hold its ground as a standard, reliable, and readable account of that phase of Norwegian travel which it professes to describe.

BELMONT, TWICKENHAM,
   June, 1876.

CONTENTS.

CHAPTER I.

CHAPTER II.

CHAPTER III.

CHAPTER IV.

CHAPTER V.

CHAPTER VI.

CHAPTER VII.

CHAPTER VIII.

CHAPTER IX.

CHAPTER X.

CHAPTER XI.

CHAPTER XII.

CHAPTER XIII.

CHAPTER XIV.

CHAPTER XV.

CHAPTER XVI.

CHAPTER XVII.

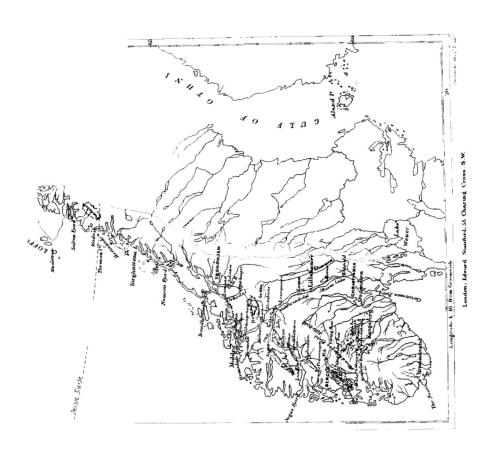

London: Edward Stanford, 55 Charing Cross S.W.

THROUGH NORWAY WITH A KNAPSACK.

CHAPTER I.

The Scandinavian coast — Christiansand — Norwegian architecture —Night in the North — The Christiania Fjord — Absence of police and passport interference — Independence of Norwegian hotel-keepers — Christiania; its streets, houses, and shops — The Klinkenberg, or Vauxhall of Christiania — Popular amusements and indications of character — Interest in English affairs exhibited by the Norwegians — Norwegian Lutheran churches — Necessity of popular instruction in science and natural history — Absence of extreme poverty and squalor in Christiania — Politeness of the Norwegians — English physiognomy — Recent development of Norwegian tourist traffic — Present hotel accommodation in Christiania — Other modern provisions for English tourists and sportsmen in Christiania — General growth of the city, and increase of wealth and luxury.

June 24th, 1856.—AFTER a stormy passage of about forty-eight hours from Hull, we come in sight of the Norwegian coast, presenting a wild broken shore of gray, rounded, rocky ridges, with smooth slippery-looking surfaces near the sea edge, where the waves run up the slopes and slide over the points of the low promontories as though they were greasy. There are no sands, no pebble beach; the breaking waves make no roar and rattle, as they do among

B

our chalk-flint pebbles ; they only slap and splash
upon the hard unwearing rocks, which are composed
of a sort of mineralogical mongrel called gneiss, a
cross between the fire-born granite and the water-
laid stratified rocks. These promontories are evidently the points of spur ridges, the outermost
extremities, the fingers and toes, of mountain giants
farther inland.

We have cargo to discharge at Christiansand,
which occupies a few hours. The aristocracy and
the proud democracy of our small community have
now fraternized, and the saloon and fore-cabin passengers, forming a united company of eight persons,
go ashore for breakfast with strong anticipations of
salmon. We are guided by my fellow-passenger of
the fore-cabin, a Norwegian stonemason, to the principal hotel. Here, after some negotiation, the proprietor consents to supply us with breakfast, which,
in the course of time, made its appearance. The
Norwegians are a deliberate, phlegmatic people, and
do nothing in a hurry.

The breakfast consists of several plates distributed
irregularly over a large table, each plate containing
thin shavings of something. No. 1, thin shavings of
raw dried salmon, of which there are repetition
plates ; No. 2, thin shavings of cold veal, also repeated ; No. 3, tongue shavings ; and No. 4, ham
ditto. I afterwards learned that thin slices are considered genteel in Norway. In addition to these are
cold boiled salmon and hot eggs, with bread, black
and white. The coffee is strong enough for a Turk
to sip with his chibouk, and well flavoured ; the

cream, worthy of Devonshire, both in quality and quantity. The charge 2s. each, stated and paid in English money.

Two hours' strolling about the town enabled us to form some preliminary notions of Norwegian architecture. Christiansand has a very colonial appearance; it looks like a place where emigrants have newly settled. All the houses are built of logs, and are at some distance apart from each other, though in lines forming streets. This separation is probably a precaution against fire. Some houses were being built and in different stages of progress, affording us an opportunity of observing the mode of construction, which is the same here as throughout Norway. Four large stones, commonly rounded boulders or glacier moraine blocks, form the foundation. These are placed at the angles of the ground plan of the building; then the trunks of fir or pine trees, rudely squared, are laid with their ends resting on these stones, and thus the wall begins. At about one foot from the end of these logs broad notches are cut to a depth equal to one-fourth of the thickness of the log, and in width equal to its whole thickness. Other logs are similarly prepared; these are laid with their ends crossing, the notch of one log sinking into the notch of the other, so that the lower face of the upper is level with the mid thickness of the lower. This is continned all round, till a thick, firmly dovetailed wooden wall is built. The crevices between the logs are stuffed tightly with moss or lichen. The roof is a framework of heavy beams, covered with planks and overlaid with sheets of birch-bark, called "naver."

Moss or peaty soil is spread upon these to a depth of several inches. A rich vegetation is common upon such roofs, and occasionally a goat may be seen grazing luxuriously upon a house-top. A cow falling through the roof on which it was grazing, and disturbing the tender converse of two lovers, is one of the incidents of an old Scandinavian story.

We sail again at about midday, and towards midnight approach the mouth of the great estuary, which, broken up by hundreds of islands and inlets, finally closes at Christiania. It is midsummer eve, and many fires are lighted on the hills, rendering it difficult to distinguish from them the "*Faerder*," or *farther* lighthouse, which marks the outer point of the Christiania Fjord. But lighthouses are little needed on such a night as this, when there is no darkness, though the day has gone.

We are all on deck to-night, passengers and sailors, leaning on the bulwarks and looking towards the north. It is eleven o'clock, and the sun has but lately set. We can see exactly where he is below that line of distant hills upon the shore. They were dull gray two hours ago, but now they have a tint of deepest purple, and their outlines are wondrously sharp. There is a thin film—a mere transparent veil of cirro-stratus or halo-cloud out there—a sheet of what would be thin fog but that it is some two or three miles high. The colours of the sunset cling to this, and the sun below the horizon throws a clear and definite light upon it as upon a screen. It marks distinctly the position of the sun, and thus we are able *to* watch him gliding on slowly from the west to north, sinking in the meanwhile a little more. Now it is midnight, and the subterranean sun due north. There is light enough to read a newspaper if it face the north. Just over the sun is a vanishing semicircle of buff light; westward it grows to orange, and from this orange zone broad bands of browning red stretch upwards and outwards. On the eastern side the buff tint melts and darkens into a fresh cool gray. Farther on, in a widening circle, extending upwards and eastwards and westwards to the south horizon, all these colours melt away gradually to neutral gloominess. There, at the southern meeting place of sea and sky, both are mingled in one heavy leaden semi-darkness. This is the region of night: still farther on over the bending sea men have been burning gas and candles for the last three hours or more. We have all learned book-wise that it is so, but here the southward darkness is visible. So are the sunny midnights of the opposite north. There is the sun, obvious though unseen: his body hidden by the earth's rotundity; but the lighted atmosphere, visible beyond the distant mountain tops, shows both his presence and position in the region of continuous summer day.

Thus visible all at once from the ship's deck are evening and morning, night and day; sunrise and sunset seen together, though definitely separated by the north midnight glow, the character of each marked most distinctly and shown in curious contrast. Why there should be such difference I am not able to explain; why the sun's rays in passing westwards should tint the sky with warm, languid, evening colours, while those spreading upwards at the same moment towards the east should look so cool and gray and wakeful, I cannot tell; but here they are side by side, and unmistakably contrasted.

We dwellers on a misty island all read and dream of the bright sky of the sunny south, of its clear blue zenith and golden-hazed horizon; but when we live beneath it for awhile and gaze upon it daily, its fiery dazzling beauty overstrains the senses, and the eye soon tires of its glare; but in this modest twilight of the north, the gentle "gloamin'," there's a tempered fascination that never wearies us; it grows continually in loveliness even unto midnight and its next day's reawakening. It bears the same relation to the gaudy southern sunlight that affection does to passion. There is no reaction, no craving for the shade.

Painters have represented nearly all kinds of sky effects. Turner, like an eagle, has dared to face the sun in his full glare and to place him in the middle of his pictures, showing us how we see a landscape with sun-dazzled eyes, when everything is melted into a luminous chaos and all the details blotted out with misty brightness. Danby, and many others, have painted sunsets gloriously; a few antique early-rising Dutchmen have accurately copied particular cases of sunrise. Such a midnight as this would be a glorious subject for a painter worthy of it, and to the artist himself a most valuable study of the characteristics of evening and morning light.

We all linger on the deck long after midnight, then one by one descend, myself the last of the passengers. I had scarcely reached the cabin door, when I heard the mate call to the captain to look over the starboard bow at a ship on fire. Of course I hastened upon deck again, and looked over the starboard bow forthwith. We soon perceived that it was not a ship on fire, but the moon reddened by the veil of misty cloud, rising behind a ship on the horizon, and looking like a dull lurid flame over the deck and between the masts and sails. It was the half-moon, of huge apparent size, rising point upwards out of the eastern leaden-gray part of the sea. She had a dull, scowling visage, as though angry with the sun for cheating her of her nocturnal supremacy. The form of the moon was curiously distorted by the unequally refractive power of the strata of air through which her different parts were seen, the lower limb being unusually lifted and flattened upwards, as though it were soft, and had been dubbed against the hard metallic horizon.

June 25th.—We awake in the Christiania Fjord, which hereabouts is studded with islands, and bounded by a gray rocky coast that grows more fertile and beautiful as we approach the city. In the immediate neighbourhood of Christiania the scenery of the fjord has a varied and bright summer aspect of much beauty, such as an Englishman is little prepared to find in latitude 60°. I am tempted to call it the Como of the North, but hesitate, as the sky may not always be as bright and blue as on this morning.

Land at Christiania, and am positively embarrassed at finding myself so utterly unmolested in a foreign country. Nobody demands my passport, nobody seizes my knapsack, and no obsequious touter offers

to conduct me to the very best hotel; but I am left
entirely to my own resources and devices. One of
the saloon passengers, an Englishman who has come
to Norway to kill time and salmon, is standing near
with his portmanteau on the ground and similarly
desolate. "Where are you going?" "Don't know.
Where are *you* going?" "Don't know." "Let's go
somewhere." "Very well." At the conclusion of
this dialogue the stonemason joins us and suggests
Hôtel du Nord, to which we blindly agree, and all
proceed thereto. We ultimately discover the host,
who receives us blandly in his little room.

After some consideration he consents, in excellent
English, to receive us, indicates the direction in
which a room may be found, and casually refers to
the fact that a bell may be connected with some
part of its walls, suggesting at the same time the
possibility of somebody coming to wait upon us if
we should happen to ring it.

This was evidently a little preliminary fencing of
dignity: he had probably encountered some stray
specimen of those wretched libels upon true Englishmen—the vulgar rich, who are distinguishable from
English gentlemen by their rudeness to tradesmen
and servants, and are sufficiently degraded to believe
that lavish expenditure can justify insolence. Some
of these, common enough "up the Rhine" and at
Chamouni, may have found their way to Christiania;
but be that as it may, our host gave us at once to
understand that he was a gentleman and expected to
be treated accordingly, and would on such conditions
reciprocate. I was delighted to meet with such a

landlord, and my companion, the salmon-fisher, equally so. We came to an understanding speedily, and then found him a most polite and attentive host.

After a breakfast similar to that at Christiansand, we make exploration of the city in company with Andersen the stonemason, who kindly offers to act as guide : he is proud of his native city, even after New York and Liverpool, and he has fair reason to be proud of Christiania. I have never seen a town of its size so free from indications of squalor and vice. I seldom visit a city without paying special attention to the slums, more even than to the palaces, and as I cannot afford to hire cabs, am compelled, even in doing the guide-book, to see some of the realities. Christiania is a remarkably white city, with wide, clean, bright-looking streets: the householders polish their windows scrupulously, furnish them with lace curtains of snowy whiteness, and keep the frames well painted. Just as the greatness of a nation depends upon the virtues and energy of the individuals composing it, more than upon the wisdom of its monarch and statesmen, so is the embellishment of a town more effectually promoted by each citizen's cleaning his own windows and house-front, than upon the erection of half-a-dozen public buildings of great architectural pretensions. The houses generally have spacious comfortably furnished rooms. They are not luxurious nor pretentious, but on the contrary they appear like the residences of well-to-do, careful people, who live within their means and pay their tailors' bills. Opposite to the Hôtel du Nord is a baker's shop,

which may be taken as a type of some of the peen-
liarities of the shops in Christiania. It appears
like a large private house. It has no shop-front,
merely the common dwelling-house windows, which
are decorated with growing flowers in pots; but the
flowers are not floury, nor does the shopkeeper look
whiter than other Norwegians. I should never have
guessed that bread was made or sold there, but that
swinging over the door is a wooden effigy of a convoluted loaf, the usual true-lovers' knot done in
bread, common here and in North Germany. Most
of the food vendors have shops of this kind. There
are a few houses with shop-fronts, but these are
chiefly devoted to the sale of fancy articles; other
shopkeepers place samples of their wares in plain
parlour windows.

On making some purchases of books, maps, and
minor matters of clothing, I found in every shop
some one who could speak English, and that generally
it was well spoken. English articles prevail at the
drapery and haberdashery establishments; the latest
devices in shirt-collars and similar articles are there,
stamped with the names of the best-known London
houses, and retailed at about the same prices as in
London.

The regular lions of Christiania, such as the Palace,
the University, a picture-gallery, &c. (for which, see
Murray's Handbook), contain little that is characteristic, beyond some of the landscapes and interiors of
what is called the Düsseldorf school, and is commonly
regarded in England as really German, although
the leading artists are Norwegians.

In the evening, we—that is, the salmon-fisher and myself—visit the Klinkenberg, which is the Vauxhall or Cremorne of Christiania. The chief entertainment is the merry-go-round, an extensive affair of the kind, elaborately constructed and placed under cover of a special building. The fee is one skilling (about a halfpenny) per ride; the apparatus accommodates some sixty or eighty people. The merry-go-round evidently holds a higher position in the social scale here than in England: fathers and mothers, comfortable-looking middle-aged citizens, sit seriously on the wooden horses, and in the mock railway cars, enjoying their halfpenny ride with all the simple happiness of little children. There were also a camera obscura, several peep-shows, and a theatre of some magnitude; in the latter a company of English acrobats, " Professor " Milner and his infant sons (all full grown), went through the usual performances; the father playing at football with his sons, walking about with a quantity of them on his head, and standing in the attitude of Ajax defying the lightning, while they made trussed fowls and " spread-eagles " of themselves, in flat controversion of all that anatomists have written and demonstrated concerning the structure and functions of the hip-joint and its ligaments. These were followed by the performances of the Chinese knife-thrower and straw-balancer, who astonished the Londoners some few years before. He was now accompanied by a fire-eating brother. At the conclusion of the Chinese performances, two English dancers appeared. Their chief effort was the " Highland fling," which

evidently enjoys the same popularity here as at the
Surrey theatre and Grecian saloon.   The price of
admission to the gardens was 6 *skillings*.   The extra
charge for the theatre was, front seat, 36 skillings;
second class, 24 skillings; back standing place, 12
skillings; the mysteries of the camera obscura and
peep-shows—cosmoramic views, in politer English
—like the delights of the merry-go-round, being
purchasable by a special extra payment.   There are
convoluted walks about the garden, with seats and
tables for refreshment after the manner of old
English tea-gardens; and among the trees and
bushes are sprinkled a few coloured lamps, looking
dull and sickly for want of darkness.

All classes of people are here, excepting the class
most numerous at our Cremorne.   Servant-girls and
their mistresses, workmen and their masters, merchants and their clerks, students and professors,
meeting on common ground and enjoying the
merry-go-round together.   Among other caterers
of refreshment is an old woman with a basket of
oranges.   I inquire the price in the best Norsk I
can muster, and understand her to reply that they
are 12 skillings each, about fivepence halfpenny.
In order to be satisfied I take one, and on tendering
a 24-skilling piece receive 12 skillings change.   My
companion protests that he shall return by the next
steamer; for his " governor " only allows him 800*l*. a
year for pocket-money, and such an income is ab-
surdly inadequate in a country where a penny orange
sells for sixpence.   We carefully watch the old
woman's proceedings in order to ascertain what class

of persons are her customers, and our astonishment is by no means diminished on finding them to be chiefly working men, who pay from 8 to 12 skillings for the exotic luxury, according to its size. In every case that we observed, the luxurious swain was accompanied by a damsel, with whom the orange was shared; and from the expression of aristocratic suavity assumed by the features of the orange suckers, and maintained as long as the orange lasted, it was evident that half an orange is "*the thing*" in Christiania. They would probably enjoy a similar social status in England if sold at half-a-crown each instead of two for a penny.

There are no policemen, *gens d'armes*, or any other official order-keepers here. There are some six or seven hundred people in the gardens and theatre, and not one questionable woman or riotous man is visible. The Norwegians are sometimes spoken of in England as a drunken people, but there is no indication here of even the earliest preliminary stages of intoxication.

After leaving the gardens we walk about the city in semi-daylight, between eleven and twelve o'clock. A few people are yet moving, but none of the "unfortunates," who have possession of our streets at this hour, are visible. In some parts of the city we walk for nearly half a mile and see no one; no police, no watchman; and we hear no sound. A city sleeping in the midst of so much light has a strange effect on the imagination; the charmed palace of the Sleeping Beauty seems to be somewhere in the neighbourhood.

The honesty of the Norwegians is strikingly demonstrated by the condition of the shop-windows. Many of them, containing articles of hardware, books, and other portable goods of some value are without shutters, the wares exposed behind common crown glass panes; and this in a capital city where we saw but one watchman in the course of a three-quarters of an hour's walk through the streets.

On our return from the gardens at about midnight we find a large party just dispersing, and on inquiry were informed that a meeting had been held to listen to a reading of the English newspapers brought by the ship that carried us. Such meetings are held periodically here, when our host, who speaks English purely and fluently, reads the English papers, translating as he proceeds. English politics, and all the incidents of our social progress, are carefully and intelligently studied by the Norwegians, who seem to be quite as familiar with the names and proceedings of our leading statesmen, as they are with those of the members of their own Storthing, or parliament. Our eminent criminals are also well known in Norway. The Palmer poisoning case had been read with much interest this evening.

June 26th.—Visit some more of the regular guide-book lions, which every conscientious tourist who knows his duty towards his Murray feels bound to do exhaustively; and besides this, I walk through most of the smaller streets of the town, and still find none of the low squalid slums that are so abundant in all our large towns and most of those on the Continent. The poorest streets are composed of clean, comfortable-looking, wooden houses; and the poorest people have a well-conducted, respectable manner and appearance. There are no blackguards visible : no people that any reasonable person of any rank could object to sit amongst in a railway carriage. The windows of the humblest houses are scrupulously clean, and filled with bright flowers in earthen pots carefully coloured with red ochre. Flowers in a poor man's dwelling are the outward symbols of most of the domestic virtues. I have had much experience in seeking lodgings in strange places, and always make first application at those houses which have well-tended flowers in the windows.

I once believed in the theory that a soft southern climate, bright skies, and out-of-door existence, had much to do with a general diffusion of politeness and external refinement among the poorer classes; and by this theory accounted for the superiority of continental poor people over our own countrymen in this respect; but what I have already seen in Christiania has altered that opinion, for the Norwegians are remarkably polite, ceremoniously so in the matter of bowing; and the best feature of this bowing is, that the gentleman bows to the poor man in just the same way as the poor man to the gentleman. I saw to-day a man who appeared to be a rich merchant, alighting from his carriage; a servant opened a broad gate that led to the house he was visiting; the owner of the carriage took off his five-guinea Panama hat, and described with it a large semicircle terminating at the knee, as is the custom here; the servant did the like, neither more nor less respectfully than did the gentleman—*ergo*, both were gentlemen.

The physiognomy of the Norwegians is peculiarly English—more so than that of Englishmen; the special characteristics of the " wooden-faced " Englishmen are seen more strongly marked here than in London. The Norwegians mutilate their faces with razors, and the pallor of their light complexions is increased by this domestic surgery.

The costume here presents very few peculiarities, being nearly the same as in London or a large German city; but white Panama hats with broad black bands prevail among the men.

The ornamentation of the Christiania churches is not very remarkable, but there is enough to show that the Northmen here have not rushed into that barbaric reaction which in Scotland led to the wanton destruction of glorious old cathedrals, the anathematizing of organs and stained glass, and the worship of whitewash.

In the tower above the belfry of the " Dom," or cathedral, a fire guardian is constantly posted, whose station commands a splendid view of the city and the fjord. To prove his vigilance, he has to call every quarter-hour from each of the four sides of the tower. In a city built so largely of wood, where a conflagration once started may become so disastrous, such a precaution is fully needed.*

* A recent fire was curiously reported in our newspapers. It was stated that " nearly three-fourths " of the city were entirely destroyed. The fire, though most serious, was not so extensive as this. Nearly three *quarters* of the city were destroyed; but three quarters, when applied to a city, do not necessarily mean three-

The hotel charges are rather high in Christiania, nearly the same as in English hotels, while the accommodation is far inferior. I paid for breakfast 2 marks, or about 1s. 9½d. ; dinner, 4 marks, or 3s. 7d. ; Christiania ale, 6 skillings, or 2½d., per pint bottle; supper of bread and cheese and claret, 1 mark 20 skillings, about 1s. 7d.; lodging, per night, 2 marks, or 1s. 9½d. ; attendance for two days, 15 skillings, or about 6d., which our host told us was quite sufficient, as he did not wish his servants to be spoiled by English lavishness. My companion had some soda-water, which cost 1 mark, or 10¾d., per bottle, though made in Christiania.

Note, 1876.—During the twenty years that have elapsed since my first visit, the development of tourist traffic between England and Norway has been very remarkable. Instead of a vessel of notorious unfitness for passenger traffic, such as that in which I sailed from Hull in 1856, there are now some excellent vessels sailing from that port to the same destination. Instead of carrying six or seven saloon passengers and two in the fore-cabin, they are now all crowded at every trip during the summer. This is especially the case with the *Angelo,* a splendid passage ship of 1600 tons, 262 feet long, 33½ feet broad, with separate dining saloon, drawing room, reading room, state rooms, special promenade, and dormitories for seventy-four first-class passengers.

fourths, for it may be divided into a dozen quarters, corresponding to our parishes. This is the case with Christiania, and about two and a half of these quarters were destroyed

This or other vessels sail weekly between Hull and Christiania, and *vice versâ*. Besides these, there are packets between Hull and Bergen, Hull and Trondhjem; between London and Christiania, Leith and Christiania, Newcastle and Christiania and Bergen, and quite a multitude for indirect routes, such as *viâ* Gothenburg, Copenhagen, Hamburg, Kiel, &c. Tourists who are victims to sea-sickness may now cross to Calais and do the rest by railway.

The still greater and really astonishing increase of steampacket communication on the coast, fjords, and lakes of Norway, will be described as I proceed.

The hotel accommodation at Christiania has developed proportionally. The "Victoria" now has almost a monopoly so far as English tourists are concerned, and the "Hôtel du Nord" has become merely its "annexe."

All the appliances of waiters, porters, chambermaids, &c. &c., are now attached to the "Victoria," besides a black board in the vestibule on which the names and numbers of the guests are inscribed. In the spacious courtyard, formerly open, a summer marquee is erected, and serves as the dining room, in which a largely attended *table d'hôte* is daily held. The smoking and reading room is a luxurious summer kiosk or conservatory, tastefully stocked with exotic shrubs and flowers, with easy chairs and marble tables amid the foliage. It is lighted in the evening with coloured lamps and Chinese lanterns, suggesting reminiscences of Vauxhall Gardens in the old days of Simpson M.C. and thin slices of ham. This hotel in its present state of development is one which even the most luxurious and fastidious of Englishmen must regard as a first-rate establishment. The charges are about the same as at the best hotels of Switzerland and Germany.

The proprietary and attendance are not quite so high-handed as of old, nor so obsequious as in hotels generally. To my taste they have as nearly as possible reached the happy medium in this respect, but due allowance must be made for the fact that on such matters I still remain a social heretic, retaining my old contempt for people who love to be flunkied, and who imagine that they increase their own dignity by adding to the number of their servants, and increasing the magnitude of their " establishments."

On my last visit I went from Hull to Bergen. Experience of both routes decides me to recommend all tourists, who visit Norway for the first time, to enter it, if possible, by Christiania. Besides the excellence of its hotel accommodation, every kind of local information is there obtainable, especially from Mr. Bennett, to whom all English tourists apply, and whose untiring courtesy, conscientious advice and aid as to routes, hire or purchase of carrioles, shooting, fishing, and every other kind of practical requirement, are invaluable.

I have only one item of adverse criticism to offer relative to Mr. Bennett's proceedings with English tourists. It is that he gives too much valuable advice *gratis*. I have seen long and carefully prepared skeleton routes which he has drawn up to meet the special requirements of individual tourists, and for

which he has refused to accept any fee. It is true
that such tourists purchase his Handbook, and possibly some of his large collection of photographs,
models, &c.; but there are cases where such purchase
is inconvenient, and there are also, I fear, a few
shabby people who give an immense deal of trouble
when they know it costs themselves nothing; while
on the other hand those who are more scrupulous
abstain from asking for what they really require,
when they see how much work Mr. Bennett is doing
without any direct remuneration. All this would be
remedied by the charge of a consultation fee, gra-
duated by the amount of trouble given. If lawyers,
doctors, &c., may receive such fees, surely an expert
like Mr. Bennett, whose advice may oftentimes save
many pounds, is entitled to make a direct and definite charge for *his* advice, and could do so without
any loss of true dignity.

The general aspect of the streets, houses, and shops
of Christiania has not visibly altered, except in general
extension, plate-glass windows, and other indications
of increased wealth. Its population has doubled
since my last visit. It was then about 40,000, and
now exceeds 80,000, with an annual estimated increase of about 2000. At the beginning of the
present century it was but 10,000.

I did not revisit the Klinkenberg, but am told that
its primitive simplicity has to a great extent departed. Human nature appears to be but slightly
affected by latitude; increasing wealth and luxury
are developing some degree of caste even in Norway.
The leading citizens of Christiania are more exclusive

than of old, and instead of riding on the wooden horses of the merry-go-round at the Klinkenberg Gardens, they now drive through the streets in cushioned broughams, and even perpetrate carriages and pairs; but they have not yet descended so low as to encase the legs of their domestics in mountebank breeches of scarlet plush, and powder their heads and shoulders with white dirt.

Wages have risen considerably in Norway, and I am sorry to say that during my last visit I observed in the towns, on the steampackets and railways, indications of intemperance in drinking that were not visible in 1856. I do not mean to say that drunkenness is prevalent in Norway, but simply that I saw more of drinking and its effects than during my former visit. Soda-water is no longer an exotic beverage at $10\frac{1}{2}d.$ per bottle. It is retailed at three halfpence, and abundantly used by all classes—a trivial but very significant indication of increasing luxury.

CHAPTER II.

The Norwegian railway — Eidsvold — A Norwegian " station " —
The Miosen lake — My friend the cook — The Scandinavian
origin of Englishmen — Knapsacks in general and my own in
particular — A pedestrian's outfit and laundry — Lillehammer
The Guldbrandsdal — The Norwegian carriole — Fladbröd
Attendance at a Norwegian farmhouse station — Eccentric
Englishmen in Norway — First taste of Norwegian hardships
The peasants' supper and bedroom at Laurgaard station.

June 26*th*, 1856.—THERE is a railway from Christiania to the Miosen lake ; I ride by it to the
terminal station of Eidsvold, a distance of about
forty miles English ; fare by third class, 2 marks 18
skillings, about 2s. 5d.

There are some special peculiarities in this little line.
It is, to a great extent, the property of a few English
engineers and contractors ; and Englishmen are astonished at the amount of traffic that is done on a single
line of rails, and at the total absence of engineering
and architectural triumphs for the world to admire
and the shareholders to pay for. I am told that it is
a most profitable speculation, as may be expected ; for
this is the great highway of Norway ; and where
people can travel at a halfpenny per mile at convenient hours, the whole population become habitual
railway travellers. What might not the profits upon
our railways become if a corresponding proportion
of our dense population made use of them ?

This railway passes through a rich fertile valley and by the side of a pretty winding river; it then plunges through some dense forests of tall pines, with stems so straight and uniformly taper that they appear like huge fishing-rods. Their bark has a fine red colour, which reflects the sunlight and fills the whole atmosphere between the labyrinth of bare poles with a warm tinge, similar to that produced by stained glass windows in the aisles of a Gothic cathedral.

Eidsvold, the northern terminal station, is beautifully situated on the river Vormen. After some inquiry, I found the inn, or station: it consists of a number of wooden houses, some containing hay, others adapted for the entertainment of cattle, and one a store well stocked with earthenware, hardware, drapery, and haberdashery. I was shown to a wooden room in one of the wooden houses, in which was a wooden box with a bed in it, and other wooden objects; had a satisfactory supper of trout, with potatoes, ale, and good brown bread, and a comfortable clean bed, without fleas, and with sheets of wholesome rough unbleached linen In the morning I had breakfast of strong coffee, bread, cheese, butter, and fresh-water herrings from the Miosen, pickled with oil like sardines; paying 2½ marks, or 2s. 3d. for all: the bottle of ale cost 3d., the rest 2s.

June 27th. — Steam up the Miosen lake in a boat belonging to the clever Englishmen, or rather Scotchmen, who made the railway. The Miosen is a long narrow lake not unlike our Windermere, but

on a larger scale; being some seventy miles in
length. The mountains that form its basin rise to a
height of about 2000 feet at their visible summits;
their form is not remarkable, but their sides, sloping
down to the lake, are covered with rich emerald
verdure, rivalling, if not excelling, our own green
fields and even those of Ireland. These slopes are
backed by fine woods of birch and mountain ash, and
dotted about them are the wooden farmhouses.
Altogether the Miosen is a beautiful lake, but not
exciting raptures. About half-way on the lake is
the site of the ancient town of Stòr Hammer—*stòr*
signifying large, and *hammer* the same as our ham
or hamlet. The ruins of its old cathedral remain,
and near it, or I believe including it, is the farm of
George Bidder, once the famous calculating boy, and
now one of the great English lords of Norway, with
a very eligible interest in that snug little railway
and the Miosen navigation.

The land hereabouts is the richest in Norway, and
the general aspect of the country very different from
what one might expect in the midst of the Scandinavian mountains, lat. 61°, the same as the ice-bound
coast of Greenland.

I took a deck passage, and found among the
natives there assembled many who spoke English
very well. I had long gossips with several, but the
most interesting of all was that with the cook, a
healthy energetic maiden, who had quite captivated
me during the day by her energetic and skilful
operations in the little galley on deck. In the
evening when her work was done, as we talked

together for a couple of hours or so, she was overflowing with loving reminiscences of an English
family whom she had formerly served ; especially of
her kind mistress : the tears rolled down her round
ruddy cheeks as she told me how her mistress tended
her with motherly care during a long illness. Many
ladies believe that servants are all ungrateful; these
ladies would be wiser were they to reflect on the fact
that the compact with a domestic involves obliga-
tions on both sides, that gratitude is due to a good
servant as well as to a good mistress.

My friend the cook was eloquent on the identity
of English and Norwegian customs, telling me how
old-fashioned people in Norway burn the Yule log at
Yule time, just as old-fashioned folks in England do,
and how they have in Norway a rhyme precisely the
same as ours :

> " A merry Christmas and a happy New Year ;
> A pocket full of money and a cellar full of beer."

She had instinctively come to the conclusion that
the English and Norwegians are of the same stock,
and listened most attentively to an exposition of my
opinion that the aboriginal inhabitants of the greater
part of Britain were the same as those of Norway,
and that the same race inhabited both countries long
before the Danish invasion of which we have historical records, and centuries before Cæsar set foot on
British ground ; though many historians have hastily
and I believe fallaciously concluded that Britain was
peopled by a Celtic race, simply from Cæsar's
description of the inhabitants of the Kentish coast,

where a local colony of Gauls might be expected to
have settled by invasion from the neighbouring continent. The descendants of the old Kentish families
of the coast are still distinguishable by their dark
eyes and hair, and Gallic physiognomy; they are by
no means of the characteristic English type. The
prisoners in the Roman slave market, whom the
punning Pope converted from Angles to Angels,
could not have been dark-haired and dark-eyed
beauties; for Italian angels (unless they be portraits
of the painter's mistress) all have blue eyes, and red,
auburn, or flaxen hair. Italian girls are liable to
fall desperately in love at first sight with flaming
red-headed Scotchmen, or Englishmen with straw-
coloured hair: the "bella barba bianca" is their
ideal of manly beauty   The young Romans of our
day, who risk their souls and do dreadful penances
for visiting the English church outside the Porta del
Popolo, go there to enjoy the felicity of breaking
their hearts for the most flaxen-haired, gray-eyed
Scandinavian specimens of English beauty: they
scarcely look at the flashing dark-eyed beauties
whom the light-haired Englishmen admire. This is
no matter of mere habit, but of original human
instinct, that was the same in ancient as in modern
Rome: had the British captives been dark-haired,
black-eyed Celts, the great Gregorian pun would
never have been uttered.

The first drunken man I have yet seen in Norway
was on board the steamer to-day. I am told that
great improvement is taking place in this respect;

drunkenness, which was once rather prevalent, is now almost extinct in Norway.

Another gorgeous northern sunset; the combined evening and morning effects were not visible on account of the hills, but the lighting up of the hills themselves was most magnificent.

I landed near Lillehammer, and walked up the hill to Hammer's hotel. Meeting the steward on the way, he introduced me to his friend Mr. Fk. Hammer, and we supped together. The hotel, built of wood, is a large one, of considerable pretensions as to style and ornament; the handsome lace curtains at the windows, and a magnificent door-mat of fir and juniper branches, are its most striking features. This fir-branch door-mat is peculiarly effective, and its odour very agreeable when bruised by the feet; the fashion is worthy of adoption in English country mansions that have a spacious entrance-hall.

There were many Swedes with leathern caps and aprons on board. They come here for work, and after a while return; wages being higher in this part of Norway than in Sweden.

After a supper of cold trout, cheese, butter, and ale, I retired to a good bed in a detached building, the window close to the road and level with it, but without shutters or anything more than the lace curtains. It was the same at Eidsvold.

The fare by the steamer, second class, was 3 marks 20 skillings, or 3s. 5d.; dinner on board, of macaroni soup and good roast beef, 18 skillings, or 8d.: this was rather under the usual charge, as I dined in the cook's galley.

June 28th.—Hook on my knapsack, and make a fair start. I pity the unhappy tourist who carries a portmanteau, or even a carpet bag, and can make no progress without a "conveyance"; who is perpetually waiting or hurrying for post-horses, or the starting of trains and diligences; who is dependent upon a laundress for the washing of his shirt; and who goes about groaning for "comfort" while travelling. A man to whom comfort is necessary, and who cannot find enjoyment in discomfort, should avoid Norway.

Before advancing on the journey I must describe my knapsack. I have had much experience in knapsacks, and made many improvements and inventions in their construction; my last invention, previous to the present one, was of zinc, suggested by a botanical vasculum, and somewhat resembling one. I walked through Wales and the Lake district with it, and found it had many advantages; but that for which it was mainly constructed was not among them, viz. relief from the heat and perspiration at that part of the back upon which the knapsack rests. Besides this, the country people mistook my mission, and were continually inquiring the price of candles.

My present knapsack is made of strong open wickerwork, curved, like an angler's basket, to the shape of the back, and lined *on the inside* with waterproof cloth, so that the bare wicker rests upon the back. A free ventilation is thus secured, which effectually carries off the perspiration. The top is closed by a leathern flap with straps. The attachment of the shoulder-straps is the same as in the Swiss and German knapsacks, viz. from the middle of the upper part of the back of the knapsack, so that the straps cross the shoulders diagonally, and require no breast-straps: which last are abominable inventions, most uncomfortable and injurious to health by pressing upon the ribs and contracting the chest. This wicker knapsack combines lightness and coolness in the highest degree; it is strong, keeps its shape firmly, and is altogether the best I have seen. It is a great mistake to make a knapsack of waterproof cloth or other pliable material; such a knapsack becomes a mere unmanageable dangling bag upon the back.

As regards the contents of the knapsack, I find that almost every Englishman carries too much: I never met one who carried too little. The common idea at the outset is, that three or four shirts are necessary. This is altogether a mistake; one on and one off only are required: both should be flannel, of large measurement, and of the best and softest quality obtainable; such as are made for rowing and cricketing. But how about a night-shirt? the reader will exclaim. The one off is the answer. But, it may be objected, they will both be dirty. Nothing of the kind! With proper management you may have a clean shirt every day. It must be managed thus:

Suppose the hour to be 10 A.M. You have walked some distance, are getting hot, and disposed for a halt. You make for the river, lake, or the first

brook or mountain torrent that crosses your path;
and such are always to be found in the sort of country
that pedestrians travel. Call the shirt on, A, and the
shirt off, B. Unhook your knapsack at a cosy nook
by the waterside, take out shirt B, and wash it in the
stream. At first the washing of one's own shirt
appears a great undertaking, but the difficulty soon
vanishes. A flannel shirt that has only been worn
one day and one night merely requires a little soap-
ing under the armpits, at the neck, and wristbands;
a little scrubbing, beating, rinsing, and wringing in
the pure water, is sufficient for the rest. When this
is done, spread out the shirt on the grass and take
your bath. If merely a shallow brook or torrent is
available, lie down flat upon the pebbles or between
the boulders, and let the water flow over you for a
quarter of an hour or so. By the time you are
dressed, your shirt will be half dry if you wrung it
out skilfully. To complete the drying, tie it to
your knapsack, and let it dangle and wave behind
you for an hour or two as you walk on.

Now let it be 5 P.M. of the same day. You are
hot, and just sufficiently tired to enjoy the luxury of
repose; you retire to the adjoining field, or into the
forest, to dress for dinner, by taking off shirt A
and pulling on shirt B. You revel in its freshness,
for it savours to the skin of the sweet clear water
of the mountain stream; you spread out shirt A, to
ventilate till the perspiration it has absorbed has
passed away; you make up your diary, lie flat upon
your back, and look through the branches of the
trees into the blue infinity above, build castles in

that region for half an hour or so, then pack up shirt
A, and do the last stage of your journey at a rattling
pace in the cool evening. Shirt A is changed to do
duty as a night-shirt, B is resumed in the morning,
in order that A may go to the wash as B did the
day before.

Many suppose that an overcoat is necessary when
travelling in a mountainous country: this is another
popular fallacy. The shirt off is always at hand to
do duty when extra warmth is required. Every
article, and every part of every article, of clothing
should be woollen; coat, vest, and trowsers, of flannel-
cloth, the linings of thin Welsh flannel. This may
appear warm for summer costume, but is less so than
it seems. In hot weather the waistcoat should not be
worn, but kept in the knapsack as a reserve for the
cool morning and evening, or the mountain heights;
the extra shirt is invaluable when benighted on a
mountain, and compelled to sleep upon a rock.
Three pairs of Shetland-wool socks are required
under these circumstances; two pairs on the feet for
extra warmth, and one pair on the hands as mittens.
One pair on and two pairs off is therefore the requisite
supply of socks, which, of course, are to be washed at
the same laundry as the shirts.

I have tried the arrangement above recommended,
and also that of carrying three or four shirts and
depending upon laundresses; in every respect, including the saving of time, the one-on-and-one-off
principle is the best. A whole day may often be
wasted in waiting for the washing of shirts.

A pedestrian should always carry a pair of forceps

for the extraction of thorns, some lint and plaster,
and a few yards of broad tape for bandage in case
of mishap, such as a sprained ankle or the like.
These are not the only surgical instruments required,
for needles, thread, and buttons are necessary for
healing the wounds to which clothing is especially
liable from rough climbing. A light thin oiled silk
cape, to be worn over the knapsack, is very useful
in wet weather; it protects the shoulders and the
upper half of the arms, which are liable to chronic
rheumatism if long exposed to the contact of wet
clothes.

These, with soap, towel, comb, tooth-brush, a
strong knife, scissors, maps, guide-books, and a stout
stick, with a long iron spike at the end, a note-book,
and sketching materials, are nearly all that the
pedestrian requires. In Norway his walking-stick
may be a fishing-rod, and he will do well to carry
some artificial flies for presents to the farmers: but
of this hereafter.

Note, 1876.—My wicker knapsack is now ex-
tensively used. Many modifications have been
made and some patented; most of these have erred
in the direction of over-elaboration. Simplicity is a
fundamental desideratum. I have found much difficulty in getting the wicker part of the knapsack
well made. It should be of the same kind of wickerwork as fishing baskets, and quite as strong. Those
I have had and seen have mostly been made of very
open wicker, the makers supposing that such is
necessary to permit the required ventilation; but

this is not the case, the strong close wicker of a fishing basket is sufficiently free of the back for all practical purposes, and has the great advantage of being strong and unyielding. One of these baskets lined with indiarubber cloth, with a flap of the same material over the lid, and properly fitted with straps, would make an excellent knapsack.

Walk through Lillehammer (or little ham), which is a large village or small town, with broad and remarkably clean streets, large wooden houses, bright windows, with white frames and lace curtains. There is scarcely a window in the main street that is not filled with flowers in bright red pots. Everybody appears to be industrious and well-to-do, and nobody rich enough to be useless.

Beyond the town the road ascends, and commands some fine views of the lake and river; seats are placed on the most picturesque points. By the side of the road I passed a mass of charcoal and ashes, the remains of a log house, recently burned down, showing the risks to which this kind of building is too liable. The road is a new one; the date of its construction, from 1851 to 1855, is inscribed upon it.

There is a fine cascade here, the Hunefoss, with a gate leading to it, but nobody to pay for opening it. As civilization advances, this and other waterfalls will, I suppose, be capitalized as in England, and 6d. charged to see the show.

Note, 1876.—I leave this remark as it stood in the first edition, in order, after twenty years' interval, to have the pleasure of refuting my own prophecy. The waterfalls of Norway have not become thus appropriated, and there are no symptoms of movement in this direction. The landowners of Norway are simple peasants, and usually what we should call very poor, but they nevertheless appear to be quite incapable of the meanness that prevails in such a place as Matlock, where the highways to the hills around the Heights of Abraham, the " Romantic Rocks," &c., &c., are farmed to local Barnums, barred with gates, and guarded by authorised highwaymen who call upon the tourist to "stand and deliver" twopences, threepences, fourpences, and sixpences each. The last time I was there I paid 3d. each for self and friends for the privilege of walking by a public-looking road up one side of an open barren hill, but instead of returning by the same path we descended on the other side. When nearly down to the main road of the valley a flat-headed ruffian stopped the way, and demanded more threepences in the most insolent manner possible. I was compelled either to pay, knock the fellow down, or walk all the way back. Having two ladies with me, I did the first instead of the second. In other parts of this same valley old lead workings are shown for twopences, on the swindling pretence that they are natural stalactite caverns.

There is no approach to anything of this kind to be found in Norway. In many cases paths are cut and bridges are made at considerable expense in order that tourists may obtain good points of view for waterfalls, &c.; but there is no begging;

no enforcing of paltry fees; no gates, except to prevent the straying of cattle. Usually a rude signpost bearing the name of the "foss," and with an arrow pointing the way, is placed prominently on the roadside. The tourist should never pass these, but follow the direction of the arrow and he will generally find that the river at the bottom of the valley, at a place quite invisible from the road, plunges over a precipice into the foaming cauldron it is carving out for itself, and then dashes forward in snowy fragments through a wild rocky gorge. He will rarely be disappointed, and usually well rewarded for his detour, as there are no catchpenny Matlock shams in Norway.

Dine at Mosshuus station on brown bread, fish, and cheese, the charge for which was 12 skillings, or 5½d. Stop for the night at Holmen station; supper of eggs and cold raw ham. There appear to be no establishments in Norway corresponding to our publichouse, the French auberge, the German gasthaus, or the Italian osteria: everybody appears to live at home. These posting stations are farmhouses. The distance from Lillehammer to this place is rather less than twenty English miles, through the entrance of the Guldbrandsdal, which extends nearly up to the Dovre Fjeld. It is one of the richest valleys in Norway and the most frequented by tourists; for whether they proceed northwards to Trondhjem and the midnight sun, or take the western country about Bergen and the Hardanger, this is the usual route from Christiania.

June 29*th.*—My bedroom is without curtains, level
with the road, and looking on to it as before.   Break
fast of bread and cheese, with wonderfully strong
coffee and rich cream, as usual.   Supper, bed, and
breakfast cost 1 mark 12 skillings, or 1s. 4d.   Walk
up the hill to Throtten, where the river spreads out
again and forms a narrow lake, on which a steampacket plies.   Like that upon the Miosen, it is well
filled; the fares being low people contrive to find
occasions for travelling.   I was overtaken here by
my friend the salmon-fisher, who drove up in company with Mr. Gould the ornithologist, and Wolff
the great bird-painter.   The two latter had commenced their experience of Scandinavian hardships
by a sojourn with Mr. Bidder at his farm, before
referred to; and doubtless had suffered such privations as Englishmen, especially naturalists, generally
do when they meet together under such circumstances.

At Christiania I had been led to believe that the
roads were so bad, that only the light carrioles
made on purpose could travel on them; but here
was a four-wheeled contrivance, drawn by two
horses, and carrying four people besides the driver
and a quantity of luggage.   An English stage-
coach, with full complement of passengers, might
travel all the way from Christiania to Trondhjem;
the road is very hilly, but not more so than some
parts of North Devon where stage-coaches are
still running.   The chief advantage of the carriole
is its lightness; where there are many fjords to
cross, it is the most convenient vehicle, as it can

be easily put into a boat. It is simply a light car, the body shaped rather gracefully, like the bow of a boat with the keel planed off, or a college-cap with the square trencher cut off, then inverted and cut in half crosswise by the ears. There are two long, thin shafts, with two wheels at one end and a pony at the other. The prow-shaped car is placed upon the shafts (with its bow backwards, of course), between the wheels and the pony. One person can just sit in the half-bowl; he disposes of his legs as he may, either arranging them horizontally on the shafts, or dangling them in the small space between his seat and the pony's tail, or otherwise, as his ingenuity may suggest. His centre of gravity is situated over a point about one-fourth the distance between the axle and the bearing of the harness; and therefore the pony supports about one-fourth of his weight on horizontal ground, the elasticity of the shafts serving as a spring. His luggage is placed on a flat board nailed to the shafts over, or a little behind, the wheels. A small boy who has to take the horse back to the station usually stands upon this board, or on the luggage, and these to some extent counterpoise the weight of the traveller and diminish the pressure on the pony's back.

Enthusiastic Englishmen usually purchase a carriole at Christiania, and add considerably to their travelling griefs thereby. Carrioles, or something of the sort, may be hired wherever there are roads for them to run upon, at the rate of one farthing per English mile, including harness. As there is so much water travelling either on lakes or fjords in all parts of Norway, the cost of carrying one's own carriole on the water is considerable. The chief advantage of a private carriole is, that the trouble of strapping and unstrapping the luggage at every station is saved.

The lake of Losna is very beautiful. It is an expansion of the river Logen, and about the same width as the Rhine; the scenery is not unlike the grandest part of the latter, where the hills are too steep to be disfigured by the ugly vine-sticks and terraces. The charge for a carriole to Elstadt by the steamer is 15 skillings; for a passenger, 36 skillings.

Having neither luggage, horses, nor carriage to look after, I started some time before the rest, and was not overtaken by the four-wheeler until about half-way to the next station, which is twelve or thirteen miles on. I arrived there before they left, and dined on raw ham, ale, and "*fladbröd.*" This fladbröd is a remarkable substance, composed of bruised oats cemented together by some means and flattened out wonderfully. It differs considerably from Scotch oatcake, being very much thinner, darker coloured, and more chippy; it is more like the material of which hat-boxes are made than anything else I am acquainted with: if you strip the paper off a hat-box you will find that it is not made of cardboard, as it appears to be, but of a thin veneer of wood: eat a small quantity of this veneer, and you will be able to form a very fair idea of the flavour of fladbröd; only fladbröd is rather more crisp and a little less resinous. It is made into circular discs from 18 inches to 2 feet in diameter; and a hungry man, who is fond of it, consumes a considerable acreage at a meal.

The view from the upper windows of the Oden station is most magnificent. The station is a large and good one, but rather embarrassing to an Englishman who brings his hotel notions with him, for there are no bells, no waiters, no servants. Like such stations generally, it is composed of several wooden buildings: the dining room is one of these, and the kitchen is over the way; therefore if you want food or drink, you walk across the road and fetch it. You may hammer on the table if you please, but having the whole building to yourself, nobody hears you, or if any of the natives do they take no notice, for they suppose that you are playing a tune for your own amusement. And yet they are not uncivil—no, nor inattentive, but they appear to have a theory that people with arms and legs can help themselves, and they allow them to do so.

Englishmen are objects of great wonderment to the Norwegians. The steward of the steamer told me of an English lady who has a farm hereabouts, who rides barebacked horses, and cuts her own timber in a silk gown; and of a Sir Something Somebody, who hired a special steampacket in order to avoid meeting five people he had travelled with; also of another Englishman, who for some years past has lived in a lonely hut with no other associate than an old woman, his housekeeper; and who spends all his time in hunting wolves and bears, but has not yet seen any.

Arrive at Vik station rather late. The distance is about twenty-three miles from the landing place, and the scenery very fine all the way; vast cultivated slopes, of the same rich verdure as the banks of the Miosen, with wooded knolls and islands on the winding river. Near to Vik the hills form a magnificent amphitheatre, a fitting council chamber for a conclave of giants, the mountain opposite representing the speaker's rostrum.

I find the salmon-fisher and the rest of the party here, and am rather inclined to crow, having done as much on foot as they had with post-horses.

June 30th.—Breakfast on fried slices of trout of extraordinary size, as large as our largest sized salmon, but of deeper colour, and remarkably full-flavoured. The trout are, I believe, caught in a neighbouring lake. Paid 1 mark 12 skillings, or 1s. 4d., for supper, bed, and breakfast.

Walk on through the Guldbrandsdal, into which several lateral valleys open, each contributing a stream to the main river, which at one place, near the battle-ground of Kringelen, forms a small lake. It was here that Colonel Sinclair and his band of Scotchmen were killed while marching on their way to Sweden in 1612. He was buried in the church of Quam close by, and a monument erected to his memory stands by the roadside: it is a small stone pillar, with a carved top, and no visible inscription.

Near to Laurgaard, just before reaching the bridge, the road passes over the lower part of a huge heap of great masses of stone, some of them blasted for road-making. They are for the most part angular and present every appearance of a terminal moraine. This is especially the case to the left of the spot where the road passes over it; the heap comes abruptly upon the greensward, with a rounded swelling outline, just as though pushed forward by some force from behind. Had the stones fallen from above there must have been an abundance of stray boulders of the same kind beyond it. Farther up the western branch of the valley there are long heaps high on the hillside, forming a ridge; these heaps, like that by the roadside, are too abrupt at the sides to have fallen from above, for had they come down with a falling impetus they could not possibly have rested there. Professor Forbes does not appear to have observed them.

Rich, verdant, sunny, and highly-cultivated slopes are the leading characteristics of this broad valley, the Guldbrandsdal. Its verdure is sustained by very careful irrigation, which is one of the most remarkable features of the farming operations hereabouts. Long troughs are made by scooping a hollow in the stem of a pine-tree; one of those troughs is laid with its thicker end close to a mountain stream, and the water directed into it; its thinner end rests in the hollow at the thick-end of the next lower trough, so that the water flows over from the first into the second. This arrangement is continued, and a little aqueduct formed: one of these aqueducts runs along the upper part of every field or range of fields. To use it, the farmer, or one of his housemen, brings a wooden trough, not channeled through as the aqueduct legs are, but with a ledge all round, so that it can form

a little pool of water. He places this just above
the part he is about to irrigate, breaks the aqueduct
by lifting the channeled log nearest to his pool trough,
and directing the stream into it. Usually he has to
shift several logs in order to bend the aqueduct
down to the required spot, but he does this very
speedily by lifting each log at one end and giving it
the required inclination. The water now fills his
wooden pool, and with a long wooden scoop he flings
a refreshing shower far and wide upon the rye, oats,
barley, pasture grass, or potatoes. Every foot of the
field is scrupulously watered thus, and when a
number of the waterers are at work, the bright semi-
circles of sparkling drops flying through the air in
every direction make a cheerful and pleasing sight
for the pedestrian in hot sunny weather such as I
have enjoyed until this evening.

Halt at Laurgaard station, and am shown into a
rough sort of kitchen, with tables, benches, a handloom, and a great fireplace, under a canopy of brick
and plaster. An old woman is sitting coiled up by
the fireplace, hybernating apparently. On one of the
benches are some young women and a dirty man
eating a plastic composition, like Roman cement,
out of a wooden bowl by dipping their wooden
spoons into it by turns. The bowl is oblong like
a butcher's tray, and contains about an ordinary
shovelful.

On my entrance they all stop feeding and stare;
the old woman uncoils and discontinues hybernation.
After consulting together they bring me fladbröd
and rusty raw bacon. The dirty man having now

finished his meal carefully sucks his knife and hands
it to me, making a bow as he presents it. The girl
sucks another knife and puts it away nice and clean
ready for the next comer. I eat a few square feet of
the fladbröd and leave the bacon. A Scandinavian
antiquity is next handed to me; it is a wooden
tankard, or rather bucket, capable of holding about
three quarts, having a carved cover, the sides plain
and about three-quarters of an inch thick. It contains beer, but as the dirty man has just been drinking out of it, and sucking the thick wooden edge as
he did the blade of the knife, I refuse the antiquity
and ask for water. This is brought in a basin, the
same sort as usually supplied in these parts for
washing.

After supper I am shown into a dirty double-
bedded room, the dirty man lying on his back
smoking in the best bed of the two. The bed left
for me is a kind of stout coffin, or egg-chest, with
some straw covered with canvas for the mattress, and
a dirty rug for the covering. The bed is close by a
window, and exactly over the head of the bed and
about 18 inches above it is a broken pane of
glass; a piece of paper is pasted over the hole, but
it only adheres by the upper part, the rest forming a
flap which accurately directs a jet of air upon the
place to be occupied by the head of the sleeper.
The window faces due north, and the wind is blowing
from the north with occasional showers. I lie down
with my clothes on, to avoid direct contact with the
earth-coloured canvas and dirty rug. I try to move
the bed, but fail; try to stop up the window, and

fail also.   The prospect of earache, stiff neck, and
rheumatism in the shoulder being imminent I reluctantly give it up, and determine to sleep out of
doors on the roadside.   With this secret intent I
return to the kitchen, inquire how much to pay, and
ask the distance to the next station.   The equa-
nimity of the whole establishment is seriously dis-
turbed by this.   The old woman uncoils again and
enters into a state of complete consciousness; the
dirty man gets out of bed, pipe and all, to see what
is the matter; the girl disappears and presently
returns with a comparatively clean male, evidently
the master of the house, who appears seriously concerned at my discontent, scolds the old woman, and
shows me to a state bedroom where all is clean and
comfortable enough, and where I sleep soundly.

CHAPTER III.

A misunderstanding, a reconciliation, a supper, a bed, and a breakfast, all for fivepence halfpenny — A sandy region and its
probable origin — Bilious hospitality — Cheating the hostess —
The Dovre Fjeld — The naturalist and the sportsman — Science
versus the Classics — The kitchen at Jerkin — Snehœtta —The
ravine of the Driv — Norwegian beer — Some etymologies —
Luxurious wild flowers — Porridge etiquette — English salmon-
fishers — Rental of rivers — Norwegian notions of English
sportsmen — The valley of the Gula — Wedding festivities —
" Tak for mad " — Costume — Modern changes in the old Norwegian farmhouse stations — Old friends with older faces, and
some departed — The future prospects of pedestrian tourists in
Norway.

July 1st, 1856.—AT about 6 A.M. the old woman, now
completely and normally roused from her last night's
state of hybernation, enters my room and kindly
suggests coffee, which the young woman brings immediately. At every place where I have slept since
leaving Christiania a small table stood by the bedside, and early in the morning a young woman entered
without any of the preliminaries of knocking, and
placed upon the table a bowl or cup of strong coffee,
and a bowl of cream ; both of which I dutifully
consumed before getting up, though I dislike break-
fasting in bed. This, however, is not considered
breakfast, but merely an awakener ; breakfast, or
frokost, being provided afterwards.

I am doubtful whether to regard this as a Norwegian custom, or to suppose that the first English tourist who visited Norway was a luxurious animal and insisted upon coffee in bed, and that the natives have concluded thereafter that such is the common high-life habit of Englishmen, and indulge every Englishman accordingly. With the exception of myself, all Englishmen who travel in Norway are regarded either as lords or members of Parliament, and it was evidently because I was not supposed to be either of these, but rather a travelling tinker, that I was located in the peasants' lodging room last night. The regular tariff for that sort of lodging is 2 skillings—rather less than one penny per night.

I had fladbröd after the coffee, and received very anxious attention from all parties: being evidently considered an M.P., this morning the people of the house were most desirous to conciliate, supposing me to have been much offended the night before. This, of course, was not the case; for, in spite of the dirt, the knife-licking, and the rheumatic window, kindness and good-will were evident throughout. If a traveller enters an inn with muddy hobnailed boots, incomprehensible rough flannel clothes, and a pack on his back, he must expect to be taken for a pedlar; and if he is treated with kindness under those circumstances, he has stronger reason to be grateful than if he had been preceded by a courier with a bag of money. There was much true politeness in the act of the dirty man when he licked the knife so carefully and presented it with a bow to the poor tramp; he knew that I should pay him nothing for licking the knife, but in doing so he did his best, according to his notions, to make it luxuriously clean and agreeable to me. I paid for supper, bed, and breakfast 12 skillings, or about $5\frac{1}{2}d$.; then walked on through a wild alpine gorge with a roaring torrent far in the depth below. After passing this gorge, which terminates at the next station, the valley widens again and the scenery changes entirely.

Curious sandbanks extend to considerable distances on both sides of the river ; these are cut through by the lateral streams, and have the appearance of the earthworks of a huge fortification. The river must formerly have spread over this valley, depositing the sand on the bed of the lake thus formed by its reposing waters. At the same time, it was cutting its way down the gorge above the Laurgaard till it drained the lake its widened waters formed, and reduced itself to its present channel.

I examined the sand, but found no shells in it. It is very fine and uniform, in all respects resembling the sand that is commonly seen to whiten the streams issuing from the foot of glaciers, and is deposited as soon the torrent meets with a quiet spreading place below. Shells are not likely to occur in such a deposit, the waters being so newly thawed and cold.

On reaching the new station of Dombaas I find an English lady and gentleman with their "tolk" or interpreter (whose functions correspond to those of a courier in other countries) engaged in a very interesting struggle. The English lady was in delicate health, and had but a small appetite. This was desolation to the soul of the good hostess, who had exhausted nearly all the resources of Norwegian cookery, and was almost broken-hearted at finding that her fair guest did not consume every dish. She evidently supposed that the lady was dissatisfied with the delicacies she had prepared, and that the plea of illness was only an excuse. We were all amused and concerned at the good woman's anxiety; but the most amused of all was the *tolk*, for he devoured all the nice things the lady and her husband were unable to grapple with. At last came the crowning effort of the kitchen; some porridge made of fine meal boiled in milk, served up with a layer of sugar on its surface, a pool of oily butter over that, and all boiling hot. This was brought forth triumphantly, and I foresaw plainly that if it failed the hostess of Dombaas would have no sleep that night. The fair patient, with the amiability of a woman, and the self-denial of a martyr, ate two or three little spoonfuls; but human nature could no further go. What was to be done? for the hostess, thus encouraged, had now evidently determined that her guest should eat the whole, though there was a good-sized Staffordshire-ware willow-pattern piedish full. Suddenly we hit upon an expedient which our unknown tongue enabled us to organize and carry out. It was that the *tolk* should stand behind the lady's chair, so that he could reach the piedish over her shoulder, and while I diverted the attention of the hostess by asking for something, he hastily, and with great glee, helped himself to piled-up spoonfuls of the porridge. Thus every time the good old lady returned she found the porridge diminished, and was delighted with her success ; expressing her satisfaction by patting her guest on the back and exclaiming " Ikke sik ! ikke sik l" ("Not ill! not ill!"). Thus all parties were gratified, especially the *tolk*.

July 2nd.—Reach the Dovre Fjeld. It is a vast undulating moorland between three and four thou sand feet above the sea level. It has no particular claims to the picturesque, and the absence of great rocky masses deprives it of any savage grandeur, though it is sufficiently desolate. The tints of the abundant reindeer moss, or rather lichen, are in many parts very beautiful; especially where a rounded heap of earth-covered boulders is overgrown with it. It is dry and crisp, forming a luxurious mountain couch; its colours vary from straw colour, through a pale buff, to a bright orange and warm red brown. Its habit is to grow on the dry well-drained spots, while peat moss occupies the swampy localities.

Though early, I halt at the Jerkin station, which is the largest and most famous on this highway from the modern to the ancient capital of Norway, and find it a bustling, rather business-like place: a Norwegian modification of a Swiss hospice. Most sporting tourists make it a resting place for some days, game being rather abundant on the Fjeld.

I find Mr. Gould hard at work, skinning and pre-paring his day's spoil, which was very considerable ; a young bird I had caught on the way was added to the collection. I was surprised at the variety of birds Mr. Gould had killed; he had, in mere numbers, more than double the amount of what an

E

ordinary sportsman, accounted a crack shot, would consider a good day's sport hereabouts. The skilful naturalist, without any of the paraphernalia of sporting—no pointers or setters with wonderful instincts, nothing but a very old-fashioned looking gun, and the bare requisites for making it go off— comes to the place for the first time in his life with a predetermination to shoot particular kinds of birds only, and those of particular ages; he walks straight to their haunts, and shoots nearly all he seeks, a far larger number than the mere bird-slayer who bangs at everything he sees. How any man can be a sportsman without being a naturalist, I cannot understand. Such a phenomenon would, I suspect, be unknown, if in the curriculum of our great Universities science and natural history, the laws and phenomena of creation, were made the leading objects of study, instead of the obscenities of *J*upiter, the foul doings of the other *divinities,* and the demoralizing details of Roman rapine and Greek treachery. The Holywell Street literature in which such abominations are gilded and sugared with the delusive glamour of poetic laudation, might with much advantage be buried in the darkness of popular oblivion, and the keys of its sepulchre left in charge of a few special antiquarians. The languages in which the nasty stories are written—or, at any rate, the stilted, pompous Latin that has been so long dead, might now be buried, and the mental health of our modern youth would be much benefited by such disposal of the pestiferous carcass. The fact that a language, spread by conquest to such an unprecedented extent, should so soon have died, and died so hopelessly in spite of popes, and priests, and pedants, is a proof of its inherent unfitness for human speech.

Among the birds Mr. Gould had shot, were some that live in England during the winter, and come to Norway for their summer vacation. Like our own species, who visit the fashionable holiday places, these birds adopt bright varied colours for their summer dress; and to secure and preserve them in their summer costume was, I believe, one of Mr. Gould's special objects in visiting Norway.

At this place I actually dine, have a joint of roast veal, with rich sauce and potatoes, besides several kinds of bread and pancakes, and concluded luxuri- ously with *café noir*, arm-chair, and slippers.

The night is perceptibly lighter here than at Christiania, and very cold.

July 3rd.—Indulge in a most extravagant southern breakfast of coffee, fried eggs, dried salmon, a kind of polpette, that Pietro, the renowned waiter of the Lepre in Rome, would be proud of serving, and some *gaufres.*

The kitchen at Jerkin is justly famous. It is a large wooden hall, a log saloon, whose rich brown smoke-tinted timbers and blazing fire, where some- thing is always frying, form a most enjoyable con- trast with the bleak waste outside. Every tourist of sound taste prefers to do all his feeding in this kitchen, and leaves the fine room over the way to the inexperienced visitors. It is exceedingly difficult to leave off eating in such a place, prepared as the appetite is by such an atmosphere, and incited continuously by the hostess, whose sole happiness evidently consists in feeding people. She oscillates perpetually between the fire and the guests, aided by a couple of sweet satellites, the most rosy-cheeked of kitchen-maids. Never a driver leaves the door, but the black bottle is brought from its lurking place, and a toss of the head, a smack of the lips, and the Norwegian grasp of thanks follows. Even after this, two or three deep inspirations may be heard, showing further how the drinker appreciates the liquor by making the most of the vapour that still lingers in his throat. I felt strongly tempted to stay another day here; but the midnight sun in the far north will not wait for me, so I resolutely pushed on; bidding a temporary farewell to my English friends, and a long one to the model hostess and her memorable kitchen.

I must not forget to mention the beautiful flowers that decorated that kitchen: every window was filled with them, and all were in full blooming condition. They were not mere Alpine plants from the Fjeld outside, but bright southern exotics that must have been brought here with considerable care and expense, and cannot be retained in such a climate without much attention. There were flowers at several of the other stations, but not equal to these. My bill for dinner, bed, and breakfast, amounted to 2 marks, or 1s. 9d.

Walking on over the Fjeld, the view of Snehætta is rather fine from its highest ridge. This mountain, long regarded as the highest in Norway, is not so imposing as might be expected from its

height, 7620 feet above the sea; but it is only 4500
feet above Jerkin, and 3520 above this point, which
is 4100 feet above the sea level, and said to be the
highest carriage-road in North Europe.

After crossing the high plateau of the Fjeld, the
road plunges into a deep valley in company with
the river Driv, which roars and foams among the
rocky masses that restrain its course. The amount
of water at this elevation gives evidence of the
extent of the Fjeld, and the quantity of snow
that is thawing around Snehætta. Many small
lateral streams pour into the valley, cutting deep
gullies in the rocks over which they fall. Several
of these flow directly from the patches of snow that
fill the hollows above. There is a curious and very
pretty effect produced by a peculiar conformation
of the mountains on the other side of the river.
Each ridge of rock runs down nearly parallel with
the valley, and forms a long, slender-pointed, high-
backed promontory; one side of the promontory
ridge being nearly perpendicular; thus a little blind
glen is formed, into which the rocky promontory
would about fit if it were reversed. These glens are
evenly curved and smooth, covered with rich grass,
and dotted with shrubs and liliputian birch-trees.
They are very numerous, much alike, and occur at
rather regular intervals, giving quite a character to
the valley and contrasting beautifully with its
general wildness: any one of them would form a
subject for a charming little picture. The scenery
is very grand all the way down this ravine to

Drivstuen. The river makes some fine cascades, and several minor ones are formed by the streamlets that tumble from the snow patches.

The character of the scenery changes below Drivstuen; where, instead of wild, broken rocks, the road passes over an almost park-like greensward.

Dine at Drivstuen on eggs, ham, German sausage, and milk, for which I pay 8 skillings, about $3\frac{1}{2}d$.

The new road referred to in Murray's Guide, and by Professor Forbes, as being commenced, is now complete, and is a very excellent one; entirely avoiding the tremendous ascent of the old road, which still remains, and is quite a curiosity in its way.

I was overtaken by two English tourists, and overtook them again at Drivstuen. One of them was a fine specimen of a sturdy old traveller; the other a young man with a green veil, which was evidently a relic of the last Derby day. I should advise other tourists who intend travelling by carriole to provide themselves with similar veils, for the dust in some parts of these roads must be choking when sitting so near to the horse's heels.

Stopping at Rise, a neat and rather smart station, I have some "öl" (ale) with my supper. It is a turbid liquid, of a reddish green colour, and from its flavour appears to be an infusion of hay flavoured with a bitter decoction of pine knots. Possibly it is the beverage made from the *molte beer*, a large red three-lobed berry, that grows wild upon the hills. The ale made from malt and hops, which is so commonly drunk on the other side of the

Fjeld, appears to be a modern innovation; it is called *Baiersk*, the Norsk for Bavarian, and is remarkably good. Beer made from berries is as old as history, and I suspect that the beer of our own country was of this kind, before the process of malting was discovered, and that the name is derived from "*beer*," a berry; probably the word *malt* is derived from *molte;* for the sweetened barley, being used as a substitute for the sweet-tasting "*molte beer*," would naturally receive its name.

July 4th.—Breakfast on eggs and ham, which to-day are "*steaked*," i. e. fried. The learned in words tell us that our word *steak* is derived from the German "*stuk*," a lump or slice; that a beef-steak therefore means a *slice* of beef. I deny this. A beef-steak originally means beef fried or broiled, or to be fried or broiled. The continual use of the verb *to steak* here forces this etymology upon one; and the use of the word steak in the north-east parts of Scotland—where a slice of salmon, if broiled, is called a salmon-steak, but a similar slice boiled is no steak at all—confirms this view. *Lax,* the Norwegian and Danish name for salmon, is still used occasionally in that part of Scotland. The Norsk verb *to boil* is "*koge*,"—anything boiled is "*kogt*," pronounced *cooked:* the *g* being generally hard, like *k*. Scholars refer us to *cuocere* for the origin of our word.

The coffee and thick cream were brought, as usual, to the bedside, and with it some wafer-cakes. Knowing now sufficient Norsk to make myself understood, I had the coffee carried back, to be taken with breakfast. I did not venture to ask for this until quite satisfied that I had got up the requisite phrase with intelligible pronunciation, lest I should be misunderstood and the coffee taken away altogether.

This day's walk was through a rich cultivated valley, with snowy mountain peaks ahead. Murray says that Schneehoetten is visible here, but unless my map and compass deceive me considerably, this must be a mistake.

A little before reaching Ovne or Aune station, there were some of the most magnificent banks of pansies I ever beheld. Several patches of above a hundred square yards were covered with an unbroken carpet of these beautiful little flowers; the variety, richness, and harmony of their colours were most exquisite ; they saturated the atmosphere far around with a delicious aroma, which was almost intoxicating in its concentration when I slept upon them for an hour or two ; the sunbeams poured upon me with a roasting heat, the rooks were cawing above and the river rumbling below; though yesterday and this morning it was freezing, and the snow patches were still visible in all the hollows of the craggy rocks above. I dreamed of oriental vapour baths, otto of roses, and beautiful princesses just imported from the snowy Caucasus, and selling by auction in Covent Garden Market at a few skillings per dozen.

Snehætta is visible near Stuen, about fifteen miles below the place where Murray speaks of it. It is a more picturesque object from this point than from the Dovre Fjeld. A number of other snowy peaks are also visible.

The women hereabouts wear a sort of cuirass of printed cotton, the black silk cap or *lue*, that has prevailed all the way from Christiania, and short white sleeves. The boys have strange skullcaps, with immense, straight, square peaks, which, projecting stiffly forward, just balance the long, straight, tow-coloured hair that hangs correspondingly behind. The men wear red nightcaps when at work in the fields, but on great occasions they are surmounted by beaver hats, evidently inherited with the farms, and having the large crown, hollow walls, and brim turned up at the sides, of the days of Beau Brummel and the Prince Regent.

I dined at Stuen in the kitchen, where four girls were dining at the same time. Between each two was a wooden bowl containing a sort of thin porridge or broth; they sat at arm's length from the bowl, and breaking off a chip of fladbröd, which they broke again and made into a bunch of several layers, they stretched out their arms and dipped the fladbröd into the curd; then describing a long sweeping curve with the hand, put the bunch of fladbrod into the mouth, where it disappeared. All made precisely the same movements; yet I saw no reason why they should sit so very far from the bowl, or why the hand should not be brought straight to the mouth; probably it is a matter of etiquette and good-breeding; the sweep of the arm certainly is rather graceful, though somewhat pompous and bombastic. The short S-shaped wooden spoon, common hereabouts, is used with the same action. Perhaps the custom may have originated from one of their forefathers having, at a remote period, dined at a German *table d'hôte*, and sat next to a fat burgomaster who commenced proceedings by tucking his napkin into his cravat to form an apron, then placed his face horizontally over his plate like a pig at a trough and shovelled the viands into his mouth, which retained one-half and let the rest fall into the plate again. A simple-minded man who had witnessed such a spectacle, would go straight home and teach his children ever after to keep their platters at arm's length, and practise the virtue of self-denial by making their food take a long deliberate journey on its way to the mouth.

My dinner of eggs, milk, and cheese, cost 8 skillings, or 3½*d.*

The scenery is very fine in the neighbourhood of Sundseth station, a deep alpine valley, with rounded wooded hills in the distance, forming huge billows of pine tops.

It is about midnight when I reach Bjerkager, which, like all these farmhouse stations, is composed of several wooden buildings. One is usually a kitchen, another a lodging-house for peasants; some are filled with hay, others are furnished for the accommodation of cows, &c., while externally there is but little difference between them. In this case I find the doors of all unfastened, walked into two or three, and disturb several cows before finding anybody else. I should have helped myself to a bed I found in one of the buildings, but being intolerably thirsty and unable to find the well or any vessel containing water, was compelled to waken the human elements of the establishment, which could only be done by dint of a terrible amount of rapping and rattling. In many places people would be sulky and ill-tempered on being roused at such unseasonable hours, but here I was served with as much alacrity and goodwill as though I had arrived at the usual time.

July 5th.—The road beyond the station commands fine views of the valley, a deep ravine thickly wooded with fir-trees, and the river dotted with pine-covered islands. There are many indications of glacier action hereabouts similar to those in the valley of the Driva, mentioned by Professor Forbes, but more extensive and decided.

The rich verdure of the Guldbrandsdal prevails over the greater part of the country through which I have walked to-day, and the fields are carpeted with sweet flowers as those of yesterday. I little expected to find this element of beauty so generally prevalent here in the far north.

On arriving at Soknaes station, am surrounded by a group of inquirers, who, on ascertaining that I am an Englishman, tell me that two Englishmen are residing here; one of whom comes forward and invites me to his room. He is a devoted angler from Oxford who has spent several summers in Norway, and is well acquainted with the language of the country. He and a friend have rough apartments here, the rental of which includes the privilege of angling in the river. Before coming to Norway I was under the impression that anyone might cast a line where he pleased in the rivers

of so wild and primitive a country, but this is not
the case; the Englishman's insatiable desire to kill
something that can struggle, or is difficult to get at,
has brought all the great rivers of Norway into the
market, not excepting those within the Arctic Circle.
They are rented by English anglers, sometimes on
long leases: and for the best portions of the most
celebrated rivers considerable sums are paid; the
usual stipulation being that the angler, besides
paying the rent, shall give all the fish he catches,
beyond those required for his own consumption, to
the farmer.

This amuses the Norwegians mightily, fishing in
Norway being one of the vulgar occupations by
which men obtain a livelihood. Our laundresses
would be similarly amused if Chinese mandarins were
to migrate annually to England and pay large sums
of money for the privilege of turning their mangles.

I spend a pleasant evening with these anglers,
who give me much information on many matters
connected with the social condition of the people.
It appears that fly-fishing was quite unknown in
Norway until it was introduced by English anglers,
and that the Norwegians are now trying to persuade
themselves that there is some fun in it; though, as
this unusually candid angler confessed, he has sometimes whipped the stream most scientifically all day
long, aided with every appliance of gaudy-feathered
flies and the most complicated tackle, and has
caught nothing; while a little boy with a common
stick, a piece of string, and a hook little better than
a bent pin, has filled a basket.

July 6th.—The road now enters the Guldalen, or valley of the Gula, the view down which is very beautiful. It is a rich cultivated valley, the river winding through a finely wooded plain, and round about green knolls and mounds that have a very complicated appearance seen from above. On descending the valley and walking a few miles down it, the structure upon which this peculiar appearance depends becomes evident.

It is due to a regular series of step-like terraces which extend throughout the whole distance of this day's walk—above twenty-five miles. The valley of the Gula is a long trough sloping and widening downwards till it dips below the salt waters of the Trondhjem Fjord, one branch of which is but the lower end or mouth of this valley descending below the sea level. At the upper part of the valley, where my walk commenced this morning, the first terrace appears. It is a flat deposit about six or seven hundred feet above the sea, and filling up that part of the trough of the valley to that height. The river cuts through it. Lower down is another, then another, and another similar terrace all cut through in like manner by the river. In some of the lower parts of the valley the upper terraces still remain. Near Melhuus station, I counted five of these rising like gigantic steps one above the other and perfectly parallel. In some parts the upper terraces are merely narrow ledges; in others they form elevated fertile plains of considerable width as well as length.

On reaching Leer station am encountered at the threshold by the bearer of a large wooden mug or

rather bucket, having the shape of a truncated cone,
and capacity of about six quarts. It is bountifully
charged with excellent ale, and placed in my hands
with pressing invitations to drink. I obey first, then
look around for explanation, and find that there had
been a wedding some days before, and that the
wedding breakfast is still proceeding. It usually
continues about a week in Norway, and during the
whole of that time beer-buckets are prominent
features of the landscape.

Among the many visitors was a party of old folks,
chiefly women, who were making a substantial repast,
and for the first time I witnessed the old Norwegian
custom of shaking or rather grasping hands all
round. It is done very deliberately, almost solemnly,
like a grace after meat. Everyone grasps the
hand of everyone else, and repeats, "Tak for mad"
("Thanks for food"). There were sixteen at dinner,
and as everyone shook hands with fifteen and repeated "Tak for mad" fifteen times, there were
$16 \times 15 = 240$ repetitions of "Tak for mad," and
120 graspings of hands.

There has been a great display of the Beau
Brummel beaver hats to-day among the men coming
from church. They wear frock-coats and hats on
Sundays, and dress-coats during the week. Both
men and women dress very neatly on all occasions,
the material being good and substantial woollen cloth.
The men wear dark gray and black, the working-dress
being in fact very nearly what we should call evening
costume, with the addition of a red nightcap.

Stop at Oust, a station which has some amount of

hotel pretensions, and have a good supper and bed. Though within a short walk of Trondhjem, which I might reach to-night, I prefer stopping here in the country, as old experience has taught me that a muddy pedestrian, without luggage, arriving in a large city at a late hour is not always well received. Professional hotel keepers generally discover that all their rooms are engaged on the arrival of such a visitor. This is very annoying at bed and supper time after a long day's walk. It matters little in the daytime, as the traveller who carries all his luggage on his back is as independent as the hotel keepers—can forage in a big town, buy a penny loaf at the first baker's shop, and eat it on a door-step, then proceed to inspect the guide-book lions and take his chance of passing some suitable hostelry on the way. Pedestrians may escape a good deal of vexation by thus timing their arrival in large towns.

Note, 1876.—I halted at Dombaas again in the course of my last visit to Norway, and at once recognized the good motherly hostess that struggled so hard to feed the sick lady. Eighteen years had altered her outward appearance, but the immortal part, her hearty womanly goodness, remained unchanged. How she fed us all and insisted upon our continuous eating is narrated in the volume devoted to this journey.

I particularly noticed one change which the lapse of years has produced. In 1856 the one English lady was an object of curiosity as well as of special solicitude; in 1874 six English ladies all arriving together,

were only regarded as an unusually large party.
Besides this, even the good hostess of Dombaas had
become more like an hotel keeper, the entertainment
of guests being now obviously a matter of business
routine and no longer an excitement. I observed
this sort of change everywhere, and felt it somewhat
oppressively, almost painfully, for it cuts a large
slice from the romance of Norwegian travel. The
domestic welcome of the peasant farmer has departed,
the participation of the family meal with the bonder,
his wife and housemen, is no more ; the smoke-bronzed
beams and log walls of the kitchen dining-room, with
its long deal table and benches, its carved and painted
cupboard and great linen chest, its hooded hearth
with chains and hook and cauldron, and other cooking
tools are now almost hidden from the tourist on these
great main highways of Norway. He is now shown
into a special apartment, which in many cases is
furnished with downright mahogany and Tottenham-
Court-Road upholstery.

I felt this most bitterly at *J*erkin, where the fine
old kitchen has become practically inaccessible to
the tourist. We were compelled to dine in the state
room over the way ; but I made a pilgrimage to the
kitchen. If weeping were in my line, I could have
done a tear or two on this occasion, and have sighed
forth the wailing words of sweet Ophelia :

" Oh, woe is me !
To have seen what I have seen, see what I see."

The grand old kitchen is now divided into a kitchen
and dining room proper by a wooden partition ; the

flowers were gone, and I stood there a shamefaced intruder who had rudely violated the realms of domestic privacy. The old man, *"Jerkin of Jerkin,"* was still there, seemingly but little older, but the hostess was invisible. The general deterioration of the whole establishment rendered inquiry for her unnecessary. There is no baby now in the painted wooden cradle, but the bright-eyed maiden who manages the household is probably the same that filled it at the time of my first visit.

Fladbröd is no longer compulsory, and rye bread has ceased to be a luxury in Norway. Huntley and Palmer, or Peek and Frean, have invaded every important station, and even wheaten bread is almost common. Had I been afoot and alone again, such enfeebling luxuries would have driven me from Norway to Patagonia, but as some of my fair companions had hypothetically assumed an inability to eat black-bread and oat-cake, and as neither my eloquence nor example could remove the illusion, I am reluctantly compelled to admit that French rolls, biscuits, tinned meats, and even mahogany furniture may improve Norway in the estimation of many English tourists.

My own particular brethren, the genuine pedestrians who really revel in " roughing it," need not, however, despair of Norway. The Tellemark remains as of old, and what that was the latter chapters of this book will tell. The changes above described have occurred only on the great highways, and even these will shortly revert to their former simplicity, as the railways lately sanctioned and now actively in course of construction will leave the old carriole roads with about the same kind and quantity of traffic as they had in 1856, and restore my description of "the good old times" to the status of "latest intelligence."

The railway between Christiania and Trondhjem is now nearly completed, and will be opened next summer. It leaves the Mjosen Lake at Hamar, diverges from the Guldbrandsdal to the Österdal, avoids the Dovre Fjeld altogether by following the Glommen to its main source, the Aursund Lake above Röros; and then by a westward detour regains the old route at Stören about forty miles south of Trondhjem. It is emphatically a tourists' railway; the portion I have traversed presents the most splendid panorama of scenery I have ever seen from any railway. For particulars, I must refer to 'Through Norway with Ladies.' This and the other railways forming a well-devised and complete system, will take all the luxurious and hurried traffic —Americans and others who are "doin'" Europe, &c., and will leave the old carriole roads to the full and healthful enjoyment of those who desire and are able to leisurely travel "through Norway with a knapsack."

CHAPTER IV.

The approach to Trondhjem — The universality of good-breeding in Norway — Influence of an aristocracy — The Cathedral of Trondhjem — Origin of Gothic architecture — Frost mummies Start for Hammerfest — The Trondhjem and Namsen fjords — A marine omnibus — Torghatten, and its mysterious tunnel — The Seven Sisters — The Hestmand — A lovesome giant's mournful story — Grand scenery of the coast — Glaciers of the Fondalen.

July 7th, 1856.—AFTER the Oust station, which has some amount of hotel pretensions, the road ascends the hills, and commands fine views of the city and fjord of Trondhjem. The city is approached by a line of warehouses very much like the Noah's-ark toys of our childhood made on a large scale : they are close to the water's edge, and appear ready to float off immediately should the water rise. The streets of Trondhjem are wide and clean, with water tanks at the corners, and only a small number of shops, but those very good. It is the universal custom here, as in Christiania, to uncover on entering a shop and continue so while making a purchase. The idea of treating a shopman as an inferior does not appear to be entertained by any class in Norway. The people here are nearly all well dressed, the ladies very gaily, with round hats and the latest London — not Paris — fashions. I have seen but one Norwegian puppy; he was one of the saloon passengers in the steampacket from

Hull. He affected aristocratic English airs, and treated his modest fellow-countryman the stone-mason so rudely that the salmon-fisher and I cut him altogether. We found on landing that he was a commercial traveller.

The different classes of society in Norway are not distinguishable by their conduct; for all are quiet, courteous, unassuming, and dignified. An English puppy, as we are all aware, is the most contemptible of the brutes, and a true English gentleman the most dignified of human beings. The Norwegians of all classes exhibit the peculiar external attributes of high English breeding in a very remarkable degree. They are, as far as I have yet seen, the best behaved people in Europe: haughtiness and cringing seem equally unknown among them. It is often argued that an aristocracy is necessary to give by example a high tone to society, but Norway is almost the only country in Europe without an aristocracy or any pretensions to such; unless it be the aristocracy of timber-merchants and fish-salters.

In one sense, it is true, the great bulk of the Norwegian people may be regarded as an aristocracy, seeing that they are the owners by inheritance of the land upon which they live.* This doubtless contributes largely to their quiet sense of dignity and independence; and, coupled with the fact that the nation has never passed through the degrading stage of feudal tyranny and serfdom, may go far to account for these characteristics. It must be borne

* In Norway, according to Mr. Laing, there is one estate for every twenty-two of the population.

in mind that while an aristocracy, by its example, diffuses refinement and elegance in society, it also inevitably engenders more or less of snobbishness or flunkyism among the naturally vulgar-minded and incapable imitators of true dignity and refinement. The peculiar absence of these pitiful vices in Norway is, I suspect, largely attributable to the fact that aristocratic influences—the aping of style, and our prevalent ideas of " station " and " social position "—are so little known.

Stopping at the Belle Vue Hotel, I found my Christiania friend the salmon-fisher there. Mr. Gould and Mr. Wolff were at a private house in the same street, the hotel being full; but we all met at the *table d'hôte*, where a good domestic sort of dinner was provided. The house is but little like an hotel ; for on arrival I was shown into a small drawing room where the mistress of the house, a graceful and elegant lady, received me just as any lady would receive a visitor coming to her house with a letter of introduction : and such is the tone of the whole establishment.

On my way to visit the cathedral I overtook a military funeral, conducted with much pomp and solemnity, and entered the cathedral with the funeral procession—a circumstance which added very much to the effectiveness of my first view of this curious old building. The exterior has a very odd, irregular, and quaint appearance. It cannot be called imposing or beautiful, but there is an air of originality and genuine antiquity about it that is very interesting. It is true that some of the most quaint

and antique-looking portions are the most modern;
having been rebuilt after fires, and the old materials
put together without any particular reference to
what they were intended for: columns being let
into walls for mere ornament, or placed in niches as
though they were statues.   I should like to bring an
archæologist who knows all about the symbolism of
Gothic ornament, and can fix the date of an edifice
by the shape of its arches, to this building, and set
him to read it without any knowledge of its recorded
history: he would make some magnificent blunders.
I suspect that Mr. Laing is quite right in stating
that " it shakes the theory of Saxon and Norman,
the round and pointed arch having been used exclusively in particular and different centuries, and
affording ground for determining the comparative
antiquity of Gothic edifices. The Norman arch in
its most florid style is connected with the Saxon in
its most simple and massive form, in a building
where the known date of the portion containing
this admixture is more ancient than the ascertained
date of those English edifices from which the theory
is derived."

Were I an archæologist, I should regard this
building as worthy of a special pilgrimage and the
most minute and careful study. If the original
design could be fully made out (and the materials
for working it out are in existence), I suspect that
it would throw more light upon the real origin and
history of Gothic architecture than any other edifice in Europe. It appears to me to form a connecting link between the Mosque of St. Sophia and

our more recent Gothic edifices. The idea of deriving the pointed Gothic arch and *nave* from the old Scandinavian shrine or sarcophagus of the sea-kings—a ship hauled ashore and placed keel uppermost—is most feasible; for if instead of placing the inverted ship upon natural pillars of the craggy coast rocks of Norway, a wooden roof with beams, ribs, &c., shaped like a ship's hull, were placed on a Byzantine colonnade and arches, with a rude Byzantine cupola at the stern end, we should have exactly what appears to have been the original form of this shrine and sarcophagus of the converted and canonized old Scandinavian king, St. Olaf. The date of its construction extends from about 1033 to 1248.

It may be thought presumptuous on my part to express an opinion, having only read the stone records, and none whatever of the many printed treatises on the subject; but still I cannot refrain from protesting against the practice of applying the name of either Saxon or Norman to the rounded arch with the zigzag ornaments and squat columns, with capitals that all differ from each other in everything but the common attribute of ugliness. These in all their varieties are unmitigated Byzantine barbarisms: the architectural refuse of the decaying Roman empire: they are but bad copies of what we may see yet remaining in Constantinople, in the subterranean temple, or rather reservoir of the thousand and one columns; and in the Mosque of St. Sophia.

Every tyro in the history of art is aware that up to the thirteenth or fourteenth century—the era of

Cimabue, Giotto, Van Eyck, &c.—the art of Europe was almost exclusively in the hands of a few wandering Greeks; the little that was done in painting, sculpture, and architecture was done by them. Cimabue, Giotto, and their contemporaries copied the Greek artists, with their gilded backgrounds, Guy Fawkes attitudes, and their other Byzantine absurdities and beginnings of beauty. The original gilded mosaic ceiling of the St. Sophia, now covered with whitewash and falling in fragments upon the thick bed of pigeons' dung on the floor,* may be taken as the prototype of the painting and mosaics of that period; and the architecture of the mosque is as obviously the prototype of everything in both Saxon and Norman architecture excepting the nave and its ship-shaped adjuncts: the pointed arch and doorway being but a transverse section of a boat or ship, keel uppermost.

The early Christian missionaries adopted the dates and many of the ceremonies of pagan festivities, as well as the forms and symbols of their worship, but gave them a Christian signification; and in like manner by combining the Scandinavian ship-temple

* Pigeons are cultivated in the vicinity of all the mosques. When I visited the St. Sophia, the pigeons were flying about the interior, and some of the galleries were yielding beneath the weight of the pigeons' dung deposited upon them. I picked up a handful of fragments of mosaic that had fallen from the ceiling. They are pieces of glass gilded or silvered on the face, and with a thin layer of glass over the leaf of gold or silver. The figures of some of the seraphim were distinguishable in spite of the whitewash, and are precisely in the style of the specimens of Byzantine art in the gallery of Florence, which are so obviously the sources of Cimabue's earliest inspirations.

with the columns and arcades of the Byzantine architecture, they probably produced the beginnings of what we call Gothic. Such, at least, appears to me the true theory of the origin of Gothic architecture; and this cathedral of Trondhjem is a most interesting illustration of it.

The family pews are very curious; they are tiers of boxes made of deal wood, like rabbit-hutches, piled one above another. A colossal figure of Christ, after Thorwaldsen, is well placed in the choir, and is very impressive; the most effective and appropriate statue I have ever seen in any church. Standing alone, and visible from every part of the building as the dominant object, its presence and influence are felt to be diffused throughout, and are finely suggestive of the living influence that should be similarly felt, and really is in a Norwegian church if anywhere.

I paid another visit to the cathedral in the afternoon, and in a kind of vault or cellar saw a large number of mummies, said to be the bodies of Norwegian kings; which I doubt, for kings can scarcely be so cheap.* They are in rough wooden boxes, or coffins, very rudely and disrespectfully heaped upon each other, warehouse fashion; most of the boxes are broken and the bodies visible. They are in an excellent state of preservation, the features being distinct and the hair remaining attached; the skin is hard and dry to the touch. They appear to have been simply frozen and desiccated, like the bodies in the Morgue at St. Bernard.

* Unless they are the Vikings, or Sea-kings.

Note, 1876.—The cathedral has lately undergone very considerable alterations and restorations. The rabbit-hutch family pews were in course of removal when I was last there, and they are not likely to be replaced.

I sought in vain for the vault wherein I previously saw the desiccated bodies of the so-called kings of Norway. I made many inquiries and could obtain no tidings of them. On referring to my original short-hand notes of 1856, I find that my visit to the cathedral was in company with some other English visitors who were travelling with a " tolk," or courier, and that the information respecting the royalty of the remains was derived from this authority. I now suspect that what I saw was merely an extensive vault containing a large number of ordinary coffins, and that the tolk invented the kings in order to increase the value of the show. Tourists who engage professional guides see many wonderful things of this sort.

I stopped this time at the Hôtel d'Angleterre. It is rather larger than the Belle Vue. The hotels of Norway are all evidently becoming more hotel-like; the private-house character so remarkable in 1856 is gradually vanishing. Commercial travellers are more numerous, and naturally exert an important influence on hotel arrangements.

July 7th and 8th, 1856.—At 11 P.M. in the still lingering daylight embark on the *Constitutione* steam-packet, bound for Hammerfest. We start at midnight, and on rising early I find that we are still in the

Trondhjem Fjord. The scenery hereabout is not very striking, but it becomes much finer in the Namsen Fjord which we reach later in the day. Here the packet winds about through narrow channels, some less than a quarter of a mile wide, and breaks into a succession of landlocked basins forming beautiful lakes with richly wooded banks and hills and islands. Many of these are much like Loch Katrine. The well-grown forests, the rich green fields and substantial farms, all under a scorching sun, are curiously contradictory to one's preconceptions of the physical geography of lat. $64\frac{1}{2}°$, but two degrees from the Arctic Circle.

Glorious sunset. Nothing can exceed the protracted loveliness of these northern sunsets. The glowing beauty lingers for hours, all the evening, through midnight, and on to the next morning.

July 9th.—Awakened at an early hour this morning by the captain (who, as well as the lieutenant, speaks English fluently), to see the mountain of Torghatten, so named from its resemblance in shape to a " wide-awake " or " sou'-wester " hat. When near to it, this peculiar shape was not very evident, though at a greater distance it is remarkably so. It is an insular granite rock, 824 feet high, perforated throughout by a very curious tunnel between 400 and 500 feet above the sea level. This tunnel is 530 feet long, 66 feet high at its eastern entrance, 250 feet high at the western entrance, and about 200 feet high in the middle. The floor slopes downwards from E. to W. from 470 feet above sea level to 400 feet. The roof of the tunnel is thus 650 feet above the sea at the W. opening and 530 at the E.

As the steamer passes, the daylight is seen clear through the body of the mountain.

(The figures now given are from recent measurements made by Norwegian surveyors. In my earlier editions I was only able to state approximate and rather contradictory estimates. The recent measurements are interesting, as will appear hereafter.) I am not aware of the existence of any other cavern of a similar kind to this, at such an elevation, and in a granitic rock. No explanation of its formation has yet been given.

Beyond this the scenery of the coast is magnificent; being composed of great chains of mountains with craggy peaks and snowy sides. The Seven Sisters is a short range of mountains rising directly out of the sea to a height of 3000 or 4000 feet, and forming an island   They make a glorious panorama as the steamer sweeps along their feet. Then the Hestmand, or horseman, rears his head from the sea, and marks the crossing of the Arctic Circle.

This Hestmando is another mountain island, shaped like a horse with a mantled rider. The head and ears of the horse from one point are quite ludicrous in their resemblance.

When I stated that no explanation had been given of the origin of the Torghatten tunnel, I had not seen the Hestmand, which is seventy miles farther north, nor heard his story narrated by a Norwegian sailor: but now the whole matter becomes quite clear. The story is as follows:

One of the younger brothers or cousins of the devil, a "Jutul," residing in this neighbourhood, went, as

he was wont to go, on a visit to his Seven Sisters.
There he met a female cousin many degrees removed
who was likewise a visitor, her residence when at
home being on an island some distance farther south.
As is usual on such occasions, the two young people
fell desperately in love with each other; and, as is
also usual, they vowed eternal fidelity. Business of
importance called the giant home, and his fair cousin
also had to return to attend on a sick brother; so,
with tears, and vows, and protestations, they mutually
tore themselves asunder, and the Seven Sisters found
the Jutula swooning on the shore from which her
lover had departed. She went home to her sick
brother, put his feet in hot water, applied a mustard
poultice to his chest, and by the aid of these and a
little aperient medicine he soon recovered. During
his illness his sister made him her confidant, and he
agreed that she should marry the Jutul of her choice;
but on his recovery his perverse nature returned, and
he determined that his sister should wed a disso-
lute companion of his, whom she had always objected
to on account of his smelling so strongly of tobacco-
smoke.

Every Jutul family has some special power or
malignant charm by which to battle with its enemies;
the specialty of this family was petrifaction. The
cruel brother exercised that power on the messengers
from his sister's lover and turned them all into rocks.
Now the lover was not aware of the brother's existence,
for the fair giantess had very improperly concealed
the fact, on account of his extravagant habits having
imperilled her dowry. Believing therefore that his

plighted one was the last of her race, and that she alone possessed the power of petrifaction, he of course concluded that she had put the stony insult on him; so mounting his steed, and shouldering his crossbow, he shot a heavy bolt at the dwelling of the *Jutuless*: his specialty being the power of unerring aim.

Her brother was bathing at the time, and it being a very wet morning he wore his sou'-wester. The bolt sped through 70 miles of air, passed through the hat of the treacherous *Jutul*, and carried away a portion of his skull; but then, impeded by this resistance, failed to make the *ricochet* the archer had relied upon, and simply skimmed the water and fell at the fair one's feet. She knew the bolt, and that none but he could have shot it. She saw her brother (who with all his faults she dearly loved) sinking beneath the wave never to rise again, and all that remained of him for her loving eyes to gaze upon was his perforated sou'-wester floating on the waters. She thought of the perfidy of the lover she had believed so true, and her heart was broken; but as she died she exercised her power of petrifaction; and herself, the floating perforated hat, her lover, and the horse he rode were all converted to fast-rooted rocks.

The Seven Sisters who witnessed the consummation of this doleful tragedy were petrified with horror.

Those who doubt the authenticity of the foregoing narrative should go to the spot and examine the evidences for themselves. There is the mounted Hestmand with his martial cloak flung over his shoulders; there is the perforated sou'-wester, and beyond it the drooping fair one, all turned to stone;

there the messengers, a long procession of low rocky islands, reaching from the Hestmand to his love, and there the Seven Sisters in stony stillness looking on.

We are told by many very eminent men that we are not to judge a narrative relating to times long past by what would be probable or improbable, possible or impossible, at the present day; but that if the narrative is minutely circumstantial and the circumstances are self-consistent, they afford internal evidence of its truth; and if, in addition to this internal evidence, we have the external evidence of monuments and localities that perfectly correspond with the narrative, these together are sufficient, and the modern current notions of inherent probability or improbability, possibility or impossibility, are not to interfere with our belief. All these conditions being fulfilled by the above legend and its monuments, we are bound to believe in the sad story of the Hestmand and his love.

As we sail along the coast, fresh scenes of savage grandeur continually unfold themselves. The great inland chain of snowy mountains is well seen about Rodö, latitude $66\frac{1}{2}°$ to $70°$. The valleys descending from these are filled with magnificent glaciers, their great crevices and blue ice being visible from the steamer with telescopes. These glaciers appear as extensive as the glaciers of the Alps: Von Buch states that some of them touch the sea; but he speaks from hearsay; there is no record of any traveller having visited and examined them. The whole region—the Fondalen—is uninhabited; a snowy waste, extending away to the Swedish frontier.

CHAPTER V.

July 9th, 1856, *continued.*—AT about eight in the evening, as we approached the Salten Fjord, lat. 67°, I observed a curiously-shaped ship, and tried to define it with the telescope. Presently it diminished to half its former size, then rose again, but this time was seemingly undermined by a sort of notch or open angle formed by one portion of it with the surface of the horizon. Further examination showed that it could not be a ship, and many opinions were expressed concerning it; but at last I discovered its real nature. It was the head of the veritable " Kraken," the great Scandinavian sea-serpent; the angle being the monster's mouth, his upper jaw only being above water. The folds of his enormously long body were seen stretching along the horizon, now rising, now sinking, all in continuous motion. At the most moderate calculation his length must have been three or four miles, from the uplifted head to the

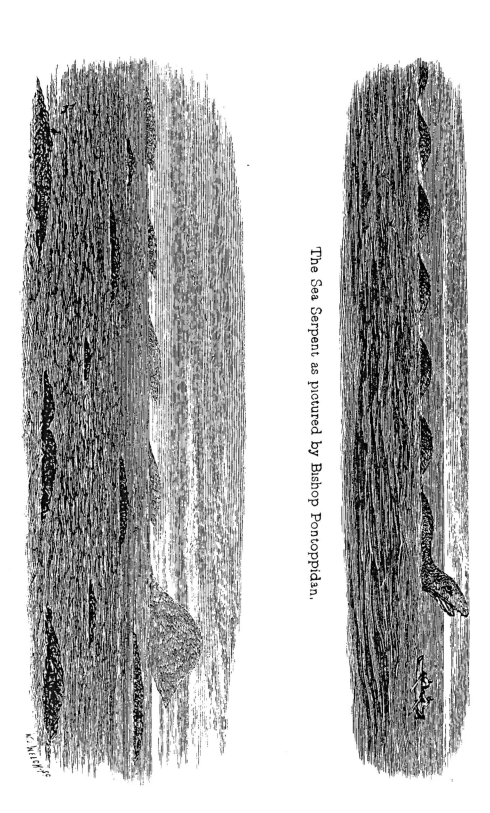

The Sea Serpent as pictured by Bishop Pontoppidan.

last visible fold; and how far the point of his tail might be from this portion I will not venture to conjecture, as this point was not displayed. It continued moving, and sometimes the greater part of it disappeared suddenly; at one moment the head almost entirely vanished, at another time only the head and the extreme caudal folds were visible, then more than half of the tail end had gone. Why, then, have neither geologists nor fishermen found any fossil or recent remains of this creature? Simply because they have not properly sought for them: the petrifactions exist abundantly. They may be found hereabouts—in the form of low rocky ridges, stretching in long lines, with spaces of sea between them, like the Hestmand's messengers. Some start abruptly out of the water and rise to fifty, a hundred, or more feet in height; these are the heads, the low ridges are the coils of the body, of the Kraken.

Towards the end of a long, clear, glaring summer's day, after the sun's rays (which here are powerful to a degree incredible to those who have not felt them) have been for eighteen or twenty hours continually pouring upon these rocks, which from the nature of their surface are excellent absorbers of heat, they become considerably hotter than the surrounding sea, and are covered with a layer of rarefied air continually ascending and waving about, and refracting the light very differently from the denser air over the intermediate sea. Now let us suppose a line of these low rocks just visible above the horizon, and between them and the spectator's eye a number of other low rocks, which he, raised on a ship's deck, looks over.   It is evident that as he moves along he will see a particular point on the horizon sometimes over an unbroken line of sea, or sometimes over one or more of these low, warm rocks, with a rarefied atmosphere above them.   Anyone who is acquainted with the rudimentary principles of optics will perceive that under these circumstances an apparently undulating motion would be given to objects on the horizon; they would appear to rise or fall, according as they are viewed through a denser or rarer atmosphere; and thus the waving of the coils of the serpent's body is accounted for.   This may be illustrated by holding a hot poker between the eye and a distant object which is seen just over the poker.

But how about the undermining of the head-rock forming the serpent's uplifted jaw?   This is as easily explained, though the principles upon which it depends are not so popularly understood.   Light may pass at any angle from a rare medium into a denser, as from air to water, water to glass, &c.: but when it has to effect the apparently easier passage from a dense into a rarer substance, as from glass to water, water to air, &c., the case is quite different.   It cannot do this beyond certain degrees of obliquity without becoming mathematically illogical and violating the consistent ratio of the sine of its angle of ordinary refraction to that of its angle of incidence. This it refuses to do so stubbornly, that rather than be thus mathematically stultified, it suffers total reflection.   It turns back altogether when consistent progress becomes no longer possible.   Hence under certain circumstances the thinnest film of air is absolutely opaque: more opaque than a dense metal, for gold-leaf allows some light to pass through it while the film of air admits the passage of no light whatever, but reflecting all that falls upon it, shines like polished silver.

By taking advantage of the remarkable power which carbon in some of its forms possesses, of clinging tenaciously to a film of air, I have devised a simple experiment which illustrates this in a striking manner. Take a piece of sheet metal, as copper, brass, iron, or any other, and hold it over the flame of a candle or lamp until its surface is uniformly blackened; then let it cool, taking care not to touch the blackened surface with the fingers. Now plunge this in a tumbler, or other convenient vessel of water, and look at it obliquely through the water: the dull black carbon surface disappears, and a bright, glistening, silvery mirror takes its place. Then take the plate out of the water, and (if the experiment has been carefully conducted) the blackened surface will be quite dry: the water has not touched the carbon, for it carried down a thin adhering film of air; it was that which shone like silver, and by its opacity concealed so completely the black surface beneath. It is because you looked very obliquely through a dense medium, the water upon the surface of a rare one, the film of air, that this effect was produced. If you take a tumbler of water, and look up obliquely through the water to its surface, the surface appears mirror-like, and reflects objects that are in the water; but your finger, held just above the surface of the water, is invisible, on account of the perfect opacity of the air under these conditions.*   Many water-beetles and water-spiders have the power of carrying under water a film of air adhering to their bodies, which appears like a coat of polished mail.   If the blackened plate be laid horizontally at the bottom of a glass vessel—such as an aquarium tank—and viewed through the sides, an explanation of the *mirage* of the desert is at once exhibited: the black surface disappears, and a mirror takes its place; such a mirror as the thirsty traveller sees upon the distant sands and mistakes for a sheet of water.   The hot sand rarefies the film of air in contact with it, the spectator's head is immersed in a denser stratum of air, and looking from that very obliquely to the rarer film upon the sand, he sees the mirror just as you may see it on the air-film of the blackened plate; but he sees it only afar off, near the horizon, and not at his feet; and as he advances, the bright illusion advances also ; the reason of this being, that the difference is so small between the density of the film upon the sands and the stratum enveloping his head, that a very great obliquity is necessary for this total reflection to take place.   Other explanations of the

* (1876.)—The public aquaria, which have become so numerous since the above was wiitten, afford a very striking illustration of this. The spectator below looking upwards to the surface of the water in a tank sees all the fishes, rock-work, &c., perfectly ieflected; the transparent air above the water surface is absolutely opaque to him, while he is distinctly visible to any spectator placed outside and above the tank.   By application of this principle a cell might easily be constructed in which all the movements of a piisoner could be freely watched by invisible warders.

mirage have been given, but this I believe to be the true one. The explanation that it is reflection from vapour will not bear examination.

The reader, however, may still be at a loss to see how this bears upon our sea-serpent and his uplifted jaw. It is thus: let us suppose one of these island rocks to have a sloping shore, or that there is a reef of low rocks close to it; these, being heated, will be covered, on their sunward side, with a film of rarefied air clinging to them for a while before ascending. Such rocks, or sloping coast, when near the horizon, will be seen at an obliquity sufficient to produce a mirage; this, the necessary obliquity, will be main-tained up to a certain height of the slope, and, so far, the dark rock will be invisible, and its place occupied by a bright reflecting surface. The light, thus' reflected, will be scarcely distinguishable from the transmitted light of the horizon, and hence it appears (unless carefully observed) that the bright part of the rock or shore is transparent, or that the rock is cut off from below: this is the gaping jaw.

This apparent uplifting of low islands and coasts, and more particularly of the long promontory slopes of islands or coasts, is a very common illusion that may be witnessed without going to Norway. The Londoner may see it well displayed on any fine summer afternoon from the deck of a steampacket going to Margate, or the Nore, or Herne Bay, when the sun has been shining brightly all day on the Essex coast at the mouth of the Thames. The Essex coast is very low, and there are trees upon it; under the conditions I have mentioned, the land becomes invisible, and the trees appear suspended in the air. Sometimes the lower half of the trees are also invisible, and only their tops are seen, cut off from the earth, and standing apparently unsupported considerably above the line of the horizon. Anyone who will carefully observe these phenomena on this or any similar coast, will, I think, be satisfied that my explanation is correct; for they are only visible under the conditions I have named, viz. when the land is warmer than the air over the sea, and they only extend to those parts seen at a great obliquity. By attentively comparing the horizon over the invisible land with that over the sea, it will be seen to be more luminous, and to resemble the film of air upon the blackened plate.

I have seen this apparent uplifting of the coast most strikingly displayed in the Greek Archipelago, and along the Mediterranean coast of Africa. The Greek islands were fantastically distorted; and at Algiers the effect was very curious; the palm-trees upon the coast seemed like balloons or parachutes flying over the sea. But, as I have said before, it may be seen on almost every coast on any afternoon of a hot summer's day; and I have been surprised to find how many people—even sailors—have seen it for the first time only when I have pointed it out to them.

The moving rocks and islands forming *my* great sea-serpent, were seen at about 8 P.M., near the Salten Fjord, lat. 67°, and I have very little doubt that he is identical with the classical "*Kraken*" of Pontoppidan and the old Scandinavian mariners.

Pontoppidan* tells us that "the Kraken is the largest creature in the world; its back, or upper part, which seems to be in appearance about an English mile and a half in circumference (some say more, but I choose the least for the greater certainty), looks at first *like a number of small islands surrounded with something that floats and fluctuates like seaweeds.*" He then proceeds to say, "If I were an admirer of uncertain reports and fabulous stories, I might add much more concerning this and other Norwegian sea-monsters, whose existence I will not take upon me to deny; but I do not choose by a mixture of uncertain relations to make such accounts appear doubtful as I myself believe to be true and well attested."

Mr. Milford† gives the following extract from the letter of an "intelligent friend at Bergen," who had made some inquiries on the subject:

"I have consulted a gentleman of much learning, and intimate knowledge of everything belonging to Norway, Stiftamund Christie, whose name is so much connected with the political institutions of Norway from the year 1814.‡ I especially asked his opinion about the sea-serpent, and he assured me that not only do the peasants feel convinced of its existence, but that he himself believes that it exists; that the Bishop of Bergen, a few years ago, published an article in an antiquarian paper, which comes out occasionally, by the directors of the Bergen Museum,

* 'Natural History of Norway,' published 1751.
† 'Norway and her Laplanders in 1841,' p. 197.
‡ His statue now stands in the market-place of Bergen.

containing information in corroboration of this belief;
that the inhabitants of the island Herröe at Sondmör
*see the serpent every year for a couple of months, in
summer, whenever the weather is fine and the sea
calm,"* &c.

I might add many other extracts of a similar kind.
All agree in describing the undulating motion of the
monster and the "fluctuating" appearance about
him. Such undulation and fluctuation are the in-
variable concomitants of the illusion described, and
are produced by the rising of the heated air.

The time of year, the state of the weather, and
the locality of the monster's appearance are similarly
confirmatory. He is usually seen in these low,
rocky, island-spotted coasts. I allude to the real
Kraken with his "mile and a half" of circumference
and some miles of length, not the puny sea-serpents
of a hundred yards' length. It is stated in some
of these accounts that boats have been chased by
the monster; but it is rather curious that such an
immense beast should never have succeeded in
catching the boats: if the rapidity of its movements
bore any proportion to its magnitude, a rower should
stand but a poor chance. I suspect the truth is that
the fear of the Kraken has been sufficient to convince
the boatman that the monster was after him, but not
strong enough to swamp the boat or kill the rower
in calm weather and in presence of spectators on
shore.

Note, 1876.—I saw no sea-serpent in 1874, but his
absence then by no means weakens my explanation,

as the conditions necessary for his existence were also absent. Instead of the clear sky and continuous solar radiation, we had mist and drizzle at the time of passing that part of the Norwegian coast which is cut by the Arctic Circle. It is here and hereabouts that hundreds, or even thousands, of glacier-planed ridges and knolls of rock running in long lines barely emerge from the sea, and where twenty-four hours of sunshine may produce the phenomena I observed in 1856, but which cannot be produced in cloudy weather.

All I have seen and heard and read, since 1856, confirms my theory of the sea-serpent, always understanding that I only refer to the veritable Norwegian Kraken of many miles in length, and waving serpentine form.

1856.—We are now fairly in the region of the midnight sun, and according to our calculations, taking the declination and refraction into account, the sun should just touch the horizon or dip a little below it. We watch it anxiously till about half-past eleven o'clock, when it is still considerably above the horizon, but we lose it behind the mountains which the progress of the steamer places to the northward. The daylight, warmed with the beautiful sunset glow, continues all night, lighting up with indescribable beauty the rugged summits and snow hollows of the wild mountains that start up from all points of this majestic coast.

July 10*th.*—Leaving the mainland and its fjords we cross to the Lofoden Islands. These are, if

possible, still wilder and grander than the mainland ·
sharp granite pyramids springing from the sea to a
height of 3000 or 4000 feet, and breaking at their
summits into a countless multitude of jagged points,
thoroughly justify Mr. Everest's comparison with a
shark's jaw. The snow lies thickly in the hollows
of these teeth and spines, but there are a few small
rich green pasture patches even here, and sheep and
goats are to be seen occasionally; but the chief
harvest of this region is cod-fish, and this harvest
was now in course of reaping. We could smell the
land as we approached it, where acres and acres of
rock were covered with the split fish lying out to
dry in the sun. Like the bodies in the vaults at
Trondhjem Cathedral, the mummification of the fish
is effected by simple drying, and " stock fish " so
much demanded for fast days in inland Catholic
countries is the result. When the drying is complete, they are stacked into heaps which may easily
be mistaken at a distance for hayricks. Near to
these stacks and drying acres—generally close upon
the shore—are huge boilers, where the cod-livers
are stewing most odoriferously. We stopped at
many of these reeking stations, and steamed between
bare granite mountains starting so abruptly from the
sea that in some parts we passed through walled-up
channels not wider than the windings of the Thames
about Richmond, and winding as much or more
than that river winds, but with sharp angular bends.
On approaching these the vessel appears to be
running hopelessly aground, and not until the bow-
sprit seems almost crashing upon tall rocks ahead,

does the helmsman pull furiously at the wheel; when the ship swings round into the suddenly discovered opening.

It must be remembered that during this journey we were not always progressing to the northward, but sometimes sailing westward, eastward, or even due southward; through channels, up and down fjords and branches of fjords; stopping at coast and island stations to pick up and set down passengers and goods; and landlocked apparently at every turn by fresh islands and promontories and shores of fjords; so that the whole journey is like sailing through a tortuous chain of ten thousand glorious lakes.

These lakes of the Lofodens resemble the Lake of Lucerne in its wildest parts, but they are still grander; for though the mountains are not so high, they are much more rugged, harsh, and savage, and the great snow patches filling the hollows at the foot of each of the spiky pyramids, add vastly to their sublimity. The wailing and screaming of the sea-fowl among the bare granite crags and right overhead, as they were startled by the steamer rounding the abrupt bends and breaking suddenly upon their solitudes, were in fine harmony with the wild desolation of the whole scene, and heightened its effect prodigiously.

Towards midnight a mist came gradually down, first hiding the peaks and magnifying the visible sides of the hills, then hanging about the masthead, and finally for a short time enveloping us altogether. It broke as we approached a station; or it may be

that we sailed through it. The effect was glorious.
Out of the misty chaos there suddenly started one
of the grandest clusters of these rugged granite
peaks. The vessel was near to the shore when the
cloudy curtain rose, the mountains sprang upon us
instantaneously like a range of phantoms, and by
the suddenness of their apparition seemed quite close
overhead and almost falling on us. The hemisphere
of gray mist that for a while had bounded our vision,
reddened as we reached its boundaries, and all the
panorama which its opening disclosed was glowing
in the ruddy glories of these incomparable midnights
of the north. I had sat up on deck all the night
before, and only went to bed in the morning during
our stay at Bodö and part of the crossing of the
channel ; yet here I am again on this bright sunny
night, drowsy and giddy with perpetual staring and
excitement, and yet incapable of sleep. I have seen
many a grand sea-coast, all the best that the Mediterranean can show, but nothing to equal this. A
fellow-passenger, and veteran tourist, who has sailed
all the world over, can remember no rival, unless it
be the Straits of Magellan. From the Seven Sisters
to the north extremity of the Lofòdens, the panorama
maintains this unrivalled magnificence.

In the early part of the day we pass close to the
channel against which the terrible word Maelström
is marked on most of our English maps. Ever since
my first school lessons in geography I have pictured
this place to my mind as a great, whirling, conical
hollow in the waters, like the den of the ant-lion,
near to which no ship dare approach, not even within

many miles. I looked for it on my Norwegian map, but it is not marked there; the rest of the English passengers were equally diligent, but with no better success, though there were three different maps among us and all on a large scale, giving minute details. We peeped at the ship's charts, and could not find it there in the portions that we examined. We then inquired of the captain, a man of much experience in these seas, who told us that all he knew about the Maelström had been communicated to him by his English passengers. He was very satirical, and cruelly hard upon us: he told us that the English had imported a great deal of entertaining knowledge into Norway, amongst which was this information concerning the Maelström; also, that the English patronized the Norwegians very kindly, and showed them how to improve their political institutions, their agricultural operations, and the build of their ships and boats: and among these practical hints and the suggestions he classed the sailing directions for avoiding the Maelström, which had been drawn up by English hydrographers for the benefit of Scandinavian mariners. We had much difficulty in getting at him at all on the matter, he was so impermeably ironical; but the lieutenant was more communicative.

It appears that the Maelström, which we read about, is an unmitigated myth. There are many *mael stroms,* or *bad currents,* hereabouts. Several of the channels between the islands are, in certain concurrent states of the wind and tide, rather dangerous for small craft; and even larger vessels, if not skilfully handled, may be drifted against the rocks. The channel where we mark the Maelström is one of these, but by no means the worst of them; in ordinary states of wind and tide it may be navigated safely in a cock-boat. There is no huge gulfing eddy anywhere hereabouts, and I believe not in any other part of the world. The ancient Greeks and Romans talk of Scylla and Charybdis, but they were a set of lubberly mariners, as the narrative of the voyages of Æneas and the other classic humbugs sufficiently show. No true sailors could have invented such a catalogue of mythical terrors as those feeble coast crawlers believed in. They made more fuss about the small bit of their petty Mediterranean lake which they attempted to navigate, than did the Phœnicians and old Scandinavians about the whole Atlantic. The passage between Scylla and Charybdis is not more perilous than going through the middle arch of Putney bridge against tide: it is just possible to get upset at Putney; but the other channel is so wide and currentless, that the idea of any danger is simply absurd. I have bathed there several times, and, though I swam about in every direction, never found an eddy that could whirl me round. Of course the travels of Æneas, &c., are only the dreams of the poet; but they describe the traditions and terrors of the mariners of the time: otherwise they would have been laughed at when written.

July 11*th*.—On returning to the mainland we seem to come upon a southern climate, though still proceeding farther north. Here are rich verdure, well-cultivated, comfortable-looking farms, and bright, smiling, sunny landscapes, backed with luxuriant woods and frowning crags. The channel from Havnvyk to Dypö, and onward for several miles, presents as fine a combination of luxuriance and grandeur as any of the lakes of Switzerland. This, and the oppressive heat, are quite subversive of one's ordinary notions of the Arctic regions; for we were now above two degrees north of the Arctic Circle. We passed several waterfalls coming from the snow-fields down to the sea: some of them having evidently only a few weeks' existence during the hot summer, which lasts about a month.

The rapidity of Arctic vegetation is here exhibited most wonderfully. The captain and lieutenant assured us that all this luxuriance had come into existence during the last fortnight: that the birch-trees now in full leaf were quite bare only two weeks ago, when they made their last voyage. In a few weeks hence their boughs will be bending under a burthen of new-fallen snow. There is no closing of the blossoms at nightfall here—no vegetable repose—no halting of the upward movement of the sap—but one unceasing development, stimulated throughout by the continuous sunbeams; and then comes the long, long winter's sleep and darkness, when all the vegetable world lies torpid beneath its coverlid of snow, until the next short one-day summer awakens it again to a wild revelry of life and growth.

We pass several fine glaciers to-day, especially in

the neighbourhood of Kastnehaven. The summer was late this year, and the quantity of snow greater than usual at this date; but the weather has been very fine ever since I arrived at Christiania: two or three showers, and one wet night, are all I have seen of bad weather in Norway.

We were disappointed of the midnight sun again to-night: there are high mountains to the northward; but the midnight glow was beautiful as ever.

July 12th.—We reach Tromsö and go ashore. It is a little trading town on an island: "ö" is the Norsk for island, and all places with that termination to their names are islands. It is only by this, or reference to the map, that one can distinguish, when on the spot, the islands from the mainland; all being so much cut up with fjords and channels. There is an English consul here; and it is a matter of etiquette to call upon the consul at such places. This custom, as tourists become more numerous, the consuls will doubtless regard as " more honoured in the breach than in the observance:" it must be already somewhat of a bore; though Mr. Holst was as polite and cordial as though we were the only Englishmen of the season.

Some of my readers may possibly imagine that Her Majesty's representative at Tromsö is a stately idler, lounging in a magnificent mahogany office, duly enveloped in brass rails and red tape, and perpetually reading a very large newspaper. Not so, by any means; dignity and usefulness go together here, as they should all the world through. The

royal standard of Great Britain waves over the door
of a homely wooden shop in the general line, where
the inhabitants buy halfpenny candles and nips of
brandy, and where you may be suited with a pair of
shoes, a Dutch cheese, or a pocket-knife; and you
may buy a horse, a bottle of claret, a bearskin, or
anything in reason, from a full-rigged ship down to
a box of matches. The representative of Great
Britain represents the greatness of Great Britain
fairly and truthfully, by driving a flourishing trade
and thereby benefiting himself and his fellow-crea-
tures around him.

Tromsö consists partly of the Noah's arks, as at
Trondhjem, and partly of some streets of well-sepa-
rated log houses. The Noah's arks, common at all
the coast and island stations in the north, are fish
warehouses—not for fishmonger's fish, but dry fish;
they are barns, where the harvest of stock fish is
stored ready for exportation. Tromsö, I believe,
does a considerable trade with Russia. We—that
is, the English passengers—crossed the water and
walked up a valley opposite the town to a Lapp
encampment, distant about four miles. I have
scarcely ever felt the heat more oppressive than
during this short walk. The mosquitoes were very
troublesome: I say mosquitoes, because it is the
fashion to give that name to every kind of troublesome gnat one encounters out of England, and to no
kind of gnat at home.

We finally reach the Lapp camp, which consisted
of two huts, one containing some goats, the other
being occupied by families of the human species.

H

Besides these huts, or wigwams, there were some
skeleton huts made of sticks, from the ribs of which
various unintelligible articles were suspended.   One
was a baby's cradle, or shell, a kind of elongated egg,
with a hole near one end; inside of this egg the
infant is deposited and closely packed with moss.
There were skin packets, containing snow skates,
and some pulks, or reindeer sledges, and other winter
utilities, now packed up and out of use.

As we approached the huts a small man with a
large supply of ragged red hair, stepped forward a
few yards, and then stood still in the sun and
perspired.   His complexion was of a yellow-ochre
tint, and his features exhibited very decidedly the
leading characteristics of the Mongolian type.

In the hut was another man with dark eyes and
hair, and features less decidedly Mongolian.   There
were some women and children, all sitting on the
ground and all perspiring. It was evident at a glance
that hot weather does not suit these people. Though
by no means corpulent, they have a considerable
amount of superficial fat pretty equally distributed
over the body like the blubber of the cetacea.   It
probably serves the same purposes, protection against
the cold, and a reserve of respiratory food; but in
this hot weather it is a greasy burthen in a state
of oily fusion, visible to the eye and sensible to the
nose.

My first impressions of these Laplanders were
very disagreeable, and I confess that my courage
almost failed me in the matter of entering the hut;
the odour, gloom, and squalor of the place, and the

certainty of many fleas disporting on the floor, made me hesitate upon the threshold and rather peep through the low door than boldly walk in. Some of us did finally venture in, myself among them.

The inmates had no notion of bidding us welcome, and seemed equally free from any sense of intrusion, nor did their faces exhibit any kind of activity beyond that of perspiring.

The hut, which at a distance looks like a stack or mound of peat, is circular, supported by a framework of wooden ribs, all bearing towards each other in the centre, and leaving an open space at the top for the smoke to issue. A rude door closes it; this is so low that one has to bend considerably to enter. The height of the hut at the centre is about 8 feet, and the diameter of the whole edifice about 15 feet. The floor of earth is strewn with twigs of fir and juniper. The fire is on the ground in the centre of the hut, and some arrangements for hanging a pot over it were visible.

The women had their hair parted in the middle and tied in a knot behind, as is common in England. Some wore skin dresses with the fur inside, others a thick woollen material with red and yellow stripes about it. Men and women both seemed to have but a single garment on their bodies, without any under-clothing; and it has somewhat the shape of our overcoats. The legs are protected with a kind of gaiter, and the shoe, or "comargo," is a large and rather handsome affair made of the reindeer skin.

After a while, on becoming familiar with their faces, they appeared less repulsive, and when they awakened into a little animation there was something pleasing in the innocent simplicity of their manner. One woman was almost pretty and might have been quite so, had she been clean, or thereabouts; she had fine black eyes and hair, and when she laughed looked somewhat like an Irish peasant girl.

After being a short time in the hut and accustomed to its gloom and odour, I could easily understand how, amid the snows of an Arctic winter, such a hovel might be an object of strong home affections to its inhabitants; how a sense of warm, dirty, loving snugness might exist among a heap of these little people, when all are huddled together on the floor round the centre fire during the long darkness of their bitter winter-time; and how the Lapp girl, who was married to a Frenchman and lived for many years among the gaieties of Paris, returned to the snows of the fjeld again when her husband died and left her alone in the dreary solitude of a crowded city.

It reminded me of a story told to me by William Chambers, who, after purchasing Glen Ormiston, was much shocked at the manner in which some of the people upon the estate were living. He found the family of a very intelligent working man all living, sleeping, and feeding together in one apartment, without regard to age or sex; he remonstrated, and did more: he built an extra room to their cottage and furnished it comfortably as a sleeping apartment. Three months afterwards he paid them another visit, and was surprised to find that the new room had not been occupied, and on asking why, was answered that it was " mair cheery-like to be a'thegither."

If a philanthropist were to erect improved dwellings for the Laplanders, with more spacious apartments, separated for the sexes, with ventilating
shafts, and mahogany chairs and tables, the little
people would doubtless desert the commodious, well-
ventilated, mahogany-furnished dwelling, and erect
one of their accustomed hovels, where they would
find it "mair cheery-like" to pig together on the
floor in their accustomed huddle of warm domestic
dirtiness.

There were several children about, who were much
better looking than their parents and appeared more
active and intelligent. No reindeer were visible;
they were on the hills among the snows, where they
remain during the hot weather to escape the gnats
that infest the valley. I saw no food of any kind in
the huts. This colony is evidently accustomed to
receive visitors, for they brought out for sale spoons
made of the reindeer horn; they asked half a dollar
or three marks each for them, and sold some at one
mark each. Their bargaining, and all their proceedings, are singularly apathetic: they seem to have
neither cupidity, curiosity, civility, nor incivility,
nor any kind of activity whatever; they are the
most expressionless people I have ever seen.

Note, 1876.—The modern progress of steam communication around the Norwegian coast has cut
away some of the interest of the Arctic journey,
as the Hammerfest and Vadso packets do not cross
to the Lofodens but keep to the mainland coast.
This shortens the journey to the North Cape, but the

sacrifice is serious. Tourists who are well supplied
with time may still see the Lofodens and see them
well by means of the small packets, which in corre-
spondence with what I may call the main-line
steamers, run in between the islands and call at
intermediate mainland stations. The smallness of
these vessels necessarily restricts their passenger
accommodation. For overworked people in need of
brain-rest, and to whom a sea voyage has been pre-
scribed, these inter-Lofoden packets afford an unrivalled means of obtaining bracing sea air, and the
most complete change of all surroundings. Such a
tourist might land at any station and remain there
until the calling of the next packet, fishing, shooting,
rowing, sailing, or basking on the rocks, or all in
turns ; or by the aid of the local fishing boats could
sail about from one island to another through landlocked salt-water channels, where no business letter
or other postal annoyances could possibly reach him.

Tromsö has made wonderful progress since my
first visit. It then had barely 2000 inhabitants.
Now its population exceeds 5000. For further
particulars I must refer to my forthcoming volume,
as I stayed there with the ladies nearly a week, and
therefore became almost naturalized.

I revisited the Lapps in the Tromsdal and found
the family considerably increased. The perspiring
patriarch was still there, but somewhat melted down
and wrinkled. Two additional huts were built to
accommodate his growing family. The old man is
reputed to be very rich. For details of our visits I
must again refer to 'Through Norway with Ladies.'

CHAPTER VI.

The midnight sun — Lapps in their Sunday clothes — Moral and religious character of the Lapps — Drunkenness no longer prevalent — A Lapp aristocrat — Adaptation of the eye to cold climates — Anomaly of climate — Alten — Fashion and gaiety in the Arctic regions — Tariff for refreshments on board the Arctic passenger steampackets, and the kind of food, &c., provided — The northernmost town in the world — Floating colony — *Alfresco* bedrooms — Live dolls — The Fjeld Lapp a considerable capitalist — The Thief Mountain — Wine in the far north — The great meridian line from the Danube to the Arctic Ocean — Migratory movements of the Lapps, and their progress in civilization — Present condition of Hammerfest — Programme of the midnight sun.

Sunday, July 12th, 1856.—LEAVE Tromsö at six in the evening. The scenery of the coast is still very grand and many glaciers are visible. At last we have open sea to the north, intercepted only by the picturesque island of Fuglö, or " Fowl Island," and we see the midnight sun. It is higher than I expected, about four times its apparent diameter above the horizon. At twelve o'clock it stood over the island, which is about 2500 feet high : we try to light cigars and paper with a small lens, but fail, though a few hours previously the experiment was successful. The band of golden glitter upon the sea, stretching from the eye to the horizon beneath the sun, is very beautiful ; but the general effect of the warm subdued light upon the scenery is not so fine as when the sun itself is behind a range of hills.

At the Oxfjord station is a good example of a terminal glacier moraine. It appears like an artificial pile of stones set up to bear the flag-staff which is mounted on its summit. Several Lapps, much better dressed than those we saw at the encampment, were sitting upon the moraine awaiting the steam-packet, and two of them came on board. During the day many other Lapps came on board; they all seemed to be dressed in Sunday clothes, made of coarse woollen material, "*wadmal*," gaily trimmed with red and bright yellow: they wore overcoats and leggings of the same shape as those at the camp. These Lapps were lionized considerably, not only by the English passengers, but also by several of the Norwegian passengers who came from the south. They showed some signs of bashfulness at being thus observed, and were even blushing with confusion when their clothes were examined; this was probably caused in a great measure by the fact that they wore their very best clothes. The first timidity overcome they became more communicative, and showed us the knives in wooden sheaths, which all of them wore attached by a thong of reindeer skin round the waist. They even submitted to be measured, blushing a good deal, and laughing somewhat among themselves. The sailors treated them with patronizing gentleness, patting them on the cheeks and shoulders and lifting them about like dolls: at which they smiled good-humouredly and blushed a little more. They appear to be the gentlest of human beings, child-like in mind as well as in stature. The height of the man we selected as an average specimen was four feet six and a half Danish measure, which is equal to about four feet eight inches English. Most of them were making short journeys; some on their way to church. They are a strictly religious people; not merely a church-going people, but high moral and well-conducted. We were told by the Norwegians on board, who know them well, that the drunkenness which was once common among them has now almost totally disappeared. Most of them can read and write.

There was one who spoke a little English and seemed to be a man of station among his people. He was five feet high and rather proud, objecting decidedly to being made an object of popular curiosity. He came on board at Kaafjord on his way to Bosekop, and was the best dressed of them all; his wife and daughter were almost handsomely dressed; their caps, or bonnets, were quite elegant artistic affairs, fitting close on the top and sides of the head, and rising at the back to a point which bends forward with a graceful curve; this was gaily and tastefully embroidered in many colours. The women's dress is a kind of tunic tied loosely at the waist, and reaching a little below the knees, edged round with a bright yellow or red band, or with a double band of both colours. The trousers, of the same drab or buff colour as the tunic, are tied rudely about the ankle with reindeer thongs; the same thongs tie the " comargo," or shoe, which is as picturesque as the headdress. These shoes, or boots, are made of rein-deer skin with the fur outside; they fit very loosely and reach to the ankles, where, being tied up with the trousers, they effectually keep out the snow; they are ornamented with red and yellow bind-ings, and the toes are turned up like Turkish slippers.

A Quain also came on board. He was about five feet two inches in height, and had a much larger head than the Lapps; his figure was thick-set, with much bone and muscle; he had a sturdy sailor-like bearing, and was evidently a more energetic but less amiable man than the Lapps. His complexion had somewhat of an olive tint, and his features were quite Tartar-like. He sturdily avoided us, and com-pelled us to feel conscious of the impertinence of practical ethnology.

The peculiar obliquity of the eye—or rather of the lower outline of the upper eyelid, which slopes downward to the nose, and forms the strongest typical characteristic of the Mongolian race or variety—was more decided in the Quain than in the Lapps. This peculiarity results from the adaptation of the eyelid to the requirements of an intensely cold climate. The gland, or "tear-pit," in the inner corner of the eye is completely overlapped by the eyelid in the Esquimaux and others of the Mongolian variety of mankind. A corresponding arrangement for the protection of the gland is also found in many of the ruminant animals that inhabit high latitudes.

The Quains are natives of Finland; although many of them have settled in Norway, especially in the vicinity of Kaafjord and the Alten valley. Both Quains and Laplanders are called Finns by the Norwegians: they are sometimes distinguished as Lapp-Finns and Quain-Finns. These Quains, or Esthonians, are usually described as having less of the Tartar countenance than the Lapps; but this was not the case with the one on board, whose physiognomy was more decidedly Tartaric than any Lapp I have seen while in Norway. The Quains are usually taller and more energetic and athletic than the Lapps. Though their dress is similar, their habits are very different; the Quain being an agriculturist, and having a fixed habitation.

The scenery of the banks of the Alten Fjord is curiously summer-like and verdant in many parts; especially upon the Kaafjord, which is the inmost branch of the Alten Fjord. This, combined with a bright sky, a scorching sun, and an atmosphere of a softness suitable for a consumptive patient, renders it difficult to believe oneself in latitude 70°, and nearly 400 miles due north of Tornea. The journey from Alten to Tornea (430 miles by the track), during the whole of which the traveller is proceeding nearly due south, presents the remarkable anomaly of a climate of continually increasing severity as he proceeds southwards. In the winter he travels from the open sea of the Norwegian coast to the head of the frozen Gulf of Bothnia. In the summer the thermometer sometimes rises to 87° in the shade, and in the winter it rarely, if ever, falls below zero, when, in other parts of the globe with the same latitude, mercury freezes. This village of Alten, with its rich pasturages, its high civilization—(largely due to copper mines)—where young ladies play the airs of Verdi's last opera, and expand their skirts to Parisian dimensions, is in about the same latitude as that in which Franklin and his comrades are probably frozen.

We saw the midnight sun again, and an hour after arrived at Hammerfest, the northernmost town in the world. After leaving the Kaafjord the grandeur of the scenery begins to decline; about Hammerfest it is comparatively monotonous and uninteresting.

In order to afford the reader full information of the cost of everything, I append a copy of the steward's account against me for provisions consumed on the way

" Han med yardl bortes."

	D.	M.	S.			D.	M.	S.
1 frokost	0	1	8		2 the	0	0	16
1 the	0	0	8		1 frokost	0	1	8
1 caffee	0	0	12		2 caffee	0	0	20
1 middag	0	2	12		1 middag	0	2	12
1 kal flk. vin	0	1	12		1 aften	0	0	0
1 aften	0	1	6		2 the ..		1	
2 the	0	0	16		1 fl. öl.		1	
1 middag	0	2	12		1 frokost	0	1	8
1 fl. vin	0	3	0		2 the ..	0	0	16
1 aften		1	6		1 middag	0	2	12
2 the ..		0	16		1 aften	0	0	0
1 frokost		1	8		2 the ..		1	
2 the ..		0	16		1 middag			
1 middag		2	12		½ fl. vin ..			
1 aften		1	6					
						7	4	8

The following is a literal translation of the above, in English words and English money ·

" He with the large beard."

	£	s.	d.		£	s.	d.
1 breakfast	0	1	2	Brought forward	0	18	9½
1 tea	0	0	3½	2 teas ..	0	0	7
1 coffee	0	0	5	1 breakfast	0	1	2
1 dinner ..	0	2	3	2 coffees	0	0	9½
½ bottle wine	0	1	4	1 dinner	0	2	3
1 supper	0	1	1	1 supper ..	0	1	1
2 teas	0	0	7	2 teas ..	0	0	7
1 dinner	0	2	3	1 bottle of ale ..	0	0	5
1 bottle wine	0	2	8	1 breakfast	0	1	2
1 supper ..	0	1	1	2 teas ..	0	0	7
2 teas ..	0	0	7	1 dinner ..	0	2	3
1 breakfast	0	1	2	1 supper	0	1	1
2 teas ..	0	0	7	2 teas	0	0	7
1 dinner ..	0	2	3	1 dinner	0	2	3
1 supper ..	0	1	1	½ bottle wine ..	0	1	4
Carried forward	0	18	9½		£1	14	11

This account requires some explanation. First, as to the title of the debtor, " He with the large beard." The steward, not knowing our names, gave us descriptive designations in his ledger. There were five Englishmen on board who were thus described : " He with the red beard," " He with the white beard," " He with the large beard," " He without a beard," and " He with a veil." The two teas which occur so frequently must not be understood as two meals, but as two cups of tea, or of " thé vand," tea-water, as the Norwegians call it. This although offered with the breakfast is charged separately.

The fare from Trondhjem to Hammerfest, by best cabin, was 15 specie-dollars 32 skillings, about 3l. 8s. 2d. English. The passage occupied exactly

six days, including stoppages.   The fare for the
return journey by the same boat was 15 specie-
dollars 27 sk., or 5 sk. less.   This difference is for
the ticket or booking of the passengers.   The charge
for any journey is made according to the mileage,
with an additional charge for the ticket.   This is an
equitable arrangement that our railway companies
might imitate.

Note, 1876.—Three substantial meals are now
served daily on all the coasting packets that have
superseded the old *Constitutione,* at uniform, fixed,
and printed tariff.   The " frokost," or breakfast, the
tariff price for which is 36 skillings = about 1s. 4d.
English, usually consists of one dish of hot fish
and one of meat, handed round by the waiter, besides
sundry shavings of German sausage, pressed meats,
&c., that are freely spread in small dishes upon the
table.   Tea and coffee are also served, but charged
separately at 8 skillings = $3\frac{1}{2}d$. per cup.   The tariff
for dinner is 60 skillings = about 2s. 3d.   It usually
includes soup, fish, two dishes of hot meat, or one of
meat and one of poultry or game ; and a dessert,
consisting of cakes, like our sponge and pound cakes,
almonds and raisins, and the fruit of the season and
locality ; cranberries, bilberries, and molteberries with
cream being the most characteristic.   Besides these
there are the usual shavings in plates on the table,
which is further decorated with growing flowers.
Delicious lobsters are freely supplied, especially
between Bergen and Trondhjem.

The tariff for supper is the same as for breakfast,

which it resembles, excepting that the regulation only promises cold meats. Tea and coffee are served with this also on the same terms. Both at supper and breakfast wine and ale are served, and preferred by many of the passengers.

Coffee is prepared after dinner and brought on deck for those who choose to take it. The wine carte is rather extensive, prices moderate, and the quality, so far as I am able to judge, is good.

It will thus be seen that in spite of " the high price of provisions," the charges remain about the same as twenty years ago, and the table has decidedly improved both as regards cookery and variety.

The fares remain the same, with some advantages in return and family tickets. For full information on this subject see Appendix. ˙

July 14*th*, 1856.—Hammerfest, situated in lat. 70° 40′, is a small town of one street, composed of the usual straggling wooden houses, some of them, however, of considerable size. There appear to be about as many Lapp inhabitants as Norwegians; or, at any rate, quite as many out of doors.

There are two classes of Lapps—the Fjeld Lapp and the Fisher, or Sea-Lapp; the former I have spoken of at Tromsö. The Lapps at Hammerfest are all fishers. Their boats are not larger than the small rowing-boats we have on our coast, and far less strongly built. These are not only their fishing-smacks, but also their family residences; serving them " for kitchen and parlour and all." They live for the most part afloat, their boats moored to the rude

quay; and it is an odd sight to see a row of these
floating families going to bed publicly, in the open
air, on a fine sunny midnight.   After a supper of
dried fish, which they pull to threads with their
fingers, they say their prayers, and then the husband
and wife tuck themselves up together under a reindeer
skin at one end of the boat; the baby, in its " egg,"
is deposited near to them, and the elder children are
concealed somewhere at the other end.   An hour
after, as I walked along the shore when the pairs of
sleeping faces alone were visible, and the silence was
complete, the scene wakened in my mind quaint
reminiscences of childish fancies of dolls'-houses, toy-
boats, Noah's arks, and the little old woman that
lived in a shoe.   The next day, as the little people
walked about in couples, hand-in-hand all so silently
and gently, speaking in a soft murmur if they spoke
at all, and with an expression both in face and gait
of such utter harmlessness and amiability, the idea
of a colony of living dolls was still more strongly
suggested.   From a little distance their dress has a
becoming and rather a gay appearance; the cap, or
bonnet, of the women is quite elegant in form, and
embroidered in many colours, sometimes being inter-
woven with gold and silver thread.   The reindeer
skins, which the fisher Lapps use for bed-covering
and clothing, are obtained from the Fjeld Lapps in
exchange for dried fish.

The Fjeld Lapp is a considerable capitalist, a flock
of 400 reindeer being, according to Mr. Laing, only
sufficient to support a family.   It is said that many
of them possess hoards of buried treasure in the shape

of silver coins, cups, spoons, &c. The captain of the steamer showed us some silver spoons and small silver drinking-cups he bought of a Lapp. The spoons had a very large bowl and a short twisted handle; the cups were ornamented with a rather elaborate pricked pattern; the workmanship of both was very rude, but the metal contained very little alloy. Still, these people are practically in a state of extreme poverty, and sometimes suffer great privations: those who have not enough reindeer to subsist upon combine the avocations of both fjeld and fisher Lapp. The number of Lapps in Norway, according to the census of 1847, was 14,464.

There is considerable variety in the expression of features of the Lapps here: some are very like idiots in feature, and, from the size and form of the head, cannot be far removed from idiotcy in mental capacity; others express considerable intelligence; but, with the exception of the proud five-feet aristocrat on board the steamer, I have seen none who exhibit any considerable amount of energy. They all have small brains, even in proportion to the body; and an expression of extreme gentleness and amiability is common to them all: they appeal to one's sympathies most powerfully.

After visiting the consul, as in duty bound, some of the party making sundry purchases of skins of white bears, silver foxes, &c., we, at the consul's recommendation, ascended a hill, called the Thief Mountain. It is about 1500 feet high, with a good deal of snow upon its sides, which has to be scrambled over with that sort of hard labour usual in ascending steep snow inclines. The heat was most oppressive even on the snow. The mountain commands a good view of the low hills and bluff headlands of the coast; which, however, are not very striking: we are told that the North Cape is to be seen from it, but this I doubt. The island of Mageroe is just visible on the horizon; but as the North Cape forms its northern extremity, it does not seem possible to see it from the south. The ascent of Thief Hill affords a very interesting opportunity of witnessing the effect of altitude on the growth of the birch. The trees at the foot of the hill are in some instances 8 or 10 feet high; but on ascending they gradually diminish to liliputian plants of 6 or 8 inches, though still having the form of mature trees.

We—that is, " He with the white beard," " He with the red beard," " He with the large beard," " He without a beard," and " He with a veil "—breakfast and dine at the chief hotel. Breakfast of tea, salmon, eggs, and cold roast reindeer, for 1 mark 12 skillings, or 1s. 4d. Dinner of salmon, hot roast reindeer, and sweetmeats: the dinner cost 1 mark 15 skillings, or 1s. 6d. each—the wine 1 mark 12 skillings, or 1s. 4d. The reindeer makes a good dish; it is something like beef, but of shorter flavour, and bears about the same relation to beef that our park venison does to mutton. The wine was excellent, and the variety rather astonished us. For the instruction of those who are curious in epicurean statistics, I append a faithful copy of the carte, which for a rude wooden inn within the Arctic Circle, appears rather luxurious:

Prus courant over Olhallens Vine, &tc.

	Per flok.				Per flok.		
	*D.	M.	S.		D.	M.	S.
Champager	1	3	0	Musak Lunel ..	0	3	12
Tokayer	1	3	0	Ditto Picardiu ..			
Lacryma Chiisti	1	1	0	Portvin gammel fiin			
Cap. Constantia	2	2	0	(fine old Port)	1	1	0
Portvin gammel fiin				Chateau Lafitte	1	0	0
(fine old Port)	0	4	0	Chateau Leaville	0	3	8
Madeira, gammel drey				St. Jullien	0	1	16
(old dry Madeira)	1	1	0	Rihnsh viin	1	1	12
Ditto	0	4	0	Haut Sauterne..	0	2	13
Portvin hvid (white				Cherry Cordial	0	3	8
Port)	0	4	0	Sherry, god	0	1	16
Sherry, old	0	3	0	London Brown Stout	0	1	12
Tennerif	0	2	0	Ditto half	0	0	20
Malaga ..	0	2	0	Ale, Edinburgher ..	0	0	20
Chateau Larose	0	4	8	Ol	0	0	8

We met some Englishmen here, and a German artist, Professor Hildebrandt, who had just returned from an excursion to the North Cape. We fraternized, of course, and our party was thereby enlarged.

The heat was surprisingly great, and the musquitoes most annoying. An odour of hot cod-liver pervades the whole of Hammerfest; and if there be any virtue in the vapour of cod-liver oil, this must be a paradise for consumptive patients.

On the outskirts of the town is the termination of the great meridian line of 25° 20', drawn from the Danube, near Rustchuk, to the Arctic Ocean. This is, I believe, the longest meridian line that has been carefully determined. It is marked by an obelisk bearing a globe, with its axis inclined to the sea

* A specie-dollar is worth about 4s. 6d.; a mark, 10½d.; a skilling, rather less than one halfpenny.

surface in the same degree as that of the earth is to
the plane of the ecliptic.   On the base of the obelisk
is the following inscription:

DET NORDLIGE ENDEPUNT
AF DEN MERIDIANBUE PAA 25° 20'
FRA DET NORDLIGE OCEAN TIL DONAU FLODEN
IGJENNEN

NORGE SVERIGE OF RUSLAND
EFTER FORANSTALTNING OF
HANS MAJESTAT KONG

OSCAR I.
OG
KAISERNE

ALEXANDER I.
NICHOLAS I.
VED UAFBRUDT ARBEIDE
FRA 1816 TIL 1852
UDMAALT AF
DE TRE NATIONS GEOMETER.

BREDE 70° 40' 11"·3.

This signifies that there is "the northern termina-
tion of the meridian line of 25° 20' from the Arctic
Ocean to the river Danube, through Norway,
Sweden, and Russia, which after the ordination of
His Majesty King Oscar I., and the Emperors
Alexander I. and Nicholas I., by uninterrupted
labours from 1816 to 1852, was measured by the geo-
meters of the three nations—Latitude, 70° 40' 11"·3."

Note, 1876.—I was rather disappointed when I last
visited Hammerfest on finding only two or three
families of fisher Lapps there, and learned that the
large numbers I saw in 1856 are only to be found
there on occasions of special immigration.   They

sail about in their boats, drop their rude anchor, and go ashore wherever they please as freely and independently as private yachtsmen. We were recompensed, however, by falling upon a great irruption of Fjeld Lapps into Tromsö. The tourist who desires to study these interesting little people must be content to catch them where he can, though he may safely rely upon finding the family in the Tromsdal as long as the old man continues to perspire and breathe. Whether his heirs will remain faithful to the old "gammer" turf hut, I am unable to say.

Sanitary progress is reaching even the Lapps; they are improving in cleanliness. Some of the gammer are now actually furnished with wooden flooring and lined inside and out with wooden planks. This form of sandwich, with turf in the middle and planks on both surfaces, makes an excellent wall for cold climates, the fibrous turf being so bad a conductor of heat.

I am told that in Russian Lapland (Finland) a fusion of races is rapidly taking place. This is also occurring to some extent is Norway, where the "Blandings folk" or half-castes are now a recognized section of the population. In the course of my last visit, I saw a considerable number of puzzling specimens of humanity, especially in fishing boats and on the Arctic coast between Hammerfest and the Russian frontier. They had the high cheek-bones, broad noses, and other Mongolian features of the Lapp, but were of taller stature and stronger build than true Lapps.

Hammerfest does not appear to me to have made

aov visible progress since my first visit, though its present population of two thousand one hundred, as compared with the seventy-seven inhabitants it had in 1801, shows considerable growth during this century. The hotel has certainly degenerated, and tourists who now look for the wine carte, which I copied as a curiosity in 1856, will be disappointed, as I was on the occasion of my revisit. I saw no obviously new buildings in the town, and the old wooden tenements appeared much older and shabbier than when I first saw them. There is, however, one exception to this in the new and luxurious mansion of Mr. Robertson, the veteran British consul, but this is out of town.

The following programme of the midnight sun will be useful to tourists whose time is limited. It includes the elevation due to refraction on the sea horizon, and of course demands such an horizon due north. With this, a day may be gained by ascending about 300 feet.

	The upper edge of the sun is visible from	The half sun is visible from	The whole sun is visible from
At Bodo	May 31 to July 12	June 2 to July 10	June 4 to July 8
Tromso ..	May 18 „ July 25	May 19 „ July 24	May 20 „ July 22
Vardo	May 14 „ July 28	May 16 „ July 27	May 17 „ July 26
Hammerfest	Mav 13 „ July 29	May 14 „ July 28	May 15 „ July 27
„ North Cape	May 11 „ Aug. 1	May 12 „ July 31	May 13 „ July 30

At the North Cape there is, of course, a perfectly free horizon, but *within* the towns named this is not the case. The above, therefore, refers to their vicinity, and to other places in their latitude.

CHAPTER VII.

A cruel defeat and humiliation — The return journey — Glaciers
of the Lyngen Fjord — A public breakfast at Tromso — A second
visit to the Lapp encampment — Moral and religious savages —
Condition of the Laplanders a proof of the high character of the
Norwegians — Snow and sunshine — The English language a
dialect of the Scandinavian — Few, if any, English words derived
from the German — When to see Arctic Norway at its best —
Bodö — The Threnen islands — The ships of the old sea-kings
— Curious change in the tone and colour of the light at midnight — Norwegian table etiquette — A new mission suggested.

July 15th, 1856.—The *Constitutione*, after two days'
stay at Hammerfest, started to return, and our English
party was augmented by Professor Hildebrandt (who
speaks English so well that I at first mistook him
for a Scotchman) and the three Englishmen who
went to the North Cape : they were students from
Cambridge, and immediately on going on board
subjected me to a severe humiliation. I should
here confess that it has hitherto been my habit to
crow over every English tourist I meet on the matter
of travelling economically ; and I had never before
found a successful competitor in this respect. During
a six months' tour in Italy, my whole expenses, including board, lodging, shoes, theatres, cafés, and
all other dissipations, besides fees to cicerone, &c.,
averaged only 18s. per week ; and yet I saw and did
everything that a conscientious tourist who obeys his
Murray is bound to see and to do. Last summer

I made an excursion, starting from London to Dunquerque and Lille, through Belgium by rail; stopping at the principal towns on the way, " doing" the hotels de ville, the churches with their carved pulpits, &c., and the picture galleries; then up the cockney portion of the Rhine, ascending the proper quantity of "fels," castles, and lateral valleys; on from Mayence to Frankfort and Nuremberg by rail; and after enjoying the artistic oddities of that old town, proceeded by rail to Munich, where I spent four days: then by coach to the Tegern-see, and on foot through the Tyrol to Conegliano; by rail to Venice; stayed four days there; and then on foot through Lombardy, visiting some of the principal cities, and the Lago di Garda, Lago d'Isea, the Lake of Como, the Splugen and Via Mala, Gorge of Pffefers, Lake Wallenstadt, and Zurich, and by Basle to the source of the Moselle; down the valley of that river to Nancy; then by rail to Paris and London. This trip occupied six weeks. I started with 15*l.* in my pocket, and brought a few shillings back; yet I visited theatres, concerts, &c., and purchased maps and guide-books besides.

After having performed such exploits, and boasted of them considerably to my fellow-passengers all the way from Trondhjem to Hammerfest, my disgust and humiliation were most intense on finding that the three students had taken deck passage at one-third the fare I was paying: they rolled themselves hardily and bravely under the tarpaulins, and slept among trunks, baskets, and barrels—and Lapps and Norwegians. To be looked down upon by my fellow-countrymen as an effeminate, lounging aristocrat, an inhabitant of sofas, a sensual sitter upon stuffed cushions while there were hard planks within reach, was more than I could patiently bear. I, who banter every friend whom I can catch in the fact of riding in a first-class railway carriage, upon the folly of paying 3s. per hour for the hire of a cushion, to be thus beaten on my own ground was the severest blow my pride could have possibly received. It was a source of great consolation, however, to find that the students did not like their deck passage: they looked very uncomfortable, and went ashore at Bodö under pretence of ascending Sulitelma; but, as I firmly believe, really to wait for the next packet and take saloon passage and claret surreptitiously.

On the return journey from Hammerfest, the sleeping and waking hours should be so divided as to see that part of the coast which was missed during the sleeping time of the last passage. The grand scenery commences again from the entrance to the Oxfjord; where, as before, a party of Lapps were perched on the moraine which supports the flagstaffs. All the stations at which the steamer halts have the Norwegian flag flying. There is, however, no necessity for any such distinguishing mark. Even in a thick mist, a sailor with a keen nose can steer directly to one of these stations at this season of the year, the odour of stewing cod-livers is so decided, and so far diffused from the centre at which it is concentrated.

At about four o'clock on the second morning of

our return journey we pass some remarkable glaciers near to the Havnes station in the Lyngen fjord : one of them very nearly reached the sea. We were near enough to examine them pretty fully, and with the aid of telescopes or opera-glasses to look down the blue *crevasses* which rib the lower parts. They exhibit the whole phenomena of glaciers at one glance : there is the snow field, or *nevé*, above, the source from which the true glacier is derived ; the deep lateral valley narrowing downwards, one of the essential conditions of glacier formation ; then the ice torrent, with its sharp billows and blue chasms filling this valley and carrying with it in its slow descent the blocks of rock forming the moraine, which when deposited at its boundaries will remain to mark its place, though the climate of the whole region should change and the ice and snow all melt away.

July 16*th.*—We made another halt at Tromsö, and all went ashore, proceeding as a matter of course to the principal hotel, the Belle Vue. The house was full—not of provisions—but of guests. We asked for breakfast, and were told by the host that he was very busy and could not give us any. We petitioned for dinner when convenient, and this was refused. We sued for wine or beer, biscuits or fladbröd, or anything digestible or indigestible containing some amount of any of the protein compounds ; but all in vain. We were made to understand that a Norwegian hotel-keeper only proposes to do a limited amount of business, and that nothing will tempt him to exceed that. We then returned to the ship and could get no breakfast there, for it was washing dav—all were engaged in the swabbing of decks and scrubbing of cabins. A little bread and some chips of cheese were at last reluctantly brought, and these we very rashly refused on account of the smallness of the quantity and the grudging with which they were served. We went ashore again, emboldened by hunger, and determined to besiege the town, to force the natives to submission and compel them to supply our wants. We were eight in number, and proceeded first to the general shop of the British consul, where we armed ourselves with bottles of ale and sauterne and lumps of cheese; then to the baker's shop, where we insisted upon loaves of bread, which were brought in ample quantity. We had, of course, neither glasses, plates, knives or forks, nor seats; but each man did his best, with his bottle, his loaf, and lump of cheese; some sitting on the baker's door-step, others standing in the street. Before our meal was finished we had a large congregation of lookers on, consisting of all the little boys of Tromsö and a considerable proportion of the adult population, who silently contemplated our proceedings from the opposite side of the street until the performance concluded, when the little boys expressed their approbation by rapturous applause.

We paid another visit to the Lapp encampment, and ascended the hills above it in the hope of seeing the reindeer, but did not find them. I observed many little things in the hut this time which I did not see before, for we were now received as old friends, with a sort of rude welcome and a more communicative spirit. The *kone*, or wife, had just gathered some wild herbs from the mountain side, which she was cutting up for soup and storing in a bag of reindeer skin. Some *komagers* and other articles of reindeer skin were in course of tanning, being laid in a pan with strips of beech bark. Among the domestic apparatus was a highly civilized copper tea-kettle, besides some other copper vessels, and a pair of ornamental mahogany bellows. The pan in which the shoes were tanning, being made of thick copper, was of some considerable money value. What would an English capitalist say of using copper for the construction of tan-pits? They showed us two vase-shaped silver cups, like common egg-cups, but a little larger, and some silver spoons with large bowls and short twisted handles; these were all of very antique pattern, with ornamental designs rudely pricked upon them.

There was a decidedly pretty girl peeling bark. We had read in many books that the inner bark of trees is used by the Norwegians and the Laplanders for food; but when we asked her whether she was preparing this for food, she seemed as much amused and surprised at the question as any Englishwoman would be. The idea of using such a material was quite new to her; but then she had never read any books of travel, poor thing, and could not be expected to know so much of the manners and customs of northern peoples as we literary and scientific folk. I found similar ignorance prevailing throughout Norway relative to the Scandinavian practice of eating horseflesh.

The more I see of these gentle savages the more I become interested in them. They are quite an anomalous race. Here they live in direct contact with the high civilization of the Norwegians, in free communication and perfect harmony with them. They are converted to Christianity, and from all I can learn have a better claim to the title of Christian than many of our own church and chapel goers; for besides attending to the outward forms of devotion, they illustrate the reality of Christianity by their genuine unostentatious humility, their loving gentleness to each other and their neighbours, their contentment and their disregard of the ambitious struggles, the greed of wealth, and all the pomps and vanities of the civilized world.

It is strange to see a people who can read and write, and who have family prayers morning and evening, still living as nomade pastoral savages; clinging in all particulars to the old habits of their forefathers, clothed in the skins of beasts, and with so much contempt for Manchester, Birmingham, and Sheffield, as to still make their own thread of the sinews of their own reindeer, their needles and pins of the bones, and their spoons of the horns. They are probably the only people in the world who do not use Staffordshire ware, and have not the willow-pattern plate among them. Whatever may have been the moral effect of reading and writing, Christianity, and the example of civilization, their influence on the industrial habits of these people is almost nothing. The brass-nozzled mahogany bellows, and the first-class copper tea-kettle, displayed as we

should display a finely-carved Indian war-club or a
Japanese cabinet, tended only to heighten the contrast between their habits and the modern usages
around them : for it must be remembered that, as
far as the Norwegians are concerned, this arctic
portion of Norway contains some of the most refined,
wealthy, and aristocratic people of the country ; the
traders in fish, who are in continual communication
as merchants with the rest of Europe, especially with
the southern Catholic portions, where the stock fish
is chiefly consumed.

The present condition of these Lapps, their peaceful, undisturbed existence, their freedom at all
periods from persecution or oppression, is a grand
evidence of the high moral character of the Norwegians. I am not aware of any other instance in the
world's history of a people so weak, so helpless for
self-defence, remaining for centuries in contact with
an energetic, civilized, and altogether stronger people,
and never having been attacked, pillaged, enslaved,
or subjected to any interference, except for the
benevolent purposes of intellectual, moral, and
religious education.

The Norwegians have recently converted them
from their strange old paganism, the worship of
Thor, with its conjurations, magical drums, and
sacrifices to the stone effigy of the hammer-bearing
god ; have taught them to read and write, and when
they fell into habits of drunkenness sent apostles
of temperance among them. The efforts of these
temperance missionaries have been highly success-

ful, and the drunkenness so common among the
Laplanders when Mr. Laing resided in Norway in
1834-5-6, is now very rare.

Those who talk about a law of Nature enforcing
with unrelenting fatalism the subjugation and destruction of an inferior race when a superior and more
highly civilized people come in contact with it, should
visit this part of Norway, and study the present relations of the Norwegians to the Laplanders. It may
be imagined that the Lapps have remained unmolested by the·Norwegians because they are so
poor as to be not worth robbing either by legal or
illegal processes. It is true that the fjeld they
occupy is quite valueless for tillage, and almost so
for pasturage; but this is not the case with the
fishing ground. The Fjeld Lapp, as before stated,
is a considerable capitalist, and, like all other capi-
talists, could not exist as such unless protected either
by morality, law, or fighting. A full-grown reindeer
now sells for about three or four dollars. A flock of
400 reindeer being the smallest upon which a Lapp
family can subsist, the average present value of the
property of each family of the pure Fjeld Lapps is
probably not less than 200l.; and this for the most
part in a readily convertible form. It is not an uncommon case for a single family to possess as many
as a thousand reindeer. If the Lapps were a sensual, drunken, or in any way improvident people,
such a state of things could not continue in contact
with open markets, money, and civilization: they
would sell their reindeer to purchase the means of

present indulgence, and rapidly sink into abject poverty and starvation. If there were many sharpers among the Norwegians —" 'cute traders," addicted to " swapping," these poor simple Lapps would long since have been tempted to their ruin.

If I were a Norwegian I should point to the encampments of these peaceful, defenceless little people as the noblest monuments of my country's honour: monuments more worthy of the nation's pride than the trophies of a thousand victories on the battle-field.

July 17th.—Leave Tromsö a little after midnight. As the day advances the weather becomes excessively hot. At its hottest, the thermometer stood at 77° in the saloon, at 92° in the *rök lugar*, or smoking saloon, a little cabin built on deck, and 108° in the sun: on shore, in the valleys, it must doubtless have been much hotter. The contrast of this glaring Italian, or, I might almost say, Brazilian sky, with the snow-clad rocks and glaciers dipping almost to the sea-edge, is very striking. It was a continual source of fresh wonderment ; one of the few scenes to which one does not become accustomed, but retains its novelty day after day.

Among the incidents on board, was a discussion on the relative importance of the study of Latin and Scandinavian as a key to English. My own opinion of the matter is, that the idea of studying any language as a means of understanding another is absurd. Every language has its own special laws and characteristics, and these are best studied in its own classics, and not in those of any other language. It is true that there are certain general laws common to all languages—the laws of thought in their relations to the faculty of speech, but these are not taught by the degrading drudgery of learning by rote the declensions of Latin nouns, the irregularities of Greek verbs, nor the barbarous and obsolete rhythm of Latin hexameters; but by the study of comparative philology, a science demanding the exercise of the reasoning powers, and the aid of a tutor that can do something more than setting and hearing a text-book lesson.

For the practical illustration of these laws, the English language is incomparably superior to either Latin or Greek, inasmuch as it is compounded of so many other languages, and has absorbed the best elements of each. It grows wherever it is planted, by virtue of its inherent fitness to the human mind and its ample fulfilment of all the requirements of thought and feeling; while the stilted Latin has withered everywhere, even on its native soil.

The common plea for the study of the dead languages, that it affords fine mental discipline and elucidates English, is merely an after-thought—a modern invention for propping up the remnants of an old barbarism. Everybody knows, and none better than those who ply this poor apology the most vigorously, that Latin was not originally introduced into our universities for any such purpose, but that its study is merely a remnant of the monkish effort to spread the spiritual dominion of Rome by making the language of old Rome and of the Church the universal medium of intellectual intercourse; an

K

effort which, in the dark ages, was successful, on account of the great advantage of having any common medium of communication between the learned few, then so widely and sparsely diffused over the world. As the Birmingham manufacturers of shoe-buckles and gilt buttons made a loud clamour, and even petitioned princes and parliaments in favour of retaining the fashions which kept up the demand for their commodities; so, in like manner, it is quite natural, and perhaps excusable, that men who have been cruelly condemned to spend their best days in the study of the classics, and who earn their livelihood by teaching them, should argue until they at last convince themselves that these, the only educational commodities they can bring into the market, are the best in existence.

This matter was discussed on board with considerable earnestness, and then came the question whether, assuming that Englishmen require to learn some other language as the basis of their own, this should be Latin or old Norsk. The matter settled down into a convivial wager of a bottle of claret; the proposition asserted on the one side being, that, taking the vocabulary of Norsk words in Murray's *Handbook*, above one-third would prove to have common English words obviously derived from them. On examination, it was found that this was the case with about half the words, and of course the affirmer of the proposition won the wager. The loser, and some of the umpires, thought it probable that the words in that vocabulary might be selected on account of their similarity to English, and another similar wager was made upon the affirmation that if the Danish dictionary be opened at random sixty times, and the first root-word in the page be taken, above twenty of these root-words should have common English words so obviously derived from them as to be admissible by all the umpires: all technical terms and words derived from Latin or French being excluded. This wager was also decided in favour of the affirmer, though it was much a closer run than the former. These experiments, easily repeated, show how nearly our language is allied to the Scandinavian; especially if attention be paid to the kind of words we get from this source. They are our common vulgar words: those which convey the most familiar ideas in the most forcible manner; those which every good writer strives to use as much as possible, and which children first learn and always prefer. Good hearty English is, in fact, a dialect of the old Norsk or Icelandic, as it is sometimes called; the language in which the Sagas are written. German is another dialect; Dutch, Swedish, Danish, and modern Norsk, are others.

During the period between the tenth and fourteenth centuries, England, Ireland, Scotland, Norway, Sweden, and Denmark, must have had a common language; for the Skalds or bards of Iceland visited these countries and there recited or sung their poems, many of which are still extant. Iceland at that period was the literary focus of Europe; her poets travelled from court to court, receiving high honours and rich gifts from princes and warriors, and then retired to their native land.

It must be remembered that these princes and warriors were not literary, book-reading gentlemen, who
could learn a classical language set apart for poetry;
but rude fighters, whose enthusiasm could only be
roused by purely vernacular poetry. The Danes
and Saxons must have spoken the same tongue, or
how could Alfred have sung in the camp of the
Danes, or even have had the exploit put upon him
by tradition? Anything beyond a difference of
dialect would have been sufficient to disable even a
literary man like Alfred from extemporizing poetry.

Without professing to be a philologist, I cannot
help expressing rather a decided opinion upon the
practice of etymologists, who, finding that an English
word closely resembles a German word, state that
the English word is derived from the German. I
do not believe that in the whole vocabulary of
English, twelve words can be found (not of modern
introduction) that have been derived from the
German. The multitude of words resembling the
German do so from having a common origin with
the German; the English and German being separate branches from the same trunk, that trunk being
the old Norsk. I do not, of course, affirm that Ger
man or old English is altogether derived from the
old Norsk; for, of course, we had the Celtic, and
some of the Roman elements introduced at an early
period, while the German has, in like manner, its
other ancient elements. If I might venture upon a
theory, it would be that all we have in common with
the German has been derived from the same source,
but has passed through a different channel. We

have received the Icelandic, or old Norsk, through Norway and Denmark, while it has reached Germany through Sweden; our deviations from the old tongue resemble the Danish, while those of the German are like the Swedish: the Danish words stand midway between ours and the old Norsk, while the Swedish stand in like manner between the old Norsk and German.

July 18*th.*—The grandeur of the Lofodens is considerably diminished on our return to them. The greater part of the snow has melted, and the rocky peaks appear diminished in magnitude, illustrating the effect of snow upon mountain scenery. I should advise those who wish to see this splendid coast to full advantage, to visit it at the beginning of *July*, or even a week earlier. The midnight sun may be seen for a month after the longest day, but every day considerably lessens the quantity of snow. The middle of *June* is rather too early, for then the weather is uncertain and the mists have not yet cleared. When time permits, the best course would be to make the northward journey about the middle of *June*, spend a fortnight about the North Cape, Hammerfest, and Alten, and then return early in *July*. By this means the wondrous rapidity of vegetation, and something of the contrast between the northern winter and summer, might be witnessed; for there is no spring or autumn here, and winter suddenly changes to summer about the middle of *June*.

The sky is remarkably clear during this part of the return voyage, and the grand ranges of mountains

far inland, with vast glaciers and snowy solitudes, are
better displayed than when we passed them before.
The melting of the surface snow is here an advantage,
as it displays the blue ice of the glaciers. The active
business-like proceeding of the steampacket, landing
and embarking passengers and goods at the many
stations on this coast of a country of classical
antiquity, render it difficult to believe that within
sight are hundreds of square miles of ever frozen
solitudes, whose desolation has never been broken by
human footsteps.

July 19*th.*—Near the Arctic Circle we passed a
fleet of " yechts : " not *yachts* by any means, but
quite of different build. They are vessels which
carry the stock fish from the Lofodens and the coast
to Bergen, where they are shipped again for their
southern destinations. These vessels are the most
quaint, antique-looking craft I have ever seen,
having immense breadth of beam with abrupt flat
sterns, and prows standing half as high as the mast.
The fish, besides being stowed below, are piled upon
the deck in a square mass almost as high as the prow
itself. The odour of such a fleet is most remarkable:
I was sleeping as we approached them, and the smell
awakened me long before we reached the outermost
vessel. They are rigged with one large square mainsail,
and a very dumpy topsail over that. They cannot be
much addicted to high speed, but appear quite indif-
ferent to any amount of sea ; and if they struck upon
a rock would probably rebound and go on ahead as
though nothing unusual had happened. The vessels
of the old sea-kings were doubtless such as these : in

ships of scarcely greater tonnage, held together by wooden bolts, without chronometers, quadrants, or even a compass, they crossed the Atlantic, discovered and traded with America, and colonized Greenland more than three hundred years before Columbus was born.

The midnight daylight was the subject of a controversy almost as animated as that on Scandinavian *versus* Latin. I had observed that a perceptible change takes place in the character of the light after midnight; that although the altitude of the sun is the same ten minutes before twelve as ten minutes after, and the amount of light probably the same, there is a perceptible difference in its character, as regards tone and colour, corresponding to the usual difference between evening and morning, sunset and sunrise. I even ventured to affirm that the change commenced at the moment of midnight, the warm tints then beginning to pass gradually into the cooler morning light. Professor Hildebrandt, the artist, agreed with me in this; while one of the English passengers stoutly contested it, maintaining that we were self-deluded : the rest were neutral. I offered to test it by a " crucial " experiment, thus:—I was to abstain from looking at any watch or clock for two or three hours before midnight, and yet to tell by the change of light the moment of midnight, within five minutes one way or other ; the sun being below the horizon or behind the hills. The experiment was tried on three successive nights, each time successfully; this success was most remarkable on the first night, when we were ashore at Bodö. According to

the united testimony of our watches and the ship's
clock, I was twenty minutes wrong; on further
inquiry, however, it appeared that the ship's clock
had not been set since we left Tromsö, which is
nearly five degrees to the west of Bodö, and as I had
proclaimed it midnight twenty minutes before the
clock, I was not above two or three minutes wide of
the true time.

We afterwards found that our friend who so
stoutly denied any difference of tint before and after
midnight, was colour-blind as regards the comple-
mentary colours of red and green: though he had a
keen, piercing sight, he could not distinguish any
difference of colour between the red cover of Murray's
'Handbook to Norway' and the green cover of Bohn's
edition of Forrester's 'Norway.' As the point at
issue was a distinction between delicate tints of red
and gray in the atmosphere, it was not surprising
that he should have been quite unable to perceive it.

During this voyage many opportunities were afforded of observing the habits of the Norwegians.
We had of course some of the upper classes in the
cabin, and there was a bishop and a member of
the Storthing among them. Spitting on the floor
is evidently a common practice in polite society.
Butter, an important article of food, is brought to
table without a separate knife. Each person re-
quiring a slice cuts it with his own knife, leaving
a smear of gravy, or whatever may be upon his
knife, as a contribution for the benefit of the next
comer. The same is the case with the cheese. Salt-
spoons do not appear to have travelled so far north.

These peculiarities may be to some extent attributable to the fact that the *Constitutione* is the worst appointed boat on the service.

We reached Trondhjem on the 21st of July, after an absence of thirteen days.

Note, 1876.—Since the above was published the subject of change of tone and colour of the sky after midnight has been further discussed, the majority of observers confirming my statement. I am not at all surprised that some should question it, for independent of the "personal equation" due to the varying power of perceiving delicate variations of tint, there is another interfering element, viz. the condition of the weather. This subject is further discussed in 'Through Norway with Ladies.'

I am glad to be able to state that the table-service in the packets has greatly improved, and the disagreeable proceedings above described were not observable during my last journey, except in the item of spitting. In this respect our Norwegian primogenitors are as barbarous as our American descendants. My attention was especially directed to this when travelling with ladies, as they were seriously annoyed by it, especially in the cabins of the Arctic steamers, where their fellow passengers lying in their berths converted the cabin floor and cushions into public spittoons, and the Norwegian ladies lacking that precision of aim which is so ambitiously cultivated by the transatlantic tobacco-chewer, the difficulty of finding safe places for bonnets and other articles of dress was very considerable.

To those benevolent people who are devoted to the improvements of others, and have a strong passion for missionary enterprise, I may suggest the organization of a special mission for the free distribution of pocket-handkerchiefs among the Norwegians; but I hereby give notice that should any of the missionaries publish 'Through Norway with Pocket-handkerchiefs' I shall demand a royalty for the copyright of title.

CHAPTER VIII.

On foot again — The pedestrian's advantages — Terraced valleys — Importance of eggs to the tourist — How to converse in a language you have not learned — The Orkedal — Probable centre of the great Scandinavian upheaval — Another explanation of the Torghatten tunnel — Fly-catchers — Tariff of refreshment for man and beast — A battle-field — Physiognomy of the Norwegians — Mercenary tenderness of the Surrendal cows — Norwegian beds and sheep-skin coverlids — I succeed in living within my income at the Quamen station — The beard provocative of refinement — Female despotism — Trout and salmon in the Surrendal.

July 22nd, 1856.—START again on foot and bend my way westward to the Orkedal. Every time I start upon a pedestrian journey I feel a sensation of escaping from imprisonment; for, no matter how free I may have been before, there is a sense of vastly greater freedom, of utter self-reliance, when alone upon my own legs, with a knapsack behind me and an unknown land before. This feeling impels me to step forward with long and eager strides, to revel in the rude, vigorous enjoyment of wild nature. It is under such circumstances that one feels the fact that simple physical existence is a positive pleasure: the mere contraction of the muscles, the inspiration of the sweet mountain air, the circulation of the blood coursing with strong vitality through every artery and vein, are all strong pleasurable sensatio ns It is at such a time as this one feels unutterable pity

for the pallid debauchee, who, by the aid of dainty
cookery and costly wines, and feeble in-door revelry,
makes such painful efforts to experience a wretched
imitation of this genuine and delicious sensuous
enjoyment.

The fortnight on board the steamer and in Trondhjem had been to me a period of effeminate, sloppy
indulgence; but now I cast all this aside and begin
the true enjoyment of travelling.   My breakfast this
morning is a pennyworth of bread, bought in the
town and carried in my pocket till hunger draws it
forth, when I sit upon a stone and eat it: never was
a banquet more delicious.

The first few miles of the route was the same as
that by which I came to Trondhjem from the Dovre
Fjeld; then the road bends over a hill commanding
a fine view of the Guldal (the reader should remember that "dal" means valley, and all places with
names thus ending are valleys) and the valley of the
Nid.   Both of their rivers, the Gula and the Nid,
are seen winding through the terraced banks I have
before described, with groups of farms upon these
small plains, churches here and there, and rich
wooded hills above.   The Lerfosse are marked by
the clouds of spray that hang above them, and one of
the falls itself is visible from a still higher point
of the road.

The similarity of the terraces in both valleys is
remarkable: it is evident that these valleys were
estuaries or fjords up which the sea penetrated,
and that subsequent upheaval of the whole country
has driven the sea back.   If such be the case, all the

valleys hereabouts must present indications of such terraces more or less distinctly marked.

The richness and beauty of these valleys contrast most strikingly and pleasantly with the wild and desolate scenery I have just left.

Several fine views of the Trondhjem Fjord are obtained from different parts of the road, which ascends many hills, and crosses bright sunny valleys that bring down to the fjord small rivers, which spread out into beautiful little lakes at several places; the banks of these lakes being rich alluvial slopes, studded with thriving farms.

I find that my note-book is quite enthusiastic concerning the scenery of this day's walk, but on re-writing I have made some deductions; as on coming upon scenery that contrasts strongly with what has preceded it, or on emerging from town to country, that there is a tendency to overrate the beauties which strike so freshly upon the mind. Had this been the last day of a long walk instead of the first, I should probably have thought much less of the scenery. Anyone who has sailed up the Rhine on the way to Switzerland, and then returned by the same route, must have been struck with the great difference in the impression which the Rhine scenery made upon him on going and returning. The enjoyment of the scenery was heightened by a luncheon on wild strawberries, which grow abundantly on the banks by the road side.

Stop at Bye station; have supper of ham, eggs, and milk, the ham cut into small pieces, the eggs beaten and put into the pan, the ham then added, and all fried together, and served as a sort of larded pancake. All tourists who venture beyond the limits of hotels, who are not utterly dependent on " waiter, chambermaid, and boots," should learn as much as possible concerning the cooking of eggs; they should know how to make omelets of eggs mixed with anything whatever, and more especially with cheese. They should be aware of the fact that albumen coagulates at a temperature of about 180°, or 32° below the boiling point, and becomes tough when heated above that; and therefore that to boil eggs delicately, the best method is to put them in boiling water, and then set the saucepan by the side of the fire for seven or eight minutes, that the eggs may be heated through to about 180°, and not to 212°. Eggs may be usually obtained where no other animal food is to be had, and they have the advantage of being reliably clean inside, even under the most unfavourable circumstances.

Am rather astonished at finding myself able to hold quite a conversation with mine host, especially as I had failed to make myself understood this morning when only asking the way. This was remarkable progress in learning a language, or it would have been if all the difference had depended upon myself; but the host is an intelligent man, while those I met in the morning were not so; and the possibility of making a little knowledge of a language go a long way, mainly depends upon the intelligence of the native who has to interpret the broken passages, and to put his own sentences into the most intelligible form.

The art of conversing fluently in a language which you do not understand is a very valuable one to the tourist : quite as valuable as that of cooking eggs; and having had as much experience in the one as the other, I may venture to give the reader a few rules to be observed, by attention to which this art may be easily acquired. First of all, do not carry a grammar, or if you do, never look at it; for in order to speak the language in a manner to be understood, utter ignorance of its grammar is a primary essential. Secondly, never attempt to ask for anything, or say anything, in the form of a sentence given for the purpose in any of the 'Familiar Conversation' books; and as a general rule avoid as far as possible the use of any sentences whatever   Thus, supposing the subject to be eggs : the grammatical tourist looks to his 'Conversations Lexicon' under that head, and finds a sentence such as this : "Landlord, if your fowls are in a flourishing condition, I shall be supremely obliged if you will do me the very great favour of preparing a few recently deposited eggs for my supper." He reads this from the book, pronouncing every word most incorrectly, and with special emphasis on the prepositions; the poor host is thereby driven to a state of desolation. All this confusion and difficulty may be avoided by stubbornly ignoring all such superfluities as articles, conjunctions, prepositions, and adverbs, and divesting the mind of all scholastic prejudices in favour of number, gender, case, tense, person, mood, and of all false sentiment respecting agreement with nominatives, &c. These impediments being removed, nothing

more is required than to use the words that are
necessary for the expression. of the main ideas;
nouns, verbs, and if quite necessary, adjectives may
be used, but you must studiously avoid all merely
connecting words that only express the relations of
words. By this means, and by taking especial care
that each idea before it is expressed shall be mentally
clear and definite, with a sharp outline and no meta-
phorical blurr or shading, nor envelopment in verbal
fog, you may speak any European language without
suffering the degrading drudgery of learning it. A
dictionary and a knowledge of the special phonetic
value of the alphabet is of course demanded. The
smallest obtainable dictionary is the best.

A preliminary rehearsal is necessary at first. You
are approaching a station or hostelry of any kind and
require supper and bed. Sit down by the road side
and think over what you intend to ask for. Pick
out from the dictionary all the nouns and verbs
required, pencil them down on a slip of paper as
your vocabulary *pro tem.*, and prearrange how you
will use them. After doing this you will have acquired a small stock of words, and just those that
will be needed again. At your next effort you will
learn a few more, and so on. *If alone* and compelled
to use the language of the country, your progress
will astonish yourself.

Many very expensively educated persons may
experience considerable difficulty in thus finding
clear and definite ideas before expressing them;
their intellects having been drugged with languages
rather than fed with ideas, they have acquired the

poisonous habit of attaching ideas to words, instead of words to ideas; their thoughts run blindly in certain phraseological grooves; words are necessary to the development of their ideas, which are tuned mechanically to the jingle of sentences.

To such people a definite idea standing out clearly before the mind in its simple nakedness has existed only in the forgotten experiences of childhood; and if many of their most cherished notions were thus stripped of the thickly-padded clothing of words, in which alone they have ever seen them, the proprietors might be shocked at their naked deformity. To many learned persons, therefore, the speaking of a language before being able to make it into sentences will be a valuable corrective exercise in unchaining the mind from the slavish trammels of phraseological despotism.

Mine host informs me that English tourists are not in the habit of taking this route, and that none have passed this way for twelve months before; but that a Scotch Englishman who manages the copper-mines at Orkedal resides there.

This (23rd July) day's journey up the Orkedal is similar to that just described. The Orkla Elv winds through a rich, terraced valley; the level of the upper terrace remaining constant, its height above the river diminishes as the valley is ascended. The walls of these terraces are in some parts nearly perpendicular, and are evidently the cuttings made by the river which flows at the foot of their precipitous slopes. It appears that all the valleys opening into the sea at this part of Norway are alike in this respect, and thus afford evidence of an upheaval of the whole of this region to a height of about 500 or 600 feet. This lifting of the mountains and their sea-filled valleys has occurred at what geologists call a recent period; probably at about the time when Cheapside, St. Paul's Church-yard, Belgravia, and all the rest of the land on which the world's metropolis now stands, formed the bed of a quiet lake; when England, Scotland, and Wales were one cluster of small islands, and Ireland another; and when the soil out of which the plodding peasantry of France are now extracting the sweet juices that we sip in claret and champagne, was being deposited under the waters of a shallow sea.

Whether it was the same great heaving of the earth that lifted the Alps from a moderate elevation to their present towering heights—that raised sea-shells to the summit of Mont Pilatus, and formed the Righi and the Rossberg out of the cemented pebbles of a shingle beach—that carried upwards with it all the sloping plains of France, and united our scattered archipelago into the two islands; or whether there was another independent centre of upheaval for the north, which exerted its greatest energy at Iceland, and then lifted the sea-bottom to the surface with such sharp and violent action as to crack the earth's crust and pour out the volcanic matter of which are formed the Snaefel Jokul, Hecla, the Sulphur Mountains, &c.—in fact, the whole of Iceland—I cannot venture to say; though it does appear the most probable supposition that the north had its independent centre of upheaval, and that was somewhere about Iceland; for the traces of Scandinavian upheaval are the most distinct at the north-western portion of Norway; they are greatest at about that part facing Iceland, and the rising appears to come from that direction.

It has appeared to me, while writing the above, that a different theory from the one on page 76 may be given in explanation of the formation of the mysterious Torghatten tunnel. It is well known and easily understood that when a rock is washed by the sea-waves it is liable to be worn away; that if the rock is of varying composition as regards hardness, the soft parts wear away the most rapidly; and thus when a hard rock is traversed by a vein of softer rock, the sea washes out that vein and thereby cuts a little cove or gully, or excavates a cavern : or if the veined rock be lofty and surrounded by water, the vein is washed out to the height of the highest beating of the waves, and a tunnel or a natural bridge is formed.

We have abundant examples of this sort of action on our own coasts ; especially on the Cornish coast, about the Lizard Point, where the rocks are composed of serpentine, veined with soft soapstone and other magnesian rocks of similar character. That fairies' playground, Kynance Cove, is a most romantic example of this kind. All who have visited Tenby know St. Katherine's rock, which at high tide is St. Katherine's island, and at low tide is beset by fair huntresses, armed, not with Diana's bow, but with hammers and chisels and indiarubber goloshes, intent upon dislodging the dianthus, niveas, venustas,

roseas, and other aquarian treasures.   This island is
perforated by a lofty cavern or tunnel, partly washed
out by the waves, and partly formed by the falling
of the undermined rock; a tunnel which has a
remarkable resemblance to that of Torghatten, with
the exception that it is not so large, and its floor is
the sea-beach; but if St. Katherine's island were
magnified, carried farther out to sea, and then up-
raised some 600 feet, another Torghatten would be
formed.

My explanation of Torghatten tunnel, therefore,
is that when the whole northern coast of Scandinavia was some 600 feet below its present level,
Torghatten was of course similarly lower; that
the floor of this tunnel was then washed by the low-
tide waves; that waves of previous centuries had,
aided by other agencies, such as frost and the gravitation of overhanging masses, formed this tunnel as
an ordinary sea cavern, and the great upheaval had
raised it to its present place.   If this supposition be
correct, the beating waves will have left traces of
their action round about the island at the tunnel's
level.   Had I thought of this when upon the spot, I
should have made an effort to go ashore and examine
the tunnel, of which we have only such vague
descriptions.

Note, 1876.—Since this was written the tunnel
has been carefully examined and measured.   The
measurements are stated on page 75.   These, so far
as they go, are confirmatory of my explanation of its
origin, which I am told was adopted by the explorers;

but I have not yet been able to obtain a copy of their report. The original tunnel appears to have been considerably modified by subsequent falling of fragments of rock from the roof, which is still subject to such disintegration, and the floor of the cavern is covered with débris.

1856.—The Orkedal is a warm and sunny valley in the summer season, and by no means suggestive of the far north. The little lake in which I took my bath to-day was at one end quite carpeted with water-lilies; its beauty being suggestive of many a pattern for our carpet makers. The blue dragon-flies were fluttering over the surface of the water, laying their eggs, and making the most of their short life in the air, while their ferocious larvæ below were devouring everything within reach. On the banks there were growing in great profusion two species * of those curious plants, the *Droseræ*, or sun-dew, their leaves bristled over with the gluey hairs, upon which small flies were struggling or lying dead. Botanists are still puzzled to decide whether these plants, and their southern relatives, the *Dionæ*, or Venus flytrap, really catch the flies to feed on them, or whether they merely perform the functions of the " catch-'em-alive " papers that abound in London at the same season.

At the stations hereabouts a printed placard is placed upon the walls of the travellers' room, in which

* One, the *Drosera rotundifolia*; the other having a long oval or nearly lanceolate leaf with a long footstalk, and whose specific name I am not acquainted with.

is stated the regulation price of various requirements. As this is rather interesting, I have made a copy of it, and the following is a literal translation :

TARIFF.

For Lodging, Provisions, &c., at the Inns ("giestgivergaard," literally lodging-giver-farms) of the South Trondhjem District.

	£	s.	d.
For a chamber with bed for one night *or day*	0	0	4½
Ditto, with ditto for servant	0	0	2¾
"Warming-up" a chamber and lighting with two candles per ditto	0	0	4½
One portion of hot meat, with bread and butter	0	0	5½
Two portions ditto ditto	0	0	9
A portion—slice of bread and butter, with cheese, meat, or a " pair " of eggs	0	0	3½
A large cup of coffee, with cream and sugar ..	0	0	2¾
A small cup ditto ditto	0	0	2
A large cup of tea-water with cream and sugar	0	0	2¼
A small cup ditto ditto	0	0	1½
A *spolkom* of ale (about a pint)	0	0	1½
One ditto of sweet milk	0	0	1
One bottle of ale	0	0	2¾
One *bog* (a book or quire) of hay	0	1	0½
A " botte " of chaff	0	0	1½
A feed of hay	0	0	1½
Stabling and attendance for one horse per night or day	0	0	2¼

Soudre Trondhjems Amt,
    20th June, 1855.   K. ARNTZEN.

July 24*th*.—The Orkedal continues beautiful to the end, and the road passes over a fjeld into the Surrendal. The weather is painfully hot to-day; and I was rather surprised at seeing a lizard: one of the small olive-coloured species that are so abundant on the field boundary walls and dusty roads in Italy.

I passed over a battle-field hereabouts where thousands of the slain (ants) were stretched in death, some headless, some bereft of limbs, and others cut in half. This is the third time in the course of my pedestrian experience (the other two were in Switzerland and Italy) that I have found about a hundred yards of the road strewn with bodies, and fragments of bodies, of ants. I suspect that they resemble human beings, even in the matter of making great wars; for it is difficult otherwise to account for such scenes, where the evidences of violent death are so abundant and the victims have not been eaten by their destroyers.

In the Surrendal there are terraces again; and as this valley has its outlet farther south, in the fjord on which is Christiansand, it affords evidence of the extent of the upheaval.

The people I have seen since leaving Trondhjem are remarkable for their clear complexions, blue eyes, fine square foreheads, and highly developed coronal region of the brain; all characteristics of the best type of the Northmen. There was less uniformity of physiognomy on the way from Christiania to Trondhjem than in these valleys, and still less among those who came on board the packet; where, indeed, the variety was very considerable. I observed there on the coast a considerable number of men of a very remarkable type, having extremely large and low heads, indicating great intellectual and animal energy, but only moderate controlling moral power. Such men go on well when they have pretty much their own way, and are not surrounded with very strong temptations, but are terrible when thwarted or tempted to evil enterprise : they are like the grizzly bear, a heavy quiet beast when undisturbed, but horribly ferocious if wounded. I fancied that these might be the descendants of the fierce sea-kings, to whom danger was delight, and who helped themselves so freely to whatever was left near the coast by any of the other inhabitants of Europe.

Here in the Orkedal and Surrendal, not one of these bull-headed men was visible; none but the mild, high-headed family.

The horses in the Orkedal and Surrendal are very fine animals, larger than those of the Guldbrandsdal and Dovre Fjeld. The cows are remarkably inquisitive ; they followed me along the road, peeped into my knapsack and pockets, and licked my shoulders and back. The horses exhibited a similar docility. This tameness and absence of fear among the cattle is a safe indication of a kindly disposition of the people.

In my original notes is a long paragraph overflowing with sentimental tenderness relative to these affectionate cows, that have followed and overwhelmed me with such loving licks; but I do not transcribe it, as upon further reflection it is evident that the licking was mere cupboard love; for all the cattle in inland and especially mountainous districts, have a strong propensity for salt, and these were merely licking the deposits from the sea spray that had fallen on my clothes during the recent voyage. The discovery of this explanation of their licking was mortifying to my feelings : man wishes to be loved for himself alone, and the spontaneous manifestations of these pastoral, unsophisticated cows seemed at last to respond to the heart's fond yearnings; but, alas! even the cows of Surrendal were licking me for the salt I carried.

I stopped for the night at the Quamen station, where I had supper of the fine deep-coloured trout fried in a lake of butter. Having finished the first bowl of milk and called for another, the hostess brought me a bucket of beer, very turbid and green, like the water of an ill-conditioned aquarium. I tasted it, of course, and tried to drink it, but failed. It may have been made from the *moltebeer*, a red three-lobed berry that grows wild upon the hills; but it tasted like an infusion of hay, salted.

At the other end of the bench on which I had my supper, the farmer, or " bonder," and his " housemen " were taking theirs; it consisted of a dark-coloured stiff porridge, made apparently of rye meal, dabbed on a board, and had the colour, consistence, and appearance of Roman cement. The party were ranged round the board, each having a bowl of milk, some fladbród, and a wooden spoon, with which he dug out a lump of cement.

My bed was of the genuine native Norwegian construction, an oblong box standing on four legs by the side of the supper bench, and filled with straw; over the straw a sort of blanket or rather rug, a canvas sheet above this, and a sheepskin for covering. I have no objection to this sort of bed when it is well made, and even prefer straw to feathers, if the straw be well laid and fresh; rough sheets, also, are better than smooth; and a sheepskin properly prepared, with the wool well cleaned, is the most luxurious of coverlids; but this remark does not apply to recent sheepskins that still retain the odour of a neglected butcher's shop.

July 25*th.*—Breakfast on the remains of my supper, which is left on the wooden bench by the bedside, and another bowl of milk. The charge for supper, bed, and breakfast is 5 skillings, $2\frac{1}{4}d$. Of course I demand particulars, and find that the lodging is 2 skillings, and the food 3 skillings.

Quamen is beyond the South Trondhjem district, and therefore the above-quoted tariff does not apply here.

I have had many curious experiences of moderate hotel bills, but this surpasses all. Once in Italy I had a supper of macaroni, stewed rabbit, salad, bread, cheese, and wine, and this with my night's lodging cost $4\frac{1}{2}d$.: the lodging cost 2 soldi, or $\frac{3}{4}d$., the wine $\frac{3}{4}d$. more, and the banquet 3*d*. There was abundance, and the charges were made on the most equitable principle; for the meat, the bread, and the cheese were weighed in their dishes before they were put on the table, and weighed afterwards; the loss of weight being charged to the consumer: a clean cloth was laid, and a neatly folded napkin provided.

I may mention, for the information of refined and fastidious people who regard the unshaven beard as a coarse institution, that I have observed that the practice of using table napkins among the poorer classes is exclusively confined to the countries where the beard or moustache is worn. The table napkin is parent to many other refinements: for example, the method before alluded to of cleaning knives and spoons by sucking them is less likely to be popular where napkins are at hand and abundant; neither is the hostess or the servant so strongly tempted to wipe plates, &c., with the corner of a dirty apron, or, failing that, with the skirt of a dress or petticoat: practices by no means unknown to the British Isles.

The people of the Surrendal appear to be all of the same family, they resemble each other so closely in feature. They are evidently poor, and the farms are small and indifferently cultivated. I am beginning to find that Mr. Laing's description of the comforts and well-being of the Norwegian peasantry is rather rose-coloured.

Smoked salmon is one of the commonest articles of food in all the valleys through which large rivers flow; it is invariably eaten raw, and the difficulty of breaking through this custom and getting it cooked is immense. At Honstadt, where I dined to-day, 'raw smoked salmon was brought to me, and I very diffidently suggested to the hostess that I should prefer it fried a little. She would listen to nothing of the kind, and told me many times over that it was *rökd* (smoked), that she liked it *rökd* without frying, and her husband liked it the same; and she intimated that if I did not like what she and her husband and other people did, I must be a disreputable character. This sort of despotism is common to women of all nations, and its universal existence is my main argument against strong-minded women who advocate a female House of Commons.

There are several pretty waterfalls in the Sur-

rendal formed by the tributary torrents that pour
into the river. The trout and salmon are very
abundant: I saw them darting about in the water
and leaping at the falls. This must be a very paradise for anglers; but it appears that anglers are
spoiled in Norway. He who in England would be
in ecstasies at catching ("killing," I believe, is the
proper word) a score or two of trout, averaging a
pound weight each, looks with contempt on such
small fry when here in Norway: anything under a
20-lb. salmon is considered "slow" and cockneyish.

CHAPTER IX.

The rich man's debt of courtesy to the poor man — Boating on the fjords — A storm — Luxurious quarters — Haymaking — An attempt at extortion — Outside piety and its usual accompaniments — The farmers' carts — A startled nightingale — The Norwegian *Ranz de vaches* — A corner of the earth unvisited by Englishmen — The Romsdals Fjord — Veblungsnaes — Preparations for royalty — The glories of the Romsdal — The Mongefoss — Model glaciers and avalanches — The traces of ancient glaciers and avalanches probably confounded by geologists — Gammel Ost — The Vermedals Foss — A recent development of travelling facilities in this part of Norway — Projected and authorized railways.

1856.—AT Surrendalsören I tasted some of the troubles to which vulgar tourists are exposed, for this being the port station of the fjord, my pedestrian independence ceased, and I had to go up and down, begging and waiting for a boat and a couple of boatmen; for these, like hotel keepers and all other people in Norway whose services are to be paid for, seem to make a principle of convincing you that the obligation is on the side of the person receiving the services, not of him who receives the wages: and there can be no doubt that they are in the right in most cases, especially where the employer is much richer than the servant.

Thus, let us suppose the case of a professional man who has an income of 1000*l.* a year, or say 3*l.* per day, which is about 6*s.* per hour for a working

day of ten hours: he employs a labourer, and pays
him 6s. for two days' work; or, otherwise stated,
he gives the produce of his one hour's work in
exchange for twenty hours of the labourer's. It is,
of course, true, that, owing to the superior skill
and intelligence of the professional man, his one
hour's work is equal in value to the twenty hours
of the unskilled labourer: that is, when we regard
it, as we must, from a commercial point of view;
but when we look upon this bargain through the
gentler sentiments of our moral nature, we must feel
that the rich man's great advantages call for a
compensating effort of courtesy and kindness to
balance the account; for each man, if he is honest
in his work, strives all the while to do his best—
the labourer strives for twenty hours, the more
fortunately educated but for one; there is, therefore, a balance of nineteen hours of moral effort,
or striving to benefit, in favour of the labourer,
which demands, at least, the payment of moral
acknowledgment.

All that we experience of class animosities and
democratic discontent is nothing more than the
instinctive effort of the labourer to obtain the
settlement of this balance, and if it were justly
and universally paid all such bitterness would soon
be at an end. I have put the case of the professional man who earns 3l. per day. How much
more strongly must it apply when the advantage
comes by inheritance—when the rich man receives,
without any material effort on his part, such showers
of good offices from his fellow-men, who feed, and

clothe, and lodge him; who till his land, and devote their utmost skill to surround him with elegance and luxury! Truely the rich man who is not kind and courteous, and thoughtful of the feelings of his less-favoured fellow-men, is the most ungrateful animal that lives : for even the caged tiger is gentle to the attendant who brings his daily food.

I know of nothing more luxurious than a boat ride after some days' walking. Any kind of riding is enjoyable then ; but to lie down in the stern of a boat that is gliding over smooth water, and to revel in beautiful scenery without any effort, when the muscles are capable of positively enjoying repose, is the most enjoyable of all. My destination was the Bolsaet station, about two Norsk miles from the starting point. The first half of the journey is along the narrow arm of the fjord which runs up into the Surrendal, then out into the main fjord, and across another and wider branch. While in the Surrendal Fjord we kept close to the precipitous rocks with which the richly-wooded mountains that dip into the fjord terminate. The scenery is fine throughout. I had hesitated whether to walk along the shore for the first Norsk mile to a small station marked on the map, and did not regret taking the boat upon seeing the sort of ground I must have gone over. It would have been, not a walk, but a scramble and a struggle through a pathless and precipitous pine forest : the seven English miles would have cost at least seven hours of severe toil.

The luxurious lounging before spoken of was only of about two hours' duration, for a storm arose just as we commenced crossing the wide part of the fjord; the rain poured heavily, and the wind ahead rendered all our best efforts at the oar necessary to make any headway at all. I was surprised at the manner in which so small and light a boat could weather such a sea; the short sharp waves were breaking continually, but she shipped scarcely any.

These boats are cunningly built: the thin strip of bulwark slopes outwards, instead of rising perpendicularly, so that a breaking sea catches them underneath; they jump at it, but scarcely any water comes over. Nevertheless, had I been alone in such a walnut-shell, I should have prepared for swimming and run for the nearest shore; but seeing that the boatmen kept their course without any uneasiness, I of course was satisfied that all was safe. After some three hours more of hard pulling, we got across, and landed at about midnight; then I found that Bolsaet is merely a boathouse and some cowsheds, and that Baekkan, or Bekken, near Thingvold, the station for sleeping, is four miles farther on. This was not altogether unwelcome news, for, the rain having ceased, such a walk I knew by old experience to be about sufficient for the purpose of clothes-drying.

The road passes across a wild and desolate moor, with a few stumps of spectral trees that start up here and there out of the misty semi-darkness; for now the nights are just beginning. At about 1 A.M. I reached quite a charming villa, that I could not have ventured to suppose to be a station but for the well-displayed sign. I knocked, and waited

awhile, when two young ladies — I am using no
hyperbole, no complimentary phrase of mere for-
mality, when I say two ELEGANT young ladies —
bade me, with the best-bred politeness, to enter, and
showed me to a well-furnished room. There was
nothing of the wooden, peasant farmhouse character
about anything; and I rubbed my eyes to be sure
that I had not fallen asleep on the wild moor, or
been enchanted by the spectral stumps. A supper
of veal and milk, with real wheaten bread, served
with courtly politeness by the elegant ladies, was of
so decidedly material and solid a character as to
convince me that it must be reality.

My bedroom was not a straw and sheepskin affair,
but quite an elegant apartment, containing a tent
bed with lace curtains, and a stuffed eider-down
tumble-off cushion coverlid; such as you have on
your bed at night, and pick off the floor in the
morning, in Germany.

I felt the want of a few phrases on this occasion,
in order to apologize properly for disturbing these
young ladies at so late an hour; for, to be candid, I
must confess that my method of conversing in an
unknown tongue works better in rural than in polite
society.

July 26th.—Coffee brought to my bedside, as at
the Guldbrandsdal, with the addition of white biscuits; and afterwards a breakfast of veal and tea,
with wheaten bread again, which I had not seen
since leaving Trondhjem. At breakfast the courtly
attendance of the two elegant young ladies was
repeated; there was a servant, but the ladies only

waited at the table. It is the old Norwegian custom, that the lady of the house, or her daughters, of whatever rank, •shall wait upon the guest: this is the very climax and perfection of hospitality, though rather embarrassing to an Englishman, who feels it his duty to attend upon the ladies. The contrast with my last night's lodgings at Quamen was very curious and amusing.

Crossing another branch of the fjord to Angvik, I walked for some miles through the rain over a dreary moor. The people here make hay, not only while the sun shines, but in the midst of the rain: they place a long rail on a series of legs about 6 feet high, a sort of hay-horse, and throw the grass or hay across it; evidently to keep it from soaking on the swampy ground.

At the station of Haegheim I encountered the first example I have met with in Norway of an attempt at petty imposition. I called for a bowl of milk, for which the hostess demanded 4 skillings, or nearly twopence; the usual charge being 2 skillings, and sometimes only one. I threw 2 skillings on the table, and looked fierce; the woman picked up the 2 skillings and slunk away to the adjoining room, where a lazy-looking man was sitting; a grumbling dialogue followed, from which, and the physiognomy of both, I inferred that the poor woman was honestly disposed, but her husband forced her to overcharge the guests. On leaving the house, I observed written over the door in conspicuous letters some proverb or motto about fearing God. I have unhappily found it a rule, without any exception, and applicable in all countries, that people who parade their religion outside, and set up pious sign-posts in their actions or conversation, are mean, selfish, and dishonest.

On reaching the Fanne Fjord grand scenery recommences. The apparent uplifting of the coast into the air, referred to at page 85, was very strikingly exhibited about the promontory on which Molde stands.

At the Lönsaet station, where I stopped, I met a very intelligent Norwegian who spoke English, and who gave me many useful hints as to my future route. Among other things he told me of a waterfall which he considered the finest in Norway, but of which no mention is made by Murray or in the 'Road-book' published by Bohn: it is the Skiggedal Foss, which I determine to visit if possible. At this station there were German beds again, and in the morning café au *lay*, as a wretched punster calls it.

July 27th.—I started by boat again, and crossing the Fanne Fjord, walked over the isthmus from Dvergsnaes to Söllesnaes. It is a flat country, an alluvial deposit, partly moorland and partly pastoral. At one part, the road, after an abrupt turn, comes in a line with a broad grassy avenue of remarkably park-like character. Far away in the distance I heard a melody so wild and shrill that it seemed scarcely possible to be produced by human voice; but after walking about half a mile along the green avenue, I came upon the singer, a girl, who, amidst a community of happy ruminating cows, was lying down and warbling most wonderfully. Her face was

M 2

turned away from me, and as my steps were noiseless
upon the soft grass, I came quite near to her, and
lying down, remained unheard and unseen, listening
to her singing. The old Greeks, who understood
such matters very well, represent the sirens with
sweet voices as well as pretty faces, and tell us that
their voices were the most potent with their victims.
They were right : there is a wonderful fascination in
the tones of certain voices, and this was one of them.
I fell into a most romantic and sentimental mood,
without seeing the face of the sweet warbler. She
sang a kind of *ranz de vaches;* but the " yodl " was
much wilder, more shrill and rapid than any I have
heard in Switzerland ; the sudden breaking from the
lightly-touched contralto notes into the piercing liquid
falsetto, was marvellous for sweetness and rapidity
some of these falsetto notes seemed to me higher than
any I had ever heard produced by the human voice.
Unhappily, before ten minutes had passed since I
had listened thus at leisure, she turned her head and
saw me. In an instant, she sprang upon her feet,
and bounded like a startled hare into the wood hard
by. She disappeared entirely, hidden by the tall
stems of the pine •trees. I waited for some time,
hoping that she might take courage and return ; for
I felt that it would be too impertinent to follow her.
But she continued invisible—did not even peep
from her hiding place ; so I walked mournfully and
slowly away, looking back very often ; but the cows
were ruminating all alone, and no more " yodling "
was heard. I wished for riches and leisure, that I
might linger hereabouts, and learn where she lived

and all about her, make her acquaintance, and then
employ great masters to cultivate her voice and teach
her all the mysteries of music.   I cannot say whether
she was pretty, though I feel morally certain that she
must have been.   I only saw that she had large,
bright eyes, which seemed to flash with terror as she
started up, and that her figure was slight, as she
bounded into the wood.

Soon after this, I arrived at the little cottage station of Sollesnaes, where the hostess, a simple woman,
on learning that I am an Englishman stepped back
a short distance to examine me at full length, then
called her husband and two children to look at the
" Engelsk "; and they examined my hat, boots, and
knapsack, with intense interest.   It is really refreshing to find a corner of the earth unvisited by Englishmen.   I doubt whether even a Scotchman has been
here within the memory of a generation; for the very
few visitors who come down the Surrendal and over
to the Fanne Fjord, all go, of course, to Molde, the
great town of the district, and proceed from thence
to the Romsdal.   I am no lover of great towns, and
usually skip them, unless Murray imperatively insists
upon their lions.

The little promontory I had just crossed is " nobody's way to nowhere."   With the host and his son,
I rowed across the fjord to Alfarnes.   The boat was
smaller and slighter than any in which I have yet
crossed a fjord, and a squall arose, more vigorous than
the one I before experienced.   The water did come
over the sloping bulwark this time, and the little boy,
who pulled bravely for above an hour, began to cry

with fear; not, however, until after catching a dozen
or so of "crabs," and tumbling each time over the
seat.   It is very difficult to row among these sharp
short waves, and I found my hands severely blistered
and bleeding at the journey's end.   The poor man
only demanded 16 skillings for his two or three hours'
hard work, and the boat had to be taken back again.
In such a case, the value of the small stock of fish-
hooks, artificial flies, needles, steel pens, and pencil-
cases I had brought with me, was proved; a present
of a few of these things being received with immense
delight.   I should advise all tourists who propose
penetrating to the less-frequented parts of Norway
to carry a few such portable trifles.   On the main
highways, the coin of the realm is the best; but in
such places as this, a little present, which is not a
mere business payment, but a friendly offering of
gratitude and good-will, is estimated far beyond its
uttermost value.

Note, 1876.—Since 1856 commercial travellers
have carried Birmingham and Redditch goods so
completely throughout Norway that such presents
have lost their value.   The best modern substitutes
for them are portraits of Queen Victoria in the shape
of *new* English silver coins.   These are very accept-
able, as presents from Englishmen, and will generally
be treasured as keepsakes, or worn as ornaments.

1856.—My dinner at the station where we landed
was a thorough Norwegian repast, consisting of the
Roman cement, with butter, and some sour curd.   I

now learn the reason of that strange sweeping motion of the hand and the stretching out the spoon at arm's length, which I have observed to be the universal habit of the people when eating this compound : it is because the curd, being a sort of new cheese, draws out into strings, which otherwise would fall upon one's clothes. No charge was made for this, and when I offered 8 skillings, about $3\frac{1}{2}d.$, the woman of the house was amazed at my prodigality, and thanked me most cordially by the expressive Norwegian mode of shaking, or rather squeezing, hands.

After this crossing of the water, came another crossing of the land—an isthmus like the last; but the road now skirts a narrow branch of the fjord, studded with rich wooded islands, and backed by the purple and snow-patched mountains of the Romsdal. The landlocked termination of the fjord forms one of the most beautiful lakes I have ever seen; a splendid subject for a picture. Crossing the Romsdals Fjord, which well deserves its fame for stern and rocky grandeur, I found that Veblungsnaes is not merely a single farm station, but an actual wooden village of forty or fifty houses, with a real hotel. I made my way to the principal apartment of this hotel, which was furnished in a most reckless manner, with real mahogany chairs, French-polished, big table, and little tables, and sofa of the same, with horsehair cushions, and a carpet.

July 28th — Veblungsnaes is the port of the Romsdal, the most famous of all the valleys of Norway. The Norwegians are proud of it; it is pictured in the 'Christiania Illustrated News'; they make special excursions from all other parts of the country to visit it, and every Englishman is told whatever else he misses he must see this, and his expectations are raised to the highest. Such vaunting heraldry of scenic fame is a severe trial to any place: it is like making a man mayor for the third time; unless really great merits are possessed, criticism is sure to be ruinously severe.

This day's journey has proved, however, that the Romsdal can safely bear this terrible ordeal of much-repeated praise. It throws its gauntlet of defiance even at the feet of the mighty Alps; it combines in one valley so many of the elements of savage grandeur. It is more like Glencoe than any of the valleys of Switzerland, but on a very much grander scale, with snow and ice and countless waterfalls superadded. Not only in the physical aspect of its dark, frowning rocks, but in the gloomy record of slaughter does it resemble Glencoe; being closely associated with the story of the 900 Scotchmen who landed at Veblungsnaes, marched up this valley, were surprised, and all but two slain. When I started, the conical peaks of the mountains were buried in threatening clouds, then came a storm of rain and hail, then the body of the clouds dissolved, leaving only some ragged fragments of white mist, which clung about the torrent gullies of the mountain sides and then slowly melted into sunshine. All the torrents and cascades were at work and doing their utmost. Every kind of waterfall is here —from the rapids and roaring leaps of the Rauma, which runs through the bottom of the valley, to

Staubbachs innumerable, Giessbachs, Reichenbachs, twin Handecks—representatives, in fact, of every type of waterfall, and rivals to the grandest of some of them.

On the left side of the valley as I ascended, the Romsdals Horn, a mountain of extraordinary steepness, springs out of the valley up to a height of about 4000 feet, like a monstrous shattered steeple; and a labyrinth of similar ragged cones is near to it. Farther on a mighty wall of rock rises directly from the road, till its notched and rugged edge seems to scrape the blue sky. This wall varies from 1000 to 2000 feet in height. In some parts of it great scars are visible, where huge masses have scaled off and thundered down; these fragments may be seen below, cumbering the river-bed, and forcing its waters to roar and foam through the alleys between them. The course of the road has been turned to wind round such blocks; and in some places the blocks themselves have been blasted, and the road cut fairly through them. Above these blocks an overhanging cornice may usually be seen, with a scar below it from which the block was detached. The heap of massive ruins below, the scar a thousand or two feet above, and the cornice overhanging the scar, have a tendency to prevent the observant pedestrian from selecting these otherwise tempting boulders for resting places or sketching seats, for in spite of calculable probabilities, the idea that another crash is just about to occur is irresistibly suggested.

To enumerate the waterfalls of the Romsdal would

be rather a serious task; there are a dozen or two that would each support half-a-dozen hotels, and be perpetually sketched, photographed, and stereoscoped, if they were anywhere up the Rhine. If they were in Scotland, in addition to all this there would be lodges built opposite to them, with mirrors to show the waterfall overhead and all round the room at once, and sliding panels to start open and disclose the view unexpectedly. In Ireland there would be a score of gates on the roads leading to them, erected for the sole purpose of supporting juvenile mendicants, who would rush to shut them as the tourist loomed above the horizon, in order to be paid for opening them when he approached. But here they pour and dash down their own chosen courses, the wild, unfettered creatures of God's bounty. Here we may gaze upon them undisturbed, and revel in the wonder, gratitude, and veneration that such a scene awakens, by reminding us that He has so fitted our faculties to His works around, that every object or action in the universe has in it some element of grandeur or of beauty capable of filling our souls with joy. There are those who tell us that this world is a festering heap of wickedness and corruption; but true and wholesome religion tells us that the man who would fit himself for the reception of a higher manifestation of his Creator's bounty in another world, must first train his soul to be capable and worthy of fully enjoying the heavenly elements of this.

The most abundant and characteristic waterfalls of the Romsdal are those which come from an unknown source somewhere, and pour over the grand rock on the left. The finest of these is situated about half-way between the Flatmark and Horgheim stations: it is called the Mongefoss. Looking up, with an effort that strains the neck, to the frowning wall of rock, a torrent is seen, pouring apparently out of the blue ether. It bends smoothly over the topmost edge, as blue as the sky itself, lustrous and crystalline with the light that shines clear through it; then it is lost, having made a first plunge of a hundred feet or so down into a boiling cauldron, which it has pounded out of the rock by its everlasting thumps; but again it reappears, shattered to snowy fragments, and striking the rock once more, spreads out and tears down a long, rugged slope, in white fleeces of broken water. At every resisting ledge, clouds of fine spray and mist are dashed forth; the sunlight tinting them here and there with bands of the glorious iris. Then a great ledge bars its path, and it bounds upwards and forwards into the free air; and thus bruised and battered to mere water-dust, so fine and light that it struggles even with the slight resistance of the air, it descends with slow, unvarying speed, some 400 or 500 feet more: then it showers upon another slope of rock, spreads into a multitude of little rills and disappears again, till at last it rushes under the road to join the Rauma, and keep its company to the all-absorbing sea.

This fall, to my taste, is finer than the Staubbach: it does not shoot forward clear of the rock in one leap; but its beauty is rather increased by this.

Both in height and quantity of water it is far superior to the Staubbach. Omitting the first fall into the upper basin, and only considering that portion which is seen falling down the face of the rock in a continuous mass of broken water, it must be somewhere about a thousand feet in height.

I am aware of the difficulty of judging the relative merits of waterfalls—especially such falls as these—for they depend so much upon the circumstances of the weather. Doubtless, I saw the falls of the Romsdal under their most favourable aspects, so much rain having recently fallen; but this is no rare case, for, according to current report concerning the meteorology of the mouth of the Romsdal, it rains there on an average somewhere about always.

Note, 1876.—A second visit to the Romsdal confirms all my first enthusiastic impressions of its indescribable magnificence.

I leave the figures of my original estimates of the elevations to prove that there was the opposite of exaggeration in my description, and now give some of these as recently measured.

The Romsdals Horn rises to 5090 feet above the sea, or about 4690 feet above the valley at its foot. The wall on the left side rises in some places to nearly 4000 feet above the road. This is the case where the Mongefoss pitches over the wall of the Mongejura, the unseen summit of which is 5000 feet above the valley.

The Dontefoss and some other minor falls have a visible descent of more than 3000 feet.

1856.—In nearly all the breaks and hollows of the dark precipitous rocks are patches of snow, some of them so low as almost to touch the cornfields: for amidst all this savage sublimity there are rich substantial farms. These farms are due to the table-lands of the terraces, of which there are two very distinctly marked, but not so lofty as those in the other valleys before mentioned.

Beside the snow patches there are liliputian glaciers in abundance, where the whole history of glacier formation is shown at a glance. There are the snow fields above, filling a basin from which dark peaks arise; the basin has a downward opening, or notch, leading to a little steep, trough-like valley, that closes in below. In the upper basin the snow surface is thawed by the sun, the water sinks into the spongy mass below, freezes again on its way, and binds it altogether as a seeming solid, but capable of yielding to the pressure of the mass above and the expansion of re-freezing; this pressure forces it through the notch of the upper basin into the lower. As it passes over the bend from the lesser to the greater declivity, it is split upon its surface by the bending, and the blue crevices are formed. In squeezing so forcibly through the notch it polishes the rock forming its sides, and the fragments of stone that are torn away or fall upon the ice become bedded into it, and when they reach the portion that slides upon the rock, they groove it with parallel lines that will mark the places where these glaciers have been, if in future ages they should cease to exist.

There are other snow basins which fail to form true glaciers, owing to the want of the trough-like valley below that closes in at its lower part. Yet in these there is evidently a downward flow, or advancement of the ice and snow which is forced through the notch; but. this notch communicating with a long straight trough like a water gully, the foremost of the advancing mass bends over till it becomes detached, and then forms an avalanche instead of a glacier. Several of these small avalanches came down during my walk: I mistook the first for a water cascade, until its cessation, and the thundering rumble which followed, undeceived me.

In these I found an explanation of the snow patches nearly level with the cornfields; for each of the avalanches deposits itself as a sort of talus, or sloping delta-shaped heap, at about that part of the terrace which must have been the shore of the ancient fjord. All these avalanche tracks are smoothed by the falling snow and ice and stones; they are probably scratched and grooved likewise, but this I cannot positively affirm, as they were on the opposite side of the river.

I am not aware that the attention of geologists has been directed to this sort of avalanche action, as distinguished from glacier action. In our own country, and in almost every part of Europe, traces of ancient glaciers are found, or supposed to be found. These traces consist of smoothed rocks with parallel scratches, and heaps of stones that have come from some distance, and yet present no traces of being water-worn. The smoothing and grooving are attributed to the slow-moving ice, and the heaps are supposed to be the moraines, or the stony accumulations commonly found at the sides and terminations of glaciers.

Now here we have side by side with these small model glaciers as many small model avalanches, each with a regularly established track. If all the snows of the Romsdal hills were melted, I have little doubt that a modern geologist would confound the avalanche with the glacier tracks; he would find smoothed and grooved rocks on both, and a heap of angular stones at the termination of the smoothed rock. These would, according to received views, be regarded as the beds of former glaciers, and the remaining terminal moraine.

In this valley the confusion would not lead to any serious speculative error, for the difference in the causes producing either a glacier or an avalanche in this particular locality is so small—merely the form of the trough—that general conclusions respecting former climate would not be affected by the mistake. But there are cases where the distinction between the former existence of glaciers or avalanches would materially affect a grand hypothesis. It is inferred from the indications alluded to, that there existed what is called a glacial epoch, when the greater part of Europe, or even of this hemisphere, was subject to a much colder climate; and if all the observed smoothing, and groovings, and heaps were produced by glaciers, it must have been so; for in order to produce a glacier there must be snow remaining through-

out both winter and summer. If, however, these
markings are but the vestiges of avalanches, a very
small difference of climate may account for them;
as regular periodical avalanches may be produced by
the winter snow of any hilly country, though that
snow should be all melted away by the heat of each
returning summer. Among the causes capable of
bringing about such a result, surface configuration
is a more potent one than climate.

My dinner at the Horgheim station consisted of
"smoerogbröd" and "gammel ost," bread and butter
and old cheese: charge 8 skillings, or $3\frac{1}{2}d$. The
gammel ost is a celebrated Norwegian dish, and this
at Horgheim the finest example of it I have met with.
It is a peculiar sort of cheese, made, I believe, with
goat's milk mixed with herbs and sugar. When new
it is very detestable, but after many years' keeping
it decomposes, and forms a sort of condiment rather
than food. It is sprinkled in a moist powder, upon
bread and butter. When in perfection, it is neither
mouldy, moist, nor mitey; it is of a uniform pale
brick colour, just capable of crumbling, and has a
rich anchovy-pastish flavour with a faint suggestion
of parmesan. If Fortnum and Mason, or Crosse and
Blackwell, were to import some of this, put it into
eccentric jars, and charge a sufficiently high price for
it, our epicures would run into ecstasies about it
until they discovered it to be the cheap food of poor
peasants.

I stop at Ormein station, opposite to which is the
Vermedals Foss, a fine triple fall with a large quantity of water and of moderate height. It further

differs from the characteristic Romsdal falls by rushing over a moderate slope which is richly wooded, instead of pitching down a bare precipice.

July 28th.—Raining again. The character of the valley now changes; the road ascends and passes along the slope of a hill; the river is far below in a deep gorge, instead of being nearly level with the road as at first, and begins to make cascades itself. One of these, about a quarter of a mile from the station, is sufficiently fine to tempt me down the path to see it even here, where one becomes so dainty and critical concerning waterfalls.

At the next station, Nystuen, there was a large assemblage of the peasantry from all the country round waiting to see the Crown Prince, who was hourly expected here in the course of a tour through the country. They were dressed in their best, the men with fresh clean red nightcaps, and the women with bright kerchiefs round their heads: all along the road I found family groups standing by the wayside. The horses were waiting at this station, where the whole party was to make a relay. A little beyond the station I met the *cortège*, which consisted of about a dozen carrioles and one leather-looking gig or chaise, in which the Prince was driving.

Note, 1876.—My route between Trondhjem and the Romsdal bv the Orkedal, Surrendal, and that broken ground across the branching fjords and tongues of land between Surrendalsören and Veblungsnaes, was a very unusual, almost untried, route for English tourists at that time; but since the publication of 'Through Norway with a Knapsack,' many have followed it, and therefore pedestrians must not now expect to astonish the natives nor to obtain supper, bed, and breakfast for $2\frac{1}{4}d.$, even at Quamen station. The carriole road is good throughout the Orkedal and Surrendal, and the stations have developed considerably.

Still greater changes are in prospect; the Royal Commission of 1875 having authorized a line of railway to run along these valleys wherein I met not a single tourist, and where none had preceded me during twelve months before. This branch will leave the main line from Trondhjem to Christiania at Melhus, there cross the Gula, and follow almost exactly the course of my walk. The main line portion to Melhus is already finished; the Orkedal branch is to be commenced in 1884, and completed to Surrendalsören in 1888. These are the dates as laid down in the general project for the whole system of Norwegian railways, but I shall not be at all surprised to find these and other dates considerably anticipated in consequence of the success which I believe will follow the opening of the first portions of the system.

I have met several tourists who have traversed the Orkedal and Surrendal, and all speak most admiringly of the scenery. These valleys cannot fail to develop still further as a popular route between Trondhjem and the Romsdal, though few are likely to go over my walk between Surrendalsören and Veblungsnaes, as the facilities now afforded by the steam navigation of the fjords reduce the whole journey to a few hours' voyage. In 1856 there were no steamers on any of these fjords.　One had been started on the Sogne Fjord, but was abandoned as unprofitable.　Now they are plying on all the important waters of Norway.

Even the Romsdal itself will presently be invaded by the locomotive.　The projected line commences on the coast at Aalesund, will thread its way over a curiously peninsular and broken stretch of land, amid many fjord-mouths in very amphibious fashion, passing Oskog and Svilte, then coasting the Romdals Fjord to Veblungsnaes, and proceeding up the Romsdal over the watershed between it and the Guldbrandsdal (at Lesjevand, the reputed lake of two outlets), then along the Guldbrandsdal to Lillehammer.　The line from Lillehammer to Veblungsnaes is to be commenced this year and finished in 1883; that between Veblungsnaes and Aalesund to commence in 1884 and finish in 1887.

CHAPTER X.

Lost on the fjeld — False alarm — The "Cock of the Mountain"
— Risks of solitary mountaineering — Out for the night — Hard
work on an empty stomach — Difficulty, delusion, and disappointment — Semi-starvation and its effects — The pastor of
Lom — The social position and influence of the Norwegian
clergy — The "pocket-pistol" a dangerous weapon — How to
cross the Kjolen Fjeld.

July 29th, 1856.—I PURPOSED starting this morning
from Molmen station, where I slept, and cross the
Kjolen Fjeld to Skeaker, but a continuous drizzling
rain, and a thick mist hanging on the hills, induced
me to follow the advice of my host, an intelligent
man, who urged me very earnestly not to attempt
it under such circumstances.

I therefore make a short day's walk through comparatively tame scenery to Hoset station, from which
there is another track over the fjeld.

July 30th.—Start at about 7 A.M., and make my
first attempt to cross a roadless Norwegian fjeld
without companion, and with no other guide than
map and compass.

After crossing the river, climbing the slope, and
passing over a plain of reindeer moss, I walked up a
long wild wooded valley and reached some huts, or
saeters, rather sooner than I anticipated from the
position they have on the map, according to which

the track over the fjeld here turns off to the left. I
crossed a bridge just erected, and found a track
taking nearly the course required. It was but an
ill-defined one, and after awhile it vanished completely on a wild rolling moorland, over which I
then steered by compass alone. After a few miles
of this, I reached a ridge of mountains, and ascended
one of them to take a general survey, in the hope of
seeing on the other side a lake which is marked on
the map, and which would serve to verify my
bearings. The lake, or rather a pair of twin lakes
are there, but I was beyond their western extremity,
instead of being at their east end or beyond it, as I
had calculated. This was very puzzling, and I lost
confidence in my map—not in myself of course.
Only those who have wandered alone over trackless
mountains can understand the painful feeling of
having relied upon a map, and then finding it deceit-
ful; it is like being jilted after a long and confident
courtship. The sense of doubt and confusion, the
hesitation as to whether to consult the map any
more, or, if consulting it, to look for details, or only
to rely on general bearings, is indescribably perplexing and vexatious. I had started with perfect
confidence, the track seeming so clear: during the
first half of the distance it followed a little rivulet,
at the Loordalen saeters it turned at right angles,
and over a ridge to a lake, and then over another to
the long valley of the Vaage Vand. There seemed
no possibility of mistake, so that I did not even take
the common precaution of filling my pockets with
food, and on passing the saeters made no halt for

milk; though my breakfast had been only a few chips of fladbröd and some "*smoer*," pronounced "smear," a good expressive English name for Norwegian butter.

After a halt, and considerable hesitation between choosing the east or the west end of the lakes, I determined upon taking a middle course, and crossing the stream that unites them. Even this was some miles to the westward, down a steep stony slope, then through a wilderness of bog, to the wide pool-like stream about 3 feet deep with soft bog at the bottom. After this I found, still farther to the east, a little valley forming an outlet to the easternmost of the twin lakes. This, according to my map, or the reading I then made of the map, should lead at once to the Vaage Vand, and nearly to Skeaker. I pushed on at a rapid pace, over rough boulders with deep holes between, with the object not only of speed, but of drying my clothes, which were wet to the shoulders; for the crossing of the stream was half wading, half swimming, with great difficulty in keeping my knapsack above water. Another motive to exertion was the pang of hunger, for being now about four o'clock in the afternoon the idea of dinner-time was irresistibly suggested.

During this walk I had an adventure or two. At one time, while admiring the utter desolation of the whole district, and concluding that hereabouts must be the summer home of the few remaining bears and wolves that occasionally visit the farmers of the Romsdal, a huge beast sprung up at my feet so suddenly, and with such fearful rustle, that all the bones of my skeleton seemed loosened in their fleshy imbedment by the start I made. It was not a bear, however, but merely a huge capercailzie, or "cock of the mountain," or "horse of the woods," as it is called. According to the usual accounts of this bird, it is so wild and wary that the sportsman has great difficulty in approaching it, but this started so close to me, that I must almost have trodden upon it. It appeared larger than a turkey, with huge wings and tail; and the noise it made in rising was tremendous: a bear would have been far less startling at first sight. These birds are, I believe, quite extinct in Britain, though formerly abundant in the wilder regions of the Scottish Highlands.

I should not advise other tourists to venture alone over a fjeld like this; for, independently of the danger of losing the way, and being overtaken by the mists, there is a considerable risk of sprained ankles, when the path is lost. The slopes of the hills are covered with loose angular stones, heaped together several layers thick, with deep holes between them. To cross such ground as this, it is necessary to step carefully, but firmly, upon the angular summits of these blocks; some practice is required to keep one's balance and to do this safely, as the stones are often loose, and they rock, or even turn over, when trodden on. When they do thus turn, a fall is almost inevitable; grazed knuckles and bruised knees and shins follow as a matter of course; but if the foot should slip down one of these crooked holes, and the whole weight of the body pitch upon it, a sprained ankle or a broken leg is

quite to be anticipated. Such a mishap is bad
enough under any circumstances; but here, where
no human being comes within hail for months together, to crawl for miles and miles over broken
rock and bog, dragging a dangling limb, and,
after hours of struggling agony, to faint and die in
the wilderness without one farewell word or glance
of sympathy, would be worse than being shot down
and galloped over on a battle-field, where you go in
for that sort of thing and are paid for it.

I know of how little avail are all these prudent
reflections, when the fresh mountain air is blowing
in one's face and the early day is wakening, when a
reckless self-reliance is engendered, and all thoughts
of possible suffering and weakness are driven out by
the sense of iron strength that the purified blood
carries with it to every limb.   These influences, and
the prospect of a vigorous battle with exciting
obstacles, tempt one's footsteps from the dusty
road to the crisp springing heather and the wild
craggy mountain peaks.   I never start upon a
walk in a mountainous country without making
sage resolutions to be most cautious; but all these
wise resolves are broken before half the journey is
done.

On this occasion, I soon found that I had got into
something like a scrape; for, on reaching the end
of the little valley, or gorge, it was evident that it
did not lead to the Vaage Vand, with a church
upon its banks, as marked in my map, but to a long
dreary valley with a small stream winding through

it, having no lake nor any traces of humanity. It now became evident that I had gone altogether wrong ; and the possibility that it might be myself, as well as the map, that made the mistake, was suggested, but not without an inward struggle ; for we all have our weaknesses and vanities, and one of mine is that I am a skilful mountaineer, and can find my way without guides over the wildest and most difficult of passable passes. I have done it often in the Swiss and Tyrolese Alps, even where glaciers stand in the way, and the limits of the snow-line have to be passed, and but seldom made any serious blunder. It therefore wounded my pride most terribly to be almost forced to the conelusion that I had gone about 10 miles too far east ; for at such a distance from the proper track there are marked upon the map two lakes, connected by a stream just corresponding to that with the soft bottom that I had waded through ; the easternmost of these lakes having an outlet running down a narrow valley just in the direction of that I was following ; this stream is tributary to another, winding through a long valley, that looks dreary even on the map, though it has one farm marked at its eastern end, some ten miles farther, and beyond the limits of my vision. This farm is called Skard-vangen. My theory now is, that the saeters at which I arrived so much sooner than I expected, were not the Loordalen saeters marked in mv map, but some others there omitted ; that I turned off too soon, and that all the easting I made to get round the lakes was so much additional aberration.*

According to this, I was now, at five o'clock P.M., about as far from my destination as I supposed I was when at the saeters at ten in the morning, with the disadvantage of having no track to follow, and an unknown amount of difficulties and obstacles to overcome; for a range of mountains of considerable elevation still lay between me and the Vaage Vand. I continued southward, finding a faint track, then passed some cows which all followed me, and jostled each other for the privilege of licking my hands, or my hat or shoulders. They evidently mistook me for their milkman, and expected their evening treat of salt. Finally, we—that is, I and the cows— reached a little saeter, a wretched hovel, filled with dirty men and a most abominable odour, vile enough to annihilate a fourteen hours' appetite.

They told me that my way was along a lofty ridge, which was visible in the far distance, running nearly east and west. It was about nine o'clock, and the sun just setting; for this being the 1st of August, the sunny nights are past.

* This proved to be the fact, as I afterwards ascertained by inspecting Muuck's map, where every farm and saeter is marked, and the configuration of the hills and valleys carefully given. I could not have made the blunder if I had had that map. Mine was only a road map—very good of its kind, but not sufficient for such solitary mountain wanderings. In Muuck's map the saeter and the side track crossing the river by which I was first led astray are both marked, the saeter by a dot, and the track by a thin line proceeding towards Gardmo. The twin lakes, whose boggy ligament I crossed, form the Roko Sjo, shown as two distinct lakes in some maps and united in others.

Just before meeting the cows, I was much surprised at a bird of a light gray colour, and rather larger than a grouse, which ran before at a few yards' distance uttering a curious scream. At first, I thought I must be near its nest, and that this was a device to draw me away, such as some birds will attempt; but it continued running before me, proving that it could not be so. Being desperately hungry, and having no prospect of supper, I took out my small revolver to shoot at it, and when just about doing so, I saw the explanation of its conduct. A large falcon, or small eagle, was wheeling round heavily over my head, and the poor frightened bird at my feet was seeking protection. To have shot it would have been like murdering a child ; so I fired every barrel at the dark enemy above, and succeeded in frightening him away.

After ascending to the first ridge, I found the track, which soon led to another valley, and from thence up the side of another mountain to a higher ridge. The night was now sufficiently dark to render it very difficult to keep the track : as long as it continued on rocky ground it was easy enough, the angles of the stones being white where the lichen had been worn away by the feet; but whenever it broke upon a patch of reindeer moss, it was so far obliterated as to be no longer traceable. I had to cross such patches continually, and then to zigzag to the right and left till I came upon the stony track. This added considerably to the distance, which was computed by the men at the saeter as four or five hours' walk. At one spot, where a large moor had to be crossed, I wandered aside for above half an hour, being misled by a heap of stones which I supposed to be a track-beacon, such things being common hereabouts. It is erected for this purpose, but it marks another track which led me quite away from my course.* Being now in a prudent state of mind, I turned back to the point at which I lost the track and went on zigzag till I again found it. I toiled on thus over angular blocks, through bogs, and across small streams, with mist and some rain, for about six hours; when, a little after daybreak, I reached another ridge, from which the Vaage Vand and the Otta were at last visible.

The lake is of considerable size, some twenty-five to thirty miles long. I was at a great height above it, probably 2000 feet, and the descent very steep. Seen through the morning mist and my expectations, the lake appeared to terminate at the point directly below me, and the river there to begin, and continue onwards to the right through a long, flat, shingle valley. As the church and the station where I hoped to find some food are marked in the map at about the junction of the river with the lake, I determined to make a direct descent down the steep slope, which, being thickly wooded, could be safely descended by clinging to the stems and branches of the trees, and swinging down from one to the other. Having been twenty hours without food or rest, I

---

* The track I followed is on the south side of the Finna and the Huna Sjo. On Waligorski's and Wergland's map it is marked on the N. side. The heap of stones referred to was at the head of the lake, and the path I came upon bent round it.

found the requisite exertion very severe; I was faint
and giddy, made false steps, and missed my hold
occasionally: every such slip brought out a bath of
cool perspiration on my forehead, and seemed to jolt
all the viscera of my system; but the prospect of
food and lodging below urged me onward in my
staggering scramble. At last I emerged from the
wood upon an open slope of loose sliding drift, and
saw below me a good road and, to my amazement,
the lake continuing to the right for many miles;
for what I had supposed to be a valley of shingles,
with the river in the middle, was the body of the
lake. I am at a loss whether to attribute this
illusion to the ripple of the lake reflecting the north-
eastern daylight, and thus appearing like pebbles,
or to an uncertainty of vision resulting from long
fasting and fatigue.

I saw the spire of the church far away to the
right, near where the valley seems to close, about
five miles distant. This was a terrible shock to my
empty stomach; but gathering up the remnants of
my strength, I slid on my heels down the loose slope,
with a rattling accompaniment of the surrounding
stones, came upon the road at last, and walked on
till I reached the end of the lake, and the church.

There were some houses in the valley, at one of
which I made inquiries, and learnt that the station
is close by the church. Feeling quite assured that
food and rest were at hand, I did not even ask for a
bowl of milk at the house where I inquired; but
upon reaching the church, with the station standing
visibly near it, as described, I found a broad and

rapid river between us, and the bridge a mile farther down, so that there were two more miles to walk, and the bridge to cross. This was the last straw upon the camel's back, and almost broke me down. Although I had been scrambling, and climbing, and struggling, rather than walking, for nearly twenty-four hours, and had taken neither food nor rest, I felt no sense of muscular fatigue, but a terrible giddiness, that made me reel and stagger along the road like a drunkard. When I reached the bridge, which was paved with planks having some spaces between them, the running water below seemed to carry away with it all my remaining senses. I fell down in a sort of semi-conscious reeling swoon, and remained lying on the planks until the giddiness somewhat abated. I then managed to get up, and staggered on at a rapid pace to the station. It is a poor place, but inhabited by kind people who appeared rather surprised and alarmed at my appearance and at what I managed to tell them of my journey. They brought bacon, fladbröd, and milk. I only proposed to eat very little, but found myself unable to take any solid whatever; so, after a draught of milk, I went to bed, and slept soundly for about four hours.

On awaking, I found a stout gentleman sitting at my bedside. He was the pastor of Lom. A Norwegian pastor is not merely a preacher; he is clergyman, physician, magistrate, arbitrator, and general friend and father, to whom all his scattered parishioners appeal. In a country where there are none but peasant farmers—no aristocracy, no gentry, no towns or villages, no shopkeepers, no professional class—a highly educated man must be strangely isolated, and, unless endowed with the true spirit of Christian benevolence, must be one of the most miserable of men; but, if suited to his work, he may be one of the happiest, for his opportunities of doing unmistakable good, and of witnessing the full fruits of his good deeds, are almost unlimited. Most of these Norwegian pastors are, I believe, excellent men, and render great services to the people around.

In the present instance, the paternal relations of the good pastor of Lom were illustrated in my case, for he sat at my bedside, where he had evidently been watching for some time, as though he feared that some fever or other ailment might result from the over-exertion, excitement, and fasting; for the farmer had told him how far I had come, and how I staggered into the house, and sat down greedily to eat, but failed to swallow a mouthful. I had similar apprehensions myself before going to sleep, not so much on account of fatigue undergone—for I had done many foolish things of the like kind before under the intoxicating influence of the mountain air —but my alarm was suggested by the peculiar symptoms, the utter absence of any sensation of muscular fatigue, and the existence of an odd desire to keep on walking or half running. This, of course, was unnatural, and a symptom of nervous derangement; fatigue being the monitor appointed to warn us from destroying our bodies by excess of labour, and anything deranging that sense is a serious mischief.

I always have protested, and always will protest, most urgently, against the insane folly, so prevalent among all classes, educated and uneducated—medical men included—of using stimulants as a remedy for fatigue, as means of continuing excessive labour, and as a whip to drive the brain or body on to further exertion. Whatever may be argued in favour of the use of such things at other times, there cannot be a doubt that this most common use is necessarily pernicious, for there is no other remedy for fatigue than rest. The sense of fatigue, reverently regarded—as it should be—is the voice of our Creator calling upon us to stop: to cease in a course of action that will damage the wondrous mechanism He has entrusted to our care ; for no man who has studied the structure of the human body, and has studied it with all his faculties, religious as well as intellectual, can fail to see and feel that it is not only a matter of policy and prudence, but also a solemn and holy duty, to guard this gift of his Creator from violence or pollution. What, then, can be more foolish and impious than wilfully to use a drug for the purpose of destroying that warning sense of fatigue, and urging oneself on to the direct violation of the solemn message of command that it conveys? There are no circumstances whatever, actual or conceivable, under which its use for such a purpose can be defended. We are sometimes forced to make an effort beyond the ordinary and desirable limits of our strength. If this be of short duration, an effort of the will is sufficient to carry us through it, unless the will has been made the perverted slave of drugs.

If the required period of effort exceeds the sustaining power of a healthy will, then it reaches the period at which a stimulant will be followed by reaction; and this reaction may in some cases be the bearer of death.

Let us suppose, for example, that the difficulty I have just narrated had been a serious one—that mists and snow had surrounded me, and another twelve hours' work had been necessary—a brandy flask, such as tourists commonly carry, if used in the usual way, would have justified its title of pocket-pistol by being an implement of suicide. I should have taken a sip at the commencement of the difficulty, and pushed on vigorously; then another sip a few hours after, when the first reaction commenced; then another sip at a shorter interval to overcome the next and greater reaction, and so on with shorter intervals, longer sips, and increasing reaction till the brandy would have been exhausted. I might have kept up in this manner somewhat beyond the time at which I staggered and fell on the bridge; but, instead of rising after ten minutes of repose, I should have sunk into utter prostration, from the reaction which necessarily follows such morbid excitement. Had the place been the wild mountain, with the snow upon the ground, I should probably have fallen into that sleep of death that comes over men under such circumstances. I have observed that in most cases where travellers have been found dead in the snow, an empty flask—a discharged pocket-pistol—has also been found by their side. On the other hand, without the pocket-pistol, I should

o

have been forced to repose before the vital energies had become exhausted beyond the possibility of battling with the cold and hunger, and thus might have slept a few hours, even on the snow, without much serious mischief, and then have struggled on with effort and halting, even for twelve hours more; for the powers of endurance of the human body are immense, when exerted in harmony with their own natural laws.

There is a time, however, when brandy or such-like stimulant may be of considerable service : that is, when the labour is over, and the nervous system is in such a state of irritable excitement as to render sleep difficult to obtain. With some temperaments, this is apt to be the case; then the brandy used for the opposite purpose to that of stimulating to further exertion—viz. as a means of calling forth the only possible remedy for over-exertion, repose—may be of great value. If, therefore, the brandy-flask be carried at all, the only safe time to use it is at the journey's end, when in some cases it may be useful; though, as a general rule, I believe that it is better not to use it even then, for the sleep obtained by its means is but a feverish slumber, followed by headache and depression on awakening.

The reader must not suppose that I am preaching a teetotal homily; for while convinced that the habitual use of any artificial stimulant, even of tea and coffee, when used so regularly as to engender a craving for it, is pernicious, I believe that the occasioual moderate enjoyment of wine, simply as a matter of indulgence (sensual indulgence if you will,

for we are sensual animals as well as moral and intellectual beings, and can gain nothing by denying
it), is permissible, and, perhaps, beneficial; for the
necessities of business and the general competition
for self-advancement are apt to render us more cool
and calculating than is healthful for the mind, and
therefore a moderate amount of convivial generosity
may be a useful moral medicine; an alterative
much to be desired.

Instead of suffering any illness or serious lassitude,
I found upon awakening no worse symptoms than a
ravenous appetite, the remedy for which was provided
in the homely fare remaining on the rough plank by
the bedside. After disposing of this and thanking the
good pastor for his kindness, I started at about two
o'clock to walk on up the valley of the Otta to Mork,
where he told me I should find comfortable quarters
and "very good people." Mork is about twenty
English miles distant from this, the Skeaker station. I
walked this at a brisk pace without any fatigue, which
would not have been the case had I carried and used
a spirit-flask on the day before. Such a dangerous
weapon has never cumbered my knapsack or pocket.

Note, 1876.—My troubles on the Kjolen Fjeld arose
entirely from the mistake of turning off too soon, and
not from any intrinsic difficulty of the route. I have
since met other tourists who, with the aid of a guide,
have crossed to Skeaker in the course of a fair day's
walk. I recommend others who propose to cross
from the Romsdal to Skeaker to start from Molmen
rather than Hoset, especially if they come *up* the

Romsdal, as the track from Molmen is nearly straight and follows a little river during the first part of the journey. They may thus establish their bearings by this part of the course without any confusion arising from compass variation, and then continue in the same direction after leaving the river, and thus hold on to Skeaker. If, however, they start from Hoset they must keep stubbornly to the Ljordals Elv, avoiding the temptation of the bridge, till they reach the Ljordals saeters, there halt, and if without a guide make inquiries. Attention to these points will render a guide unnecessary, but for the reasons already stated it is dangerous to travel alone over this or any other of these solitary fjelds where human help is so far beyond reach.

CHAPTER XI.

A proud Norwegian beauty — Household charity a substitute for poor-rates in Norway — The good people at Mork — The family big box of the Norwegian farmer — The Lia Vand — Formei extent of the Nord Fjord's glacier — Saeter life — A damsel at bay — Collecting of the goats and cows — Cheese-making — The supremacy of woman and the inferiority of the male sex at the saeter — The head of the valley and the snow fields — Difficulty in selecting the pass — Climbing powers of Norwegian horses — The Stiggevand and ice cascades of the Justedals Sneæfond — Grand and desolate scenery — Head of the Justedal Paternal advice to young mountaineers.

August 1st, 1856.—THE valley of the Otta is very grand and desolate, approaching in some parts to the grandeur of the Romsdal. Much of the road passes through dark wild woods of pine, with many fallen and shattered trunks lying about at the feet of the living trees, giving to the whole the primitive aspect of a new, unsettled country. Hitherto, the valleys I have passed through appear cultivated up to the limits of profitable fertility; but here there appears to be much neglected land left waste for want of population.

As I sat upon a boulder by the roadside, busily occupied in making the diary of my last day's wandering, some people approached and passed, whom I scarcely noticed; then one of them stopped in front of me. On looking up I was startled by a strange apparition. A tall, elegant, and most beautiful girl, about eighteen years of age, was standing before me; she held in one hand the end of a long stick, a young pine-tree stem stripped of its bark; the other end being held by an old blind man, curved almost to the ground. His abundant hair was perfectly white, long and straight, and wild; his eyelids and lashes were also very long and white, and his forehead high and deeply wrinkled. His dress was very coarse and poor, and his whole aspect was expressive of the deepest humility and dependence, combined with a certain amount of venerable gravity. She, on the contrary, was the personification of absolute pride— of innate, unassuming pride—a pride that is unconscious of its own existence, that makes no effort at dignity, and has no thoughts of dignity, but is instinctive dignity itself. I had excited her curiosity, and when I looked up she was examining me. I was so much amazed, that I must have stared at her considerably; but that made no difference: she continned her calm scrutiny, utterly unmoved, as though I were a beast in a cage, or a mineralogical specimen. One don't mind the scrutiny of rude peasantry, especially when it is accompanied with wonder and admiration; but to be examined so very calmly—to be treated as a "specimen" by such a beautiful creature—stirred up the fragments of pride that exist somewhere in my own constitution; and it may be that I looked almost fiercely at her, but still made no impression of any kind. She was neither confused nor indignant, but simply concluded her survey of the specimen, then spoke a word to the old man, and walked calmly on. He tottered after her, clinging to the other end of the white stick, which was at least 10 feet long. She was a perfect specimen of what we regard in England as the high Norman aristocratic type of beauty. Her face was a long oval, of geometrical perfection; her eyes were deep blue; her forehead was high and white; her nose, long and straight; every feature, in short, was unexceptional in form and symmetry. Her hair was flaxen, and her complexion clear, with very little colour. She was dressed with much care and neatness: a clean kerchief smartly tied over her head, and a black cloth jacket closely fitting her beautiful figure. She was quite different from any of the people I had seen hereabouts; her face and hands were utterly clean. She was probably the daughter of some farmer, and the old man the family pauper.

In Norway there are no poor-rates, but the farmers have to support the aged poor as inmates of their houses. These old people generally do some light work, such as gathering wood and the like. The custom is primitive and has many advantages. Charity thus becomes an active virtue, dwelling at the fireside of home—" it blesseth him that gives, and him that takes," for in kindly treating such a pensioner a happy influence is spread throughout the house, and the little children are trained in the exercise of practical benevolence by a course of practical instruction that no maxims or sermons can substitute; for moral training can only be effectual when carried out by means of actual exercise in deed and feeling: mere ethics only inform the intellect.

A man may be profoundly versed in the principles of art, and yet unable to paint a picture.

On arriving at Mork I found that the pastor's encomium on the " good people " was well merited: the hostess was overflowing with goodness. The arrival of a guest threw her into a state of excitement quite unusual among Norwegians; she brought out a vast array of pans, containing cream, soft cheese, milk and porridge, piles of fladbród and crisp flour cake; a ham, that seemed to have been smoked for years, was unhooked from the rafters, eggs were set a-frying, and the coffee berries turned out and roasted forthwith.

She was one of those really kind women who love to see people eat, who sincerely believe in the helplessness of man, and that he must necessarily perish unless a woman is near to minister to his comforts; and she was full of sympathy for a solitary wanderer whose mother was so far away. She made many inquiries, all of which I answered as fully as my Norsk allowed; then she showed me the big box containing her Sunday clothes and wedding dress, and a great stock of domestic apparatus. Her name, " Thora Olsdatter," and her husband's, or father's, " Live Olsen," were written upon it in gay letters, and the inscription bordered with brightly painted flowers. All the panels of the room doors were also painted with vases bearing bright flowers, in which the primary colours decidedly prevailed.

The big box thus emblazoned with the family name is a common and prominent object of Norwegian farmhouse furniture. It is usually 8 or 10 feet long, about 3 feet wide, and 2 feet high, and the treasures it contains are most miscellaneous. Suspended from the lid are caps and ribbons, a large watch, and other trinkets; at the bottom is a store of neatly folded bed clothes and towels, table-cloths, &c. There are side shelves and fittings for shoes and men's clothes, coffee berries, and pepper, and the very few other exotic luxuries used in a Norwegian household.

I am now becoming reconciled to sheepskin coverlids; when they are perfectly clean, as the one I have here, they are most luxurious, the soft wool, in its natural state of curliness and elasticity, touching the skin more tenderly than any woven fabric.

I had much difficulty in pressing upon the good Thora Olsdatter any payment. She considered the steel pens and paper of needles I had given her to be an equivalent for the board and lodging, and when I explained that they had nothing at all to do with it, she refused to take more than one mark and a half.

I find that Mork is not marked at all on Munch's map, though it is in Waligorski's.

August 2nd.—Start again for the fjeld, on my way towards the snowy solitudes of the Justedal. The track which I select passes up a wild valley, where the walking over loose stones reduces one's best pace to about two miles per hour. Then the valley widens and the river expands into a fine specimen of a wild mountain lake, called the *Lia Vand* in Waligorski's map, and the *Lida Vand* in Munch's, but not correctly laid down in either. Beyond this lake the track passes over a glacier moraine of great extent and unmistakable character. The river struggles among its boulders, and at other parts slides smoothly over the grooved and polished rock-bed of the glacier itself, which must have covered this ground at quite a recent period, for the river has not had time to obliterate the footsteps of its predecessor. This glacier was doubtless but an extension of the great Nord Fjord's glacier now existing a little higher than this, and from which the river is derived. This glacier has gradually receded to its present position at the head of the valley, leaving at every stage of its retreat a ruin of rocks from its deposited moraines.

The reader will understand that I have now quite left the region of stations and farmhouses, and must either sleep on the rock or find a "*saeter.*" It is towards one of these that I have been steering all day long, in accordance with the directions of Thora Olsdatter. The Norwegian saeter corresponds to the Swiss chalet; it is a little wooden hut, built upon a mountain pasturage, that is only open from the snow during a few weeks of the summer. At this period the cows and goats are driven up, and left to roam upon the pastures during the day; at evening time they are collected by an offering of salt, then milked, and the cheeses made. They make *cheese* while the sun shines here during the short summer. Every tourist who visits Norway, and would study the Norwegians, should have some experience of saeter life. I gladly availed myself of this opportunity of spending a night in the saeter attached to the farm of my good hostess of Mork. There were several of these wooden huts dotted about a dreary moorland, from around which high peaks of glacier-bearing mountains rise. I found some men asleep in one of the huts, and upon awakening them they offered to provide me with food and lodging. As there appeared to be many saeters, and these attached to different farms, I inquired whether the one they proposed for my lodging belonged to Mork; whereupon the men looked curiously at each other, and one of them, with a significant grin, quite unintelligible to me, asked whether I particularly wished to lodge in the Mork saeter. I replied, " Yes," very decidedly; for these fellows were a dirty-looking set, and I was certain that even a saeter, if it belonged to Thora Olsdatter, would be clean. My decided answer provoked a general laugh, and they escorted me in procession to a hut at some distance from the rest, knocked at the door and called to the inmate, who, for some time, made no answer; but at last a blooming lass—a ruddy, muscular, rural beauty— opened the door, and looked forth with a frown of stern maidenly defiance. After a volley of banter, which she received very contemptuously, I was introduced as a traveller who had come all the way from England to visit her saeter, and lodge there for the night. I was received very haughtily at first, until I frowned severely at the scoffers, and told her of my coming from Mork as the guest of Thora Ols., who had sent me hither. She then bade me welcome, and immediately I entered shut the

door unceremoniously upon the grinning swains outside, who were seeking an excuse to come in likewise.
She supplied me with supper of cheese and fladbröd,
and showed me the bed from which she had just
risen, which was to be mine; explaining that she
had slept during the day, that her work .was about
to commence, and would last through the night:
she then disappeared.

In the course of an hour I heard a wild " yodl,"
very loud, but not very melodious. The damsel was
returning with a flock of about thirty goats and some
six or eight cows. She took a little bag of salt from
the hut, and, before she had fairly cleared the threshold, was the axis of a pyramid of goats, who were
crowding round her, and leaping over each other's
backs for the privilege of licking her hand after
each dip into the salt-bag. She repelled the goats
as energetically as she had repelled the men, but
more mercifully; for she thrust the ends of her
fingers into the mouth of each before giving it the
buffet of dismissal. The tact she displayed in preventing any of the obtrusive animals from obtaining
more than one lick of salt was remarkable: a second
application was met by a grasp of the horns, and a
thrust that drove the upreared aspirant staggering
backwards a yard or two; she must have distinctly
known the features of each individual goat to pick
them out so certainly. The cows were next treated
in like manner, then seized by the horns and ears, as
the goats were seized before, and each one dragged to
its proper stall in an adjoining building, not distinguishable exteriorly from that designed for the bipeds.

This milking was a work of some time, for the brave damsel was quite unaided in this scuffle with her flock, and in all the subsequent operations of milking and cheese-making. She was queen and mistress of her own domain and family, and her efforts seemed pretty equally divided between the cares of internal administration and the repelling of the external male invaders, whose gallantry seemed entirely confined to teasing her, and led to no suggestion of aid in her really arduous labours. The men seemed, in fact, to be merely a set of idle, useless, inferior beings; earnestness and energy being exclusively female attributes at this altitude. It may be that the men were idle because it was Sunday, or that they had come up to the saeter-land on a visit to their fair superior; it is, however, notorious, and acknowledged throughout Norway, that in the saeter women reign supreme, and men can only exist there as tolerated intruders.

While the milking was in progress I slept upon the bed, with my clothes on, of course, as the cheese-making had to be done by my blooming hostess in the same apartment. It was a wooden room, about 5 yards long by 4 yards wide; the walls lined with shelves, on which were cheeses already made, and the materials for making more. The bed was of the usual rustic Norwegian construction—an oblong box, made fast to the wall, and partly filled with straw, over which were some coarse sheets, shawls, and a sheepskin; this one was about wide enough for a comfortable coffin. In the corner opposite to the head of the bed, and almost within arm's reach,

was the great stone hearth, covered with a stone and
plaster dome.   The other corners were occupied by
benches on which the vessels for standing and mixing
the milk with the other cheese materials were placed.
There was also a second small apartment, or rather
cupboard, for the storage of pans, pails, &c.   Everything was scrupulously clean in this particular
saeter.

Soon after sunset the sovereign mistress of the
place returned, bearing heavy pails filled with rich
milk from cows and goats.   Some lumps of wood
were taken from the store place under the bed, a
crackling fire was soon blazing on the hearth, and
the iron cauldron, filled with a mysterious mixture
of goat's milk and other unknown ingredients, from
which the green cheese that ripens in time to
" gammel ost " is made, was hooked to the black
chain over the middle of the fire.   For some hours
after, every time I awoke the sticks were blazing,
and the busy lass was there, stirring, mixing, and
watching till after midnight, or nearly to the dawn,
when she disappeared.

At five o'clock, when I started on my next day's
walk, she was at work again, making more cheese
from the morning's milking.

August 3rd.—The ascent of the valley towards the
snowy wilderness of the Nord Fjord and Justedals
Bræen is by an abominable path over the wreck of
glacier moraines, and through thickets of low beech-
trees, or rather bushes ; the elastic arms of which,
entangled with each other, continually bar the way,
and, springing back as they are bent aside, pick off

one's hat, flog one's face, and take most tantalizing liberties with the knapsack behind.

This vegetation soon ceased, and I came upon the Handspikjen Fjeld, a waste of loose stones with soppy snow between, and every vestige of the track oblite-rated by the thawing. It happened to be just the sort of place where a beaten track is specially needed. Over a rolling moor one may steer by compass; but here I arrived at the head of a valley terminating in three peaks, the centre one being just in the direc-tion which, according to the map, I ought to take; only a mountain pass is never over a peak, but always by the lowest practicable way in the hollow between two peaks. Which, then, must I take; the hollow too much to the right or that too much to the left? The configuration of the hills not being given accurately on my map, I had therefore to go by guess. It appeared that these courses led to very different places; to valleys branching off in different directions. They all led upwards to the great snow deserts of the Justedal and Nord Fjord, or to the dreary Sogne Fjeld, and downwards again to rocky solitudes filled with the ruins that the recently receded glaciers have left behind. My destination was the Justedal, the only one of these valleys that is inhabited; but the upper end of this is as desolate as the rest, the first farmhouse being so far down that I could only expect to reach it at the end of my day's walk. It was quite pos-sible, therefore, that I might take the wrong valley, and only detect my error after some hours' walking; and thus have to spend another night in a region still wilder than that where I had strayed aside before.

I ascend the middle peak hoping to make a survey that would aid me, but find that the apparent summit is surmounted by another far above and away, and that probably by another, and perhaps another still; as is so often found to be the case in making such ascents. I see little more than peaks of rock and plains of snow; the "*fond*," or motherland of the numerous glaciers of this region being visible from this elevation. I therefore descend and make for the pass which seems the most hopeful, and on approaching it am surprised and rejoiced to find upon the snow the footmarks of a horse and two men, evidently recent. The Justedal being the only probable destination of anybody, I resolve to follow the trail. I could not have believed it possible for a horse to travel over such ground had I not seen the footprints, and I suspect that none but a Norwegian horse could do it. It is a steep mountain side, covered with angular boulders varying in size from a man's head to a church, heaped together to an unknown depth, with crooked crevasses between, some filled with snow and others gaping open. Part of the climbing is to be done by stepping on the angles of the smaller blocks, or along the edges of the larger, where they are wedged in with an edge upwards, and partly over the sloping snow-covered surfaces of the largest masses. Snow climbing is always very laborious, but this sort of compound of snow, and rock, and treacherous snow-covered holes, is particularly so.

On reaching the summit of the pass a singular scene presented itself. At the foot of a vast amphitheatre of snowy mountain peaks is a gloomy basin of rock filled with the waters of a half-frozen lake. The water comes directly from the snow above. and is of a peculiar blue-white, semi-opaque, London-milk colour, common to such snow water. This lake is marked in Munch's map as the *Stygge Vand,* which I take the liberty of translating freely as the Stygian Pool. It is the head water or source of the Storelv or main river of the Justedal, and should be seen by all who venture over this wilderness.

It lies in a gloomy hollow, walled at its upper end by a dark precipice. The summit edge of this precipice is one of the shores of that vast icy sea, the Jostedals and Nord Fjords' Bræ, the largest glacier region in Europe, covering an area of more than 500 square miles, and pouring its overflow down a hundred valleys around.

The overflow here is very curious. The ice-sheet as it marches onward and outward meets the edge of the precipice above the lake, is pushed beyond it and overhangs. This cornice illustrates the plasticity of ice in a very striking manner by bending over and forming great hanging sheets that reach a short way down, then break off and drop as small icebergs into the lake, their broken edges forming a blue face to the curved cornice, from which depends a fringe of icicles. If this wall of the lake-shore had sufficient slope to hold the icy cascade without breaking, glaciers would be formed ; or if the supply of breaking masses were sufficiently great to over-

power the thawing below, the basin of the lake
would be filled up and become continuous with the
great ice and snow fields above, and might extend
onwards to the spot where I stand, or even overflow
this and push down the valley to the saeters below.
That this was formerly the case is shown by abundant evidences on every step of this day's walk, and
the latter part of yesterday's.

The soft though sharp outline of the virgin snow
standing against the blue sky just where it pours
over the precipice, is very beautiful.   There are
no birds up here, no roaring torrent, no rustling
of trees, or buzzing of insects; not even the ripple
of a thin stream, as heard on the Swiss glaciers;
but a silence that is almost absolute, and adds
vastly to the effect of such a scene, especially on
the mind of a solitary pedestrian who can linger
and enjoy just those influences to which he is the
most susceptible.   A guide is a positive nuisance
under such circumstances: the tourist is so dependent upon him that the chief excitement of
the walk is gone when there is no effort required
to find one's way and no possibility of losing it;
and he interferes with the enjoyment of the scene
by hurrying one on with the sole motive of getting over the ground.   Even a congenial friend,
however desirable in general travelling, interferes
with the feelings and reflections which such overwhelming solitude and silence awaken.

Note, 1876.—This was written several years ago
when I heartily enjoyed the excitement of a solitary

and somewhat dangerous adventure among mountains. Up to this time I had only once employed a guide, and that was for the ascent of Mont Blanc. I am now older, more prudent, and thankful that my solitary wanderings all terminated so mildly. Besides this, I now have sons of my own, and feel the responsibility of inciting young men to imitate my own youthful indiscretions. Therefore I say again, don't go alone to such places. Do without a guide if you please, but have with you a sturdy companion who can carry you on his back if you should break your leg or sprain your ankle; or return with help to pick up the pieces, if you should happen to step over a precipice when overtaken by a mountain mist and groping through its darkness.

Such a mist would render this walk very dangerous.

By reference to Munch's map I now find that the Justedal may be reached by crossing the barrier ridge on either side of that middle peak which I ascended, but this was not at all indicated by the map I had. If Munch is right, the westward side of the peak should be taken in order to see the Stygge Vand, but in any case it may be reached by following the course of the river upwards.

The hollow forming the bed of this lake affords an interesting illustration of glacier erosion. When the ice-sheet poured over the rock-wall in sufficient quantity to fill the valley below, as it certainly did, its pressure at the foot of the precipice must have been very great, producing a concentrated erosive action just where the lake now stands, and forming an icefall basin analogous to ordinary waterfall basins.

CHAPTER XII.

Glacier cornices of the Justedal ice-field — The evils of dining
The Trangedal and Lodal glaciers — Advance and recession of
the Justedal glaciers — The "Bear's Path" glacier — Fermented milk — A human candlestick — An interior — Scandinavian fleas — Scenery of the Justedal — More starvation —
The Nygaard and Krondal glaciers — Luxurious quarters and
Englishmen — How to enjoy dissipation — Centre ornament for
a dinner-table — An evening concert in Norway — The trail of
the travelling snob — Drunkenness and extortion — A mutinous
boat's crew — A walk in the dark — Startling the natives with
portable lightning — Domestic revelations.

1856.—FOLLOWING the trail of the horse, I descend
over similar ground to that on the other side of the
ridge, and soon come upon a track which on this side
is marked by occasional heaps of stones. I always
regard it as a matter of imperative duty to con-
tribute to such heaps by adding a stone to every one
I pass ; they are almost necessary on this side, for in
ascending it would be very easy to miss the particular
notch through which I had passed, and by taking
the wrong one to wander away to the upper desolation of ice and snow, and within reach of glacier
cornices, where masses of ice occasionally detach
and slide down the steep slopes of rock from which
the glacier has receded. Such cornices of ice overhanging precipitous or very steep rock-walls, with
glaciated slopes at their feet, appear to be characteristic features of this boundary of the great ice-

field, which is overflowing in every direction. When it terminates in a sloping and narrowing valley its overflow fills the outlet, and forms an ordinary glacier in lieu of the river which would have been formed by a watershed. When, on the other hand, the overflowing ice meets a precipice, it forms a bending cornice in lieu of a cascade; an icefall when the cornice breaks, in lieu of a waterfall. The glaciated slope below may have been smoothed by the cornice fragments sliding down it.

I now walk on over a wide fjeld of glacier moraine leading at last to the outlet of the Stygge Vand; a torrent of respectable dimensions, which, fed by a succession of glaciers, grows to a river, the Storelv, as it flows down the Justedal. At the point where the fjeld narrows and descends to form the bed of this valley, the torrent makes a succession of falls over walls of piled-up boulders.

From this point a considerable length of the valley is visible, and a few miles farther down I see three men and a horse reposing by the river side, and find, on approaching, that the men had been taking their dinner and siesta. I follow their example to the extent of eating some fragments of fladbrod I had brought in my pocket, but cannot indulge in the luxury of a sleep on account of the gnats and flies that swarm about my head, biting and stinging unmercifully; for within an hour or so after leaving the Stygge Vand and its overhanging snows, the plague of insects, intensified by a scorching sun, commenced. The peasants and the horse were protected by an outer stratum of hair on the one and of dirt on the others. All things have their uses.

I find that they started from the saeters about two hours earlier than I did, and it was their footsteps I saw in the snow. I walked on with them for about an hour; they complained sorely of fatigue, and at last gave up on reaching an empty saeter hut. They were surprised at my freshness, especially when I told them how far I wandered from the track by ascending the peak, which added some two hours of hard climbing over and above their day's work. I was rather surprised at it myself; for I had done some very heavy work during the last few days, without any feeling of fatigue worth notice. This, I suspect, is attributable to two causes: first, to having prudently commenced with easy stages; and, secondly, to the total absence of hotels and anything approaching to a dinner.

I have continually found that in countries where there are hotels and good dinners it is very difficult to do a fair day's walk. If any attempt at dinner is made early in the afternoon, the case is quite hopeless; and even when dinner is taken late in the evening, at the end of the day's walk, the fierce appetite thus engendered, if at all pandered by tempting dishes, is almost certain to give the stomach so much to digest that a large amount of vital energy is consumed in the process, and much unnecessary weight added to the body. This, of course, may be to a great extent constitutional; a lean, spare man would probably walk better on good dinners, but one with decided tendencies to over-assimilation, and naturally addicted to fattening, should feed on dry fladbröd, bruised oats, or stale crusts and water, if he wishes to be in the best possible physical condition. The exercise will render these sufficiently palatable and digestible to enable him to eat and assimilate sufficient.

Near to the saeter where my tired companions stopped are two magnificent glaciers, descending from the "fond," down lateral openings into the valley below. They are very near together, and would join at the lower part if they extended a little farther. The upper one comes down a straight valley, and can be seen in its whole course from the "fond"; it spreads out at its lower part, and displays magnificent blue crevasses : this is the Trangedal glacier. The next below is the glacier of Lodal. The descending branches that pour down the lateral valleys from the great frozen wilderness above are called "Jökler," or "bræ," the latter term applying also to the fond above.

The Lodal glacier exhibits the phenomena of medial moraines very distinctly and beautifully. It has travelled a long way, and bears evidence of tributary streams and much wearing away of mountains. It spreads out at its lower part, affording, by its shape, strong confirmation of the theory of Professor James Forbes, according to which the ice of glaciers is a viscous or partially fluid mass, that yields resistingly to gravitation and its resulting pressure, and flows, as water does, only very slowly. The dirty aspect of the lower part of this glacier is due to the outspreading of the two medial moraines, until they meet each other and finally join the lateral moraine. This, I suspect, is due to the rapid thawing of the lower part of the glacier during the long summer days. The ice upon which the moraine rests being protected by this rocky covering, the moraine is apparently raised, and stands on a ridge, which, becoming higher and higher and more steep-sided, the blocks at last slide down its slope, and are spread out on each side of their former position. This action, continually repeated, would in time distribute them over the whole surface of the glacier and obliterate the regular moraine bands that are visible higher up.

I walked on down the valley, the wild grandeur of which is most magnificent. At the foot of the glaciers is a long waste shore of smooth rock, which terminates in a wild heap of boulder rocks, indicating the former extent of these glaciers. One might imagine that great waves from the sea of ice above have rolled and broken on this shore, and heaped up the shingle beach beyond, and are now retreating over this smooth strand, and gathering up to curl over and break again, and then rush up as far as their former boundary.

Glaciers do thus advance and retreat; only not quite in the shape of breaking waves, nor so rapidly. For about a hundred years the glaciers of the Justedal have been retreating : this of Lodal is some 600 or 700 yards from its former moraine. In 1740 the damage to farm property in this valley by the encroachment of glaciers became a subject of judicial inquiry. Their retreat has been subsequent to this.

A few miles farther down the valley there is another fine glacier without any medial moraine, and scarcely any at the sides. The blue crevasses and great ribs of ice are very fine in this. It is called the " Biörnestegs Bræ," or Bear's Path Glacier, and nearly opposite to it are some more saeters.

Two or three miles farther down is the farm of Mjelvor, which I had fixed upon as my destination. A peasant I met on the way proved to be the proprietor of this house and of all the country round. The farmhouse is a gloomy, dirty place, but the host did his best to accommodate me ; there were some women about, but there appeared to be no mistress, for he himself served me with some buttermilk that was three or four weeks old—the cows being all at the saeters above—and some very dry raw ham and fladbröd. This very stale milk, which I had heard of on the way as one of the Norwegian beverages, but had not tasted before, is rather remarkable ; it has a tart saline taste, more like some kinds of ale than anything of milk. I suspect that it is fermented and slightly intoxicating ; that by means of the acid and casein the sugar of milk has been converted into grape sugar, and has then fermented : it is evidently used as a substitute for beer. On account of its excessive tartness, amounting to acrid pungency, I was unable to take sufficient to test its stimulating properties. My bed was made specially for me of a couple of planks across a bench, a bag of straw upon these, a sheepskin over all, and a broken window above my head for ventilation.

The family, which consisted of the master and six or seven housemen and women, supped altogether on cement, spooned, as before described, out of a common bowl. The bowl stood on a rude table or block, and they stood around it, dipping by turns scrupulously spoon and spoon about. It was dark, and the large timbered room was lighted only by a blazing band of resinous pine-bark, twisted together into a long stick or scroll, and held at arm's length overhead by an aged man with long white beard and silver hair, who stood so still and looked so withered that he seemed like a frozen mummy, fitted with glass eyes and glued to the ground as a permanent candlestick. He was the family pauper, standing in humble servitude, and waiting his turn when the general meal was done.

The red glare of the reeking brand lighted the faces of the cementivora with a copper tinge; who, as they stood around the bowl, reaching it by turns at arm's length and returning their spoons with the long sweeping curve before described, seemed like demons doing an incantation. The red light spread dimly throughout the whole of the wooden room, tinging with lurid and fitful glare the rude logs that form the walls, the brown-smoked heavy beams above, and all the dingy domestic stores suspended from them, and making the great fireplace built into the corner, and the two wooden-box bedsteads and the dilapidated handloom dimly visible. The whole scene would have made a fine subject for such an artist as Gherardo della Notte.

Scandinavian fleas are very energetic, and on this

occasion were abundant also. My bag of straw was
very ancient, and many generations of fleas must
have lived in peace within it and passed away to rest,
since the straw was last changed or the bag washed.

August 4th.—Rise early in consideration of my
bedfellows, and take only a few mouthfuls of fladbröd, resolving to make amends at the first comfortable-looking farm I should pass on my way down
the valley, which winds about amidst the wildest
imaginable desolation of black frowning crags and
glacier ruins. It is equal in grandeur to the
Romsdal, and more desolate. There are no waterfalls of any magnitude; but the icefalls—the glaciers
—well supply their place. I should recommend all
tourists coming to Norway to visit the Justedal if
possible; and, if at this season, to bring some food
with them. Being an inhabited valley, I was reckless in this respect; started early, and hungry;
walked on some miles before I reached a house, and
passed that disdainfully in hope of finding a better
one; but in this was disappointed. Finally, on
becoming more moderate in my expectations, I
knocked at the next and tried the door, but found it
bolted; all the people were away up at the saeters
or the distant " eng," or upper hay ground, on which
at this season the harvest is gathered. I tried other
houses with the same result all the day through, and
was thus compelled to make breakfast and dinner on
raw (stolen) turnips and wild bilberries, which last
grow in great abundance and are remarkably fine.

There are two other glaciers at this part of the
valley. The Nygaard glacier comes down a winding

valley, and spreads out finely below.   Like that of
Lodal, its former shore of heaped-up moraine is most
distinctly marked; the strand between this and its
present limits is a desolate plain of rock, smoothed
and grooved by the former glacier, and the stones
imbedded in it.   Below this is the Krondal or Berset
glacier.   There is a wonderfully fine amphitheatre
of rocks at the lower part of the valley.

I reached the mouth of the valley shortly after
sunset, and was surprised at finding a downright
hotel there — something absolutely luxurious — a
place where cookery is understood, and real bread
may even be obtained, and wine in abundance.   Such
being the case, I of course met some Englishmen
there: had it been a region of nothing to eat, but
plenty of copper ore, I should have found a Scotchman or two.   For my own part, I was in a very
decidedly English state of mind, after starving more
or less for the previous ten days.   Having already
relieved my conscience by confessing to the fact that
I did steal some turnips, I may explain that they
were only two, and those very small; my principal
food during the day being bilberries — very delicious,
but by no means solid and satisfactory.   They call
them *blau*, or blueberries, here; their rich colour
justifies the name, and suggests the etymology of
the Scotch name "*blaeberry*."

I had a sumptuous banquet of ham and eggs, with
bread and a bottle of claret (St. Jullien, of very good
quality); the charge for the wine was about 1s. 5d.
English.   The duty is 2d. per bottle.

The man who never had a holiday, and has none

to anticipate; who has no shop, no factory, no office
no farm, no studio—in short, no daily work to do;
but has been cast upon the world by cruel parents
with the stultifying curse of a large inheritance and
no fixed ambition—the purposeless idler, to whom
all the days of life are of equal dreariness—is
perhaps the most miserable of all human beings.
What would he give to be capable of the sensations
of a hard-worked London apprentice on Easter
Monday, or a shopman on Good Friday! He never
knew, nor ever can know, what Sunday means. I
do not, of course, allude to the dreary demoralizing
Sabbath of the modern puritan, but the bright,
happy, soul-refreshing Christian holiday. Those
who talk so much about the fourth commandment
commonly forget its first and fundamental injunction,
"Six days shalt thou labour;" for without the six
days' labour, there can be no seventh day of rest.
Daily labour is as necessary to man's happiness as
daily food is to his physical health. I have never
met a single example of an idle man who was not a
miserable man; and one of the greatest of all our
popular delusions is that of considering a forced
vocation an evil. The man who spends his life
merely in seeking enjoyment, soon finds that enjoyment is an irksome labour—a labour without holiday
or any refreshing rest. So with the man who has
claret every day with dinner; he can form no idea
whatever of the enjoyment I had of that particular
bottle of St. Jullien, and the ham and eggs at the
Ronnei station, after the invigorating hardships of
the previous week or two. It was a mighty feast—

a furious dissipation—which I shall remember for a whole lifetime.

August 5th.—I determine to stop here a whole day, for rest, luxury, letter-writing, and St. Jullien. There is something like a village here; there are gardens and fruit-trees; and my dessert after last night's ham and eggs was a branch of a cherry-tree served with the leaves and fruit upon it. I resolved that if ever I have a garden and a wife, and give a dinner-party in the summer, the dessert shall be served in this fashion—well-laden branches of fruit-trees arranged as a centre ornament, the fabric to be pulled down after dinner, and the branches handed round among the guests to pluck what they desire.

Note, 1876.—On trying to carry out this resolve while I resided at Caergwrle and had some fine cherry-trees, an unexpected difficulty rendered it impracticable. The cherries in our climate do not ripen so rapidly nor so simultaneously as in Norway. A branch gathered when the first fruit has ripened has about 95 per cent. of its cherries green and uneatable; if left until all or the majority are ripe, the sparrows will have cleared off the best.

1856.—In the evening there was much company at the hotel, and some music; the instrument, one of the ornaments of the chief drawing-room, being a grinding organ, such as the Italian boys carry about our streets: the handle was turned by the host, and the company assembled to hear it were delighted with the concert. The Englishmen

who eclipsed me by taking a deck-passage on the
Constitutione, arrived here; but I now had my
revenge, for they were too late for the concert,
while I had the privilege of hearing it all through.
This is a favourite station with yachting parties, of
which there are several every year from England.

The river of the Justedal, the Storelv, brings
down an immense quantity of glacier-worn *débris*,
which, being deposited at its mouth, has made a
fertile nook hereabouts: the deposition is going on
rapidly. I found, when bathing, an extensive sub-
aqueous plain, stretching right across this branch of
the fjord; in the course of a century or so, it will
probably be high and dry, and cultivated right across
to Marifjoeren on the opposite side.

August 6th.—Walk over rich cultivated country
between Marifjoeren and Hafslo. There is a beautiful lake at Hafslo, and a curious steep zigzag road
near Nagloren.

On arriving at Sogndalsfjoeren I found a considerable portion of the boating population either
drunk or in a state of recovery from drunkenness
(which, of the two, is rather the more disagreeable),
and I spent two or three hours vainly endeavouring
to engage a boat to take me down the fjord: for
there are no roads or even tracks, or ledges for
travelling on foot hereabouts, where the rocks dip
almost perpendicularly into the waters of the fjords.

The people at this place seem very different from
any Norwegians I have met before: they have larger
features, lower heads, and, many of them, dark hair
and eyes, and almost a Neapolitan physiognomy.
The boatmen were very uncivil, and, for the first

time in Norway, I found them bent upon making an overcharge: evidently calculating upon my being an Englishman and submitting to it. This, and the drunkenness, are partly explained by the fact that an English yacht had been there just before: English lavishness had left its usual demoralizing trail behind. After a great deal of trouble and altercation, I got a boat and two men, one of them partially sober, the other entirely drunk. In order to obtain these, I was obliged to offer 1 mark per man per mile, instead of 20 skillings, the regular fare, and this was considerably below their demand: indeed, they seemed quite unwilling to work at all.

The drunken man commenced by pulling furiously, then missed the water, catching crabs, and fell over the seat. Then a head wind blowing, very moderately, they struck altogether, tied the boat to a rock, and refused to go on unless I paid them a dollar. I took no notice of their demand, but lying down at the bottom of the boat, bade them good night. They ate dried salmon and drunk "brandevin" for about three-quarters of an hour, and then went on; but the drunken man was now quite useless; he merely splashed the water and rolled about, while the boat made a very curious course. At one moment it was nearly capsized, for they were running it ashore upon a sloping piece of rock which would have uplifted the bow and sent the stern under water; but I took the oar from the entirely drunken man and just pushed off in time. The other looked over at the deep blue water, and the steep rocks above, in a very uncomfortable manner: he was evidently frightened, and when I strapped on my knapsack and made them understand that I was quite prepared for swimming, and that I had only saved the boat for the sake of my knapsack, which was lying under the seat, he became quite civil and humble. His drunken helpmate continued as random and stupid as ever, but persisted in rowing; and as they had to keep close to the shore to escape the wind, the boat was in continual danger of running into the rocks. I sat with my arms folded at the stern, and told them that they might capsize the boat as soon as they pleased, when I should swim to a landing place and walk back over the rocks; showing my map and compass to prove that I could find the way. The partially drunken man became almost sober, and offered me some brandevin by way of conciliation; this of course I refused, but I took an oar and pulled, and we now made some progress, until after rounding a projecting arm of the mountains, when we became exposed to the full force of the wind. The comparatively sober man pointed to a track over the rocks which leads to Lunden, the station we were bound for, and I gladly got ashore at the first practicable landing place, paid them the price agreed for the whole journey, and walked on.

They had taken me about half way, and it was growing dark and raining. At about ten o'clock I reached a little village, and found that it was not Lunden, but Norum, with its church close by. It grew very dark, and I had much difficulty in keeping the track; but I walked on till past midnight, passing many houses and much cultivated land. I inquired at several of these houses, but such inquiry is a more difficult matter than might appear to any-one who is unsophisticated in matters of Norwegian domestic architecture ; for bells, knockers, locks, and bolts are equally unknown, and all the houses were in the utter darkness of a wet and cloudy night. I opened one door and called out, but got no answer ; then I stepped forward and found it full of hay. Trying another, I found that the inhabitants were cows ; then another, which was a storehouse for cheeses, pails, and agricultural implements. Walking on farther, I opened another door, stepped forward into a broad dark vacancy, and heard around me several snorers ; I called and coughed, but the snoring continued uninterrupted. After some little hesitation and compunction on the score of imper-tinent intrusion, disturbing the people, &c., I took out my box of wax vesta matches and struck a light ; this flash of light startled all the sleepers at once ; they sat up in their beds, and disclosed the fact that nightshirts are not fashionable in these parts : but they were very civil, in spite of being thus uncere-moniously startled, and told me that Lunden was some distance farther.

At one of these places I was rather startled myself. It was a hay-house partly filled, and being vacant near the door where I stood, I struck a light, when suddenly a man in the costume of Paradise arose from out of the hay close by my feet. These hay-houses in Norway correspond to the " spare rooms " of English domestic economy, and are used for sleep-ing apartments when there is a pressure of visitors.

At last I reached a house, which, after waking the host and hostess by means of my portable lightning, I found to be the Lunden station. I was kindly and hospitably received, and provided with a supper of fladbröd, and "smör," and sour milk. The house was a poor one, but there was the old simplicity and kindness I have become accustomed to associate with Norway, and which serves to compensate for deficiency of physical comfort. The altercations with the boatmen of Sogndalsfjoeren, their general conduct, and the feelings they awakened, had made a sad rupture of these pleasing associations.

The Vikings were the younger sons of the old proprietors of Norwegian coast-farms, and went abroad to seek their fortunes when the patrimonial estate could be no further subdivided. *Query.* Had the very, very, great, great grandfather of my host here such a son, and did this young Viking, once upon a time, sail up the Thames, build himself a house upon its banks, and give it the name of his old Norwegian home?

CHAPTER XIII.

The Naero Fjord — Gudvangen and the Naerodal — Out for the
night again — Mountains safer than plains for out-of-door
sleeping — Returning from church by water — Sunday costume —
A jolly boatman — Night on the fjord — The Vöring Foss — A
project for Barnum — Sailing before the wind — The station at
Utne — A wonderful cap — The origin of corrugated zinc and
iron — Deference to Englishmen — The cost of boats in Norway
— How to make an economical yachting tour in Norway — The
Folgefond — The varying saltness of the fjords, and its possible
effects on animal and vegetable life, a subject for investigation.

August 7th, 1856.—START by boat, with my host
and another man, for Gudvangen, distant 3⅜ Norsk
miles, about 24 miles English ; a good day's work.
These men were well satisfied with the legal fare.

The assistant boatman might have been trans-
ported directly to Venice, and if there upon the piaz-
zetta, crying, " Barca, barca, vucol barca, Signore,"
would not have been recognized as out of place,
except by a large round silver brooch he wore in his
shirt front. His physiognomy is of the same type
as I had observed for the first time at Sogndalsfjoeren—dark hair and eyes, large nose, muscular
swarthy cheeks, and a rather lank bony figure.*

The scenery of this fjord is very grand ; very
much like the Lake of Lucerne at its wildest portions,

---

* This physiognomy I have since found to be characteristic of the
peasants of the Tellemark and neighbouring districts.

and quite equal to it. At the distance, glimpses of the Justedal snow-fields are obtained.

The Naero Fjord, a branch of the Sogne Fjord, is grander than any part of the Lake of Lucerne. It is the grandest lake I have ever seen. The name of narrow fjord well describes its chief characteristic. It is an irregular sea-filled gorge between perpendicular rocks rising to a height of 3000 feet or more; Murray says 5000 feet, but this, I think, is an excessive estimate. The summits of the mountains are probably about that height, but not the walls that dip into the salt lake.

It was curious to see porpoises and a grampus rolling about in such an apparently inland lake as this. Eagles are not uncommon hereabouts: I saw two in the course of the day. The boatmen call them the " òrn," pronounced " earn," the same name, and apparently the same species, as the Scottish eagle.

I landed at Gudvangen in the afternoon. This is the port of the Naerodal, or narrow valley, a continuation of the same rock-walled valley as the Naero Fjord, but with a river at the bottom instead of a branch of the sea. The Kil Foss pitches over the precipice opposite the station from a height of 2000 feet. It is a fall of the Staubbach type.

I walked up this very singular and magnificent valley, between its great walls of rock, and past the curiously shaped sugar-loaf mountain that stands like an obelisk and forms one of its most remarkable features, until I reached the upper end of the valley, which is closed in by a pyramidal mountain standing bolt upright in front of the road, and apparently defying farther progress. The zigzag road over this, the Stalheims Kleven, is a fine specimen of roadway engineering, and the views from the different parts of its eighteen bends, which directly face and splendidly display the valley and fjord, are most magnificent. There are two very fine cascades, the Stalheim Foss and the Sivle Foss, which are alternately displayed in turning the opposite bends.

I started from Gudvangen at about 6 P.M., intending to stop at the next station, some two hours' walk ahead; but passed it without being aware of the fact: I only remember some dirty huts about the spot. At about eleven o'clock I reached the next station, Vinge, entered it, struck a light, and found a dirty man lying in a dirty trough: not a raised box, as usual here, but a wooden trough, lying on the ground. In another trough, on the opposite side, was an equally dirty woman; there were some children and other dirty people distributed about in similar troughs, on the other parts of the floor. The man made some surly answers to my inquiries, and did not show any symptoms of intending to rise. I was considerably disgusted, and made up my mind to walk on. It appears that this station and the one previously passed are not used at all as sleeping places, but merely for the changing of horses. Tourists coming this way all sleep at Gudvangen.

Note, 1876.—This is still the case; Gudvangen to Vossevangen being one day's carriole journey nobody stops between.

1856. Walking on a mile or two farther, I made another attempt to get a bed, which was equally unsuccessful. Close by the road was a tempting hayfield, with the new-mown hay stacked on wooden frames or horses; I spread a little of this upon the ground, and lay down by the side of one of the frames; but in a very few minutes I found—what in the dark I had not observed—that the field was a spongy semi-bog; the water soon soaked through my bed of hay and my clothes also, and I was glad to walk on again to dry myself.

In the absence of the dry, crisp heather, or reindeer moss, a nice flat piece of rock is, after all, the best outdoor bed; and it is always safer to sleep upon a mountain than upon a plain. The dews and night mist—dampness and malaria—settle in the plains and lower valleys; but upon the mountain sides and summits, when it is not actually raining or "mizzling," there is dry safe ground always to be found, and an atmosphere which may be cold and benumbing to the toes and fingers, but is not liable to engender ague or rheumatism. I found such a stone a little farther on, where the road rises, and slept comfortably upon it for a couple of hours, until the day dawned.

August 8th.—Walk on through grand and beautiful scenery, variegated with lakes and waterfalls, and lighted by the rising sun, to Vossevangen, which I reach at 6 A.M.

This station is prettily situated on the banks of a lake, with fertile country and wooded hills around, and is well provided with food; even such luxuries as white bread may be obtained here. After a supper, or breakfast, whichever it may be called, I went to bed, and slept till midday, spending the afternoon idly and luxuriously, bathing in the lake, lounging on its banks, writing letters, and fishing; but, cockney-like, I caught nothing.

August 9th.—Walk through beautifully wooded country and rich rocky glens, passing a dozen or so of waterfalls and several lovely lakes. It is Sunday, and there is a Sunday calm and brightness in the air, and over the country all around. On crossing the lake at Graven I met the people coming from church. They walked down the hill, then all embarked and crossed the lake, while I ascended the slope, which commands a fine view of the lake. The effect of this procession of boats, creeping slowly and silently over the waters, was very picturesque; the white caps and red dresses of the women contrasting finely with the dark waters of the lake and the wooded hills around.

There is decided character in the costume hereabouts: the men wear short jackets and vests, with double rows of showy glass buttons on them; some have Brummel hats, and others glazed sailor's hats. The women dress very gaily: a white kerchief is folded over the head, fitting closely to its shape; then by means of a wire or cane it is stretched over the top of the head in the form of a large flat arch, spreading far out at the sides, and terminating in large wings, while its loose remains fall down partly behind and partly at the sides: altogether it forms an elaborate and extensive specimen of millinery architecture. The boddice of their dress is a sort of open waistcoat of scarlet cloth with a bright green border, the lower part of it disappearing under the skirt, which comes up very high ; the open part of the vest is filled with a breastplate of embroidered cloth worked elaborately with brilliantly coloured wool and silk : some have bright glass beads worked in with the wool, and the more aristocratic have breastplates worked with gold and silver thread. I saw one matron, whose breast was covered by one great central star, the rays alternately of gold and silver, and the centre of glistening beads. It was altogether on so magnificent a scale, that only a stout woman could find room between the shoulders to display it all at once. Besides these embroideries the women have a brilliant supply of silver and silver-gilt trinkets; I am not sufficiently versed in jewellery to give them a name, but they may be described as cup-shaped buttons without shanks, or brooches. They wear them about the neck ; and when they have a sufficient number they make a necklace of them; while those who possess but two or three simply hang them in the front of the neck. The men also wear large silver brooches in their shirt fronts, and fasten the shirt-neck with silver-linked buttons.

The road now passes over a small fjeld on to Ulvik, a water station, where, after some delay, I get a boat with one rower, a jolly fellow with a club-foot and one eye. I help him to pull, but when he learns how far I have walked he insists upon taking the oar from me, makes a bed with his jacket and some canvas, and will not go on until I lie down comfortably for the night, which is approaching.

One by one the stars broke through the darkening curtain of the sky above, the lingering daylight of the north still shining from the sharp purple edge of the mountain ridges, while I lazily lounged on the bottom of the boat and the old man rowed on monotonously, singing the rude spontaneous music of a happy unselfish heart: then the daylight passed quite away, all the stars shone out at their very best, and several meteors trailed along the sky.

At midnight we reached Vik, the station from which tourists usually start to visit the great Voring Foss. I invited the one-eyed boatman to take supper with me, at which he was much delighted, though the supper was very rude, bread, butter, and cheese being all that the house could supply. The station is a very poor one: a small jackal to so great a lion as the Vöring Foss; but when Norway grows more fashionable, as it doubtless must, there will probably arise a considerable hotel hereabouts.

Note, 1876.—This anticipation has been to some extent fulfilled. Mr. Bennett informs us that this station has been sold to " two respectable young men who are willing to do all they can for the accommodation of travellers, and make their visit to the Vöring Foss more agreeable than it was formerly."

August 10*th*, 1856.—Proceed towards the waterfall walking first to the Eidford lake, then crossing it to Saebo.   There is a fine example of a raised beach or

terrace on this small lake. The valley above is very
wild and grand, well worthy of a visit for itself,
independently of the fall. It is terminated by a wall
of rock that seems quite impassable, reminding one
of the approach to the foot of the Gemmi pass. A
rough zigzag path up this leads to a large rolling
moor, surmounted in the far distance by the snowy
peak of the Halling Jokl. The fall is somewhere hereabouts; a mile or two from the commencement of this
moor: but it is not easy to find. I was told below that
there is a gorge to the left, and a thin thread cascade
visible from a distance, and that immediately below
this is the Vöring Foss; but that in spite of these
indications it is very difficult to find. This proved
to be quite true, and in order to save time I made
for the small farm of Hól, where, after consuming
two large bowls of milk, I engaged a little boy to
conduct me to the Foss. Most of the farmhouses
have pictures of some kind; rude prints, portraits
of King Oscar, and subjects from Scripture history,
prevail. At this establishment a great work of high
art is carefully hung upon the wall and exhibited
ostentatiously in the best available light: it is the
railway map of England from Bradshaw's 'Guide.'

I saw the fall from two points: the first, a ledge
of rock, from which the lower part is visible; the
second displays nearly the whole of it. The torrent
forming the fall flows from the melting snows of
the Halling Jokl, and traverses for some miles the
moor at its foot. There it sinks into a gully it has
cut, to the depth of some 200 feet below the level
of the moor; and thence it pitches in a foaming

mass down into a narrow gorge of fearful depth.
The place from which I first saw it was a projecting
piece of rock, not merely perpendicular, but undermined, and positively overhanging this horribly
magnificent abyss. The rock is smoothed at the top,
and slopes downwards in a most slippery manner
towards the overhanging precipice. A slater, a
chamois hunter, or a Chamouni guide, might possibly
venture to stand upon the brink, but I could not; so
I lay down and let my face hang over, and shuddered
even then. Plumb down below, a clear thousand
feet or more, with no rock or anything to break the
declivity, is the foaming pool of milky water, into
which the torrent thunders with solid, crashing
energy. The idea of sliding forward and pitching
down headlong after the manner of the water, is
irresistibly suggested, accompanied with a horrible
suicidal fascination—a sort of insane desire to do so.
On the opposite side the perpendicular rocks rise
200 or 300 feet higher.

The other point of view commanding the whole
of the fall is rather less horrible. The fall itself is
not a beautiful one, seen thus from above: it being
so much fore-shortened that its height, said to be
900 feet of clear fall, is by no means evident. The
deep, dreadful hole it has dug for itself by its everlasting pounding upon the rock, is grander than the
fall, and well worth a long pilgrimage. The cataract
is not a graceful sheet of water, nor a waving mare's-
tail fall, but a descending mass, a great lump of
water, driving eternally downwards; demonstrating
the tremendous and never-ceasing power of gravita-

tion, and seemingly intent upon forcing a passage to the earth's centre.

The cutting made by this waterfall is altogether a very remarkable one; something like the gorge of the Tamina at the Baths of Pffefers. It must be about two miles in length from the foot of the fall to its outlet at the bottom of the zigzag path up the barren mountain; its depth is above a thousand feet, and it is probably only four or five yards in width. I was sorry that I could not afford time to explore it. At the expense of a day's work and a ducking, I have little doubt that the fall might be reached by climbing and wading, and perhaps, in some parts, swimming up this gully.

It would pay very well, I am sure, to buy the farm at Saebo, and build a rough hotel there with a wooden gallery like that in the gorge of Tamina. I am no advocate for artificial adjuncts to waterfalls; but in this case, where one of the grandest, if not the one grandest fall in Europe is almost inaccessible, an artificial approach to it, displaying not only the fall but the magnificent gorge it has cut, would be perfectly permissible, and the payment of a toll for the use of the gallery (as at Pffefers) quite legitimate. The present station is not only a very wretched one, but is so far from the fall that it is a day's work, whether by horse or foot, to go to it and back again; leaving very little time for contemplating the fall and making an exploration of its vicinity. An inn at Saebo would be within a couple of hours' walk of the top of the fall, and close by the outlet of the gorge. The whole concern might be bought for a

trifle—waterfall, gorge, valley, and farm; some other
waterfalls higher up might be included, and the
mountain thrown into the bargain, as a consideration
for cash payment. It would be the grandest show in
Europe. Is there no Barnum that will bid for it,
and work it in conjunction with steam communication on the Hardanger Fjord? If not, let us form
a Limited Liability.

Note, 1876.—My suggestion has been admirably
superseded by the Norwegian Tourist Club, of which
I am proud to be a member. They have made a
path through the gorge to the foot of the fall. The
steam communication on the Hardanger Fjord is
now amply provided, but the Saebo hotel is not yet
established.

August 11*th*, 1856.—Start with a boat and rowers
for Utne; distant two Norsk miles. It is a windy,
squally morning, but the wind being aft we put up a
sail, and the boat, a very small one, rushes through
the water during the squalls at a wondrous pace. It
is a very exciting sail; the boatman holding the
sheet in his hand, keeps the sail square until the
bow of the boat is fairly buried in the water. The
men tell me that such a boat, with its mast and sail,
can be bought here for five or six dollars.

On reaching the Utne station, I was told that if I
waited for an hour I could have hot " mad," that is,
a dinner. Fearing that such unusual luxury might
corrupt me, I told them that I would not wait, but
would be glad to take anything they had ready—

expecting, of course, some fladbröd and smör. To
my surprise, a well-cooked grouse was brought in
in about ten minutes, with salad; and after it some
gooseberry-fool, with delicious cream. There were
two polished mahogany chests of drawers, besides
other furniture, and a floor so clean that it seemed
never to have been trodden on; in addition to all
this, the walls were papered. This is, to my taste,
one of the best stations I have met with in Norway.
It has no hotel pretensions, yet there is a certain air
of elegance, combined with a thorough farmhouse
homeliness and comfort, and the cleanliness of the
place is quite exhilarating. The charge for all this
was one mark, or 11d. English.

It was well worth the money, and a day's journey,
to see the work of art borne by the hostess upon her
head. It was a mighty structure of white cambric,
or some such material, similar to those already
described (page 232), but far more marvellous. The
great arch overhead spread aloft like a peacock's
tail; and, instead of depending on wire or cane, was
self-supporting by virtue of starch and a wonderful
complication of fine crimping—I believe that is the
proper term, if not I will try another, and say
"goffering." The immaculate whiteness of all its
vast expanse was in perfect harmony with the cleanliness of the whole establishment.

This station is situated at the commencement of
the Sör Fjord, which is one of the terminal branches
of the Hardanger Fjord. I walked on over a rough
path, sometimes keeping the shore, then mounting
the steep hillsides, commanding fine views of the

fjord. There is a splendid combination of savage grandeur and smiling beauty here. Lofty mountains slope steeply down to the water, thrusting forward sharp promontories, between which are sheltered bays with verdant banks of gently sloping cultivated land, and comfortable clean-looking farms dotted here and there. There is much game in this neighbourhood; Utne, I have no doubt, would be a capital station for a sportsman.

The quiet, light-haired, characteristic Norsk people prevail here. The dark Celtic-looking features which were common from Sogndalsfjoeren to Vik have disappeared again. With the true Scandinavian type of face and head, there are combined more cleanliness, better farming, and more of the aspect of comfort and simple honesty. The red waistcoats, silver ornaments, and plaited hair still prevail.

An Englishman, or a tourist of any country, is evidently a great curiosity here. Many pass to the head of the fjord, but they go by water; the land-path is quite a byeway.

The men and women were busy in the fields gathering the harvest of oats and barley. They left their work as I approached, and asked me many questions; but their manner was so simple and unobtrusive that there was no rudeness in their curiosity: indeed, many of them took off their hats and stood uncovered when I told them I was an Englishman. When they become better acquainted with travelling Englishmen, this compliment, I fear, will be discontinued.

On two or three occasions when these gossiping

halts occurred near a farmhouse, one of the girls separated from the group, ran off, and speedily returned bearing a bowl of milk, that was given me to drink as a simple offering of hospitality. One of the farmers told me that the path on this, the west, side of the fjord becomes so bad that I could not reach my destination, the Flesje station, until two in the morning. He advised me to cross the fjord, and showed me a man going over, who rowed me across and refused to take any payment.

I walked on along the eastern shore, encountering the same kind of simple curiosity and civility as before. Being recommended to stop at a house built close on the water's edge, near to Ullensvang, I found it to be the new inn of Lofthuus partly built. The portion that is finished is very comfortable, and I was served with *wheaten* bread and a good bed.

August 12th.—Proceed by boat. The boatman had been a sailor in an American brig, and spoke nautical English. He had a new boat, rather a good one, adapted for two rowers and four or five passengers, and told me that the boat, with a pair of oars, cost 7 dollars, or 12 dollars including mast, sails, and rudder. For 50 or 70 dollars—i. e. from 10*l*. to 14*l*.—a "skyter," or sloop, with a tall mast and sails, a deck, and a cabin, in which two or three persons may contrive to sleep, can be purchased; or for about 25*l*. a vessel fit for sea, in which the voyage round the North Cape might be safely made in summer time, and even the return journey to England. He pointed out to me two or three such vessels, which might pass muster at Cowes in foggy weather.

A party of four or five might start from Bergen or this part of the Hardanger Fjord, purchase such a vessel, lay in a stock of biscuits, &c., and with the aid of a gun or two and some fishing tackle, obtain the rest of their food and visit the best parts of Norway at a very moderate expense. This man, whose name is Peter Hartsberg, of Ullensvang, told me that he would undertake the piloting and management of such a vessel. I should say that four or five hardy fellows might, in this manner, start from Hull, have two months' yachting and some inland excursions, fare handsomely all the while, and return to England at an expense not exceeding 20*l.* or 25*l.* each. Idlers and coxcombs would of course require five or six times as much. With careful management the best fjords, and the voyage to Hammerfest, might be "done" in a boat that would cost but 5*l.* The only difficulty in this case would be in coasting from the mouth of one fjord to another; but by choice of weather this might be quite safely done, the distance to be traversed on the open coast being seldom more than a day's row or sail, and there are plenty of bays and harbours everywhere. The small boat has some considerable advantages over a large one; it may be rowed in calm weather, and can run close into the shore and creep behind projecting rocks, when shelter from the wind is desirable.

The purchase of a boat appears to me a far better investment than the purchase of a carriole. The best scenery in Norway is on the coast and near the fjords; the best stations are those on the fjords, and even the inland scenery is all very near the fjords. A boat will carry a good stock of provisions, besides shooting and fishing materials; and if in addition to this a tent were provided, no cabin would be needed, for the tourist might land upon any convenient rock, make up his bed, and pass the night luxuriously. This, for good swimmers, would be the most enjoyable, and the cheapest way of visiting Norway. A few lines and hooks will always afford a supply of food.

The glaciers of the Folgefond, another great ice-field, covering about 100 square miles, overhang the lower part of the fjord on its western side. From one of these, ships are laden with summer cargoes of ice for the London market by simply loosening the lower part of the glacier where it terminates on perpendicular or steep sloping rocks. The ice thus detached slides and pitches down into the fjord from which it is collected and laden into the vessels.

This arm of the fjord, though a branch of the sea, is so far from the opening of the fjord—more than 100 miles—that the saltness of the water is scarcely perceptible to the taste. One might drink half-a-pint of it without observing it to be at all salt, unless especial attention were directed to the fact. Such being the case, I was much surprised at finding that the rocks are thickly grown with seaweed, a species of bladderwrack, similar to that which abounds on our own coasts, but of paler colour. The mussels are also very abundant, but very small; they diminish in size as the water loses its saltness.

CHAPTER XIV.

The Tyssedal and Skjeggedal — Glacier ruins on a grand scale — An unvisited region and neglected waterfalls — A singular glacier and its mode of formation — Influence of the amount of rainfall in determining the height of the snow-line — Recent invasions of the Skjeggedal — Odde — Evidences of general honesty — A recently arrived pastor — Position of the Norwegian pastor — Importance of practical education to the clergy — A hunt for a lodging — The Haukelid Fjeld — A wet bed — How to pass a wet night on the fjeld — Norwegian mode of preparing coffee — A hint for English cottagers — A returned emigrant.

1856.—I LANDED at Tyssedal, situated at the mouth of the Skjeggedal, where, according to the Norwegian I met at Lonsaet, there is one of the finest waterfalls in Norway—one not mentioned in *Murray,* and apparently unknown to English tourists. The only mention I have found of it in any book is by Professor Forbes, who heard its roar (or what his guide supposed to be its roar) when crossing the Folgefond, which is above 12 miles distant as the crow flies.

I walked, or rather climbed, up the valley by a difficult track, over magnificent glacier ruins—sometimes struggling among moraine boulders, then across vast slopes of bare smoothed rocks, so steep as to be almost dangerous. In most places these steep slopes terminate in a precipice of considerable depth with the torrent roaring below. It is something like walking on a slated house-roof of gigantic dimensions. The glacier-slopes in this valley are even more remarkable than those of the Jostedal.

After two or three hours of this sort of scrambling, I came upon an oasis amidst the desolation, on which oasis are two farms. I asked for Jacob, to whom I had been recommended by the pastor of Ullensvang. Jacob is the principal farmer and owns the greater part of the valley. I found him working in the field, and he took me to his home, he and his wife bidding me a kind welcome. They are a young couple, recently married; and the house, though poor, is clean and comfortable. They gave me a supper of lake trout and ale, and a good straw bed with clean blankets and no fleas, in an adjoining building.

August 13*th.*—After breakfast of trout and coffee I started for the falls, under the guidance of Jacob. We first crossed a little lake, then went on farther to a large one, some four or five miles long: a wild mountain tarn, with precipices around. Over one of these, at the upper end of the lake, is the Ringedals Foss, called also the Skjeggedals Foss. It is a very beautiful waterfall, about 600 or 800 feet high: the stream just grazes the rock nearly all the way, spreading into a snowy sheet, and throwing out a vast amount of spray. It is something like the Mongefoss; not so high, but the quantity of water much greater: is the most beautiful fall I have seen in Norway, but not the grandest. There is no difficulty in approaching it.

We proceeded then to another fall on the north

side of the lake. After about an hour and a half of hard scrambling over rough boulders, with much rank vegetation springing between them, we came to the foot of the Tysse Strenger, as Jacob called them. They are twin falls, pitching into a common chasm. They start at some distance from each other, but in their long journey downwards are so much spread out by the resisting air, that they meet and mingle into one cloudy mass of spray below. The lighter fragments of the spray are carried far away from the body of the falls in a diminishing cloud, extending at its extreme limits to a distance of quite half a mile. This has brought about a curious result: the formation of a glacier of an entirely abnormal character. Although so late in the year, and the sun's heat so strong, the gorge at the foot of the cascade was bridged over with ice, under which the waters flowed. This, though thus undermined, was so strong, that I and Jacob walked over it with perfect safety: from it, in fact, the best view of the falls may be obtained. Like the ordinary glacier, it is crevassed; though I am not prepared to state that the crevasses are formed in a similar manner. I was prevented by a broad blue crevass— reminding me of the " bergschrund," or last upper crevass of an Alpine snow-field—from walking quite close to the falls; but was near enough to get well wetted while standing on any part of this ice-bridge, or waterfall glacier. The mode of its formation is quite evident. During the winter, the spray is of course frozen, and this cloud is so dense that it forms a great accumulation of snow, too deep for all the summer's sun to melt; thus bringing the snow-line in this small spot some thousands of feet lower than that of the country generally, and indicating in a very striking and instructive manner one of the causes (and one that has not been sufficiently considered) which determine the height of the snow-line, viz. the quantity of snow-fall during the winter. It is evident that with a given amount of summer heat a corresponding depth of snow is capable of being melted. With a constant amount of snow-fall during the winter, the height of the snow-line would vary directly with the amount of summer heat; and, on the other hand, with a constant amount of summer heat, the height of the snow-line would vary inversely with the amount of winter snow-fall.

This requires to be continually regarded in all speculations concerning the existence of a " glacial epoch," and in all inquiries as to the causes of the periodic advance and recession of glaciers in particular localities; especially in latitudes where the winter is long. All around this small permanent glacier, or snow fond, is a rank vegetation, which extends up the hillsides far above it.

On our way back, Jacob stopped and listened; we heard a rustling, and he said that it was a bear. We followed the sound, and presently found a track faintly indicated by the treading down and bruising of the herbs growing between the boulders. Following this, we came upon some bear's dung, but did not catch a sight of bruin himself. Had I been alone I should have preferred steering in the opposite direction;

but Jacob assured me that the bear, unless wounded, or its young molested, will never attack a man: that he has been within a yard of a bear, and the bear has civilly walked on. He was very anxious to track this one to its lurking place, as there is a price set upon the heads of bears by the government; he had also a personal objection to these animals as tenants upon his property.

Jacob informed me that only two other Englishmen had, within the memory of man, visited this valley; and that I was the first who had explored these twin falls: the other Englishmen having only visited the Ringedals Foss.

I should recommend all tourists who are tolerably strong on foot to make an excursion up this valley and visit these falls. The wildness of the valley itself, and its very remarkable glacier ruins, well repay the rough journey; and both of the falls are worthy to rank amongst the finest in Norway.

Some fine glimpses of the Folgefond and the fjord are obtained in looking down the valley from the upper ground near the falls. A day and a half is quite sufficient for this excursion, half a day for the ascent of the valley, and a day for exploring the falls and returning; or, with a moderate effort, it might be all done in a day.

Note, 1876.—The above account of this valley and its waterfalls is the first that was ever published. Until the time of my visit it was practically unknown to tourists. The waterfalls were not indicated in any of the maps then published, nor mentioned at all in any guide-books. In 1874 I met one of the chief government surveyors, and he told me that his attention was first directed to these falls in 1860 by a reader of 'Through Norway with a Knapsack.' He had been surveying in the neighbourhood of the Vöring Foss shortly before this, and was not aware that the Skjeggedal contained anything particularly interesting. I therefore regard the reputation of these falls with a certain degree of proprietary interest, and am rather proud of the fame they have acquired since I introduced them to the travelling public.

Speaking of the Ringedals Foss, the recent editions of Murray's 'Handbook' say that "this grand waterfall is one of Norway's gems;" and that "in savage grandeur the scene it presents probably exceeds that of the Vöring Foss, though the falling body of water is scarcely as large or solid." It is now visited by every tourist who can spare a day for doing so, although it is not on the way to anywhere else, and demands a special excursion. The steampackets of the Hardanger make special halts at Tyssedal to enable visitors to ascend the Skjeggedal; photographs and engravings of the falls are published; the Tourist Club has materially improved the track up the valley, which is now practicable for ladies, and during the season a boatman ("the genius of the lake," as he is called) is specially and regularly engaged in rowing tourists along the Ringedals Vand to reach the falls, the visitors now being far too numerous for Jacob himself to escort them.

This invasion of Jacob's solitary and previously unknown domain by an annual flock of sight-seers is one of the most striking changes which has been effected by the development of Norwegian travel since my first visit; but the British visitors to Norway have not *yet* combined to present me with a " piece of plate" and a new hat for discovering these waterfalls. The vignette on the title-page is from a photograph by Knudsen of Bergen. It affords a good idea of the general character of the Ringedals Foss, but does not fairly represent the height of the upper fall, 700 feet. This is due to its distance beyond the lower fall, the concealment of its lower portion, and the want of an object of comparison.

1856.—I walked back to Tyssedal, took boat and reached Odde, at the entrance end of the fjord, the same evening. The closing of the fjord is very fine, the station beautifully situated, and almost an hotel.

August 14*th.*—Heavy rain this morning, which supplied me with an excuse for lingering in these luxurious quarters, to write letters and get my shoes patched; for among other excesses of civilization, there was a travelling cobbler located at a small farm hard by. I also went out a-fishing in a boat, with some tackle lent me by mine host, and caught a haddock, which I brought back in triumph and had cooked for dinner as a first course; it was followed by stewed hare and jelly, with potatoes and other vegetables, white bread and pancake, and cherries for dessert. After this saturnalia, I started again, at about 5 P.M., on my way to a district where such excesses are not likely to be repeated.

I proposed to walk on to Skare, the second station beyond, and about fifteen miles distant; but on reaching the lake of Sandven, found the road so abominable that I was content to halt at Hildal, the first station. There, after the usual supper of fladbröd, butter, and sour milk, I slept in a good, clean straw bed in an upper reserved room, where there was a multitude of boxes containing the family wealth, and, besides these, a watch and some silver trinkets were hanging to nails upon the wall. The people must be very honest, or they could not trust a savage-looking vagabond stranger like myself so unsuspiciously.

August 15*th.*—Walk up the valley by a rough winding path among wild rocks and precipices tangled with pine and birch forests, among which there is many a noisy torrent and many a white cascade. I passed several clusters of poor hovels on small alluvial flats, where the river had once been a lake and left some soil behind. There are some magnificent views of many valleys seen at once, from a portion of the path where it follows a ledge upon the face of a steep precipice, and thus winds round the mountain side at a great elevation. At one part it is bounded by a wall of rock which descends perpendicularly to the river about 1500 feet below: finally it rises to the bare rocks and snow patches. Waligorski's map is quite wrong here; it places the road on the opposite side of the river.

Murray's 'Handbook for Northern Europe,'

p. 187, speaking of this route, describes the stage from Seljestadt to Skare as "the last station practicable for a carriole." This is rather amusing to read on the spot, as the path in some parts is a steep staircase, about 3 feet wide, ascending the stony slope of a mountain side having an angle of about 80°. The rude steps are about 18 inches high. Norwegian ponies and carrioles certainly do make the passage of some astonishing roads, but this one is rather beyond their powers.

The summit of the range being reached at last, the track then descends to a dark, quiet lake, at the upper or alluvial end of which is a cluster of farms, forming a sort of village, called Roldal. This day's walk has been a most magnificent one.

Inquiring of the people in the fields about a lodging, I was directed to "Robert," or to the "Prestgaard," i. e. the parsonage. A kind man in wooden shoes took me to Robert's house, when we found that all the inhabitants were away to the saeters, except a travelling shoemaker, who had taken his temporary quarters in one of the wooden huts of which the farm is composed; the rest being locked up.

We tried another house with the same result. I had some diffidence about applying to the priest, as in such a case there must be a difficulty in paying for one's entertainment; and it is rather presumptuous to call and ask for hospitality without any introduction. In this case, however, as there seemed no alternative, I did apply; not directly for food and shelter, but for information as to where

I might obtain it.   A young man came to the door and evidently wished me farther.   He told me that he had recently arrived here, and pointed to the house of Robert as my best chance.   He was very different in appearance from the other pastors I have seen.   They were all rough, farmer-looking men, of a decidedly practical turn of mind; this was a pale young man, dressed in town costume; he had recently left Christiania, having been transplanted from the refinements of city life to these rude quarters, where he must labour in obscurity with no other associates than the unwashed and untutored peasants around him.   His pallor, high white forehead, and nervous temperament, all indicated a hard student, who had probably earned honours at the university and had dreamed of intellectual fame. He appeared like a man suffering deeply from this isolation and disappointment, and very much soured thereby.   There are no fair competitors for young curates hereabouts; no amateur church decorators, nor workers of needlework slippers.

Certainly a double-refined literary education is a most unfit preparation for a clergyman who is to be placed in such a position as this.   A short apprenticeship to a few useful trades, such as carpentering, cooperage, shoemaking, and, above all, a knowledge of medicine and surgery, would be in every respect better than Greek, Latin, metaphysics, mathematics, and controversial theology.   A good knowledge of the applicable scientific improvements in agriculture would be an immense boon; for, all the pastors being farmers, their farms might thus be made models for the districts, and through them any amount of improvement could be introduced.

I tried again at the house of Robert; and the shoemaker, after some search, found a key which opened a room in which stood a bed. He also supplied me with some raw ham and fladbröd. I had by this time become independent of cooking, and could heartily enjoy a meal of raw ham and bruised oats in the form of fladbröd. The kind man with the wooden shoes accompanied me throughout my search, and did not leave me until I was fairly housed; yet I had great difficulty in inducing him to accept a small payment in return.

August 16th.—Start for a rough walk over the Haukelid Fjeld into the Tellemark, the most un-civilized region of Norway. The distance is six Norwegian miles, or about forty-three English miles. This over wild mountains is equivalent to at least sixty on ordinary roads. I therefore make up my mind to be out for the night, no saeter or halting place of any kind being marked on my map.

The man with the wooden shoes earnestly urges me to take a guide, but I determine to do it alone.

There is a rudimentary road for about a mile out of Röldal which gradually degenerates into a track about a foot wide, and presently to mere. shoe-wearings upon the rock; and even this track is lost altogether at the crossing of every bog, of which there are many. The track is really a difficult one to keep; for although not marked on the map, there are many saeters, and paths leading to them which may be easily mistaken for the track across the

fjeld.   This fjeld, like the others I have crossed,
is for the most part a dull, dreary waste : a rolling
moor, diversified with bogs, many stagnant pools or
lakes, and occasional mountain ridges.   I walked on
all day over this sort of ground, coming at about
nightfall upon a ridge of mountains.

It soon became too dark to follow the track any
farther, and the mountain side being steep and
uncertain, I sought a bed-chamber, and found a
capital one ; a sort of shallow cavern formed by an
overhanging or undermined mass of rock, the floor
of which was a nicely hollowed, clean block of stone.
I ascertained this by throwing a lighted wax match
into it ; thinking it just possible that such snug
quarters might be already tenanted by a bear, or a
family of wolves.   Having thus learned that the
premises were unoccupied, I crawled into them, put
on my extra shirt over my waistcoat, and all the
socks I possessed on my feet and hands ; then coiled
myself on the hollow floor of the stone, laid my
pistol within easy reach, in case of quadrupeds, and
using my knapsack for a pillow, soon fell asleep.
After about two hours I awoke, and found myself
terribly cold ; on further investigation, I perceived
that I was wet also : in fact, that I was lying in a
pool of water, and that water was dropping from the
rock above.   Heavy rain was falling, the air was thick-
ened with mist, and the nice clean hollow in the stone
proved to be a basin worn by the dripping from the
rock above, and evidently a regular water receptacle.

The rain and mist, combined with the darkness of
the night, rendered it almost impossible for me to

proceed: yet, being so thoroughly drenched, it was not agreeable to stand or sit still. I was on the steep side of a mountain partly covered with low bushes and stunted birch trees. After slowly proceeding a little way, a brilliant thought occurred to me: I determined to make a fire, and set to work accordingly. A withered tree offered fuel ; but after three or four hours' perseverance, I only succeeded in getting up a crackling and a smoulder: but this served capitally to pass away the time. I should advise all benighted travellers to light a fire, or to try to do so: the gathering of the fuel, the building it up with scientific arrangements for currents of air, the lighting and blowing, the awakening hopes when a flicker arises, the fluctuations of despair when all is black again, carry one through the dark hours amazingly

August 17*th*.—At daylight I found that I had wandered quite away from any vestige of the path, and therefore steered straight on by compass for an hour or two, until I came upon a track taking something like the direction of my route. I followed it to a place called Flathyl, a small settlement of wooden huts, where I might have obtained lodging and food, but my besetting sin of stubbornness would not allow me to do so: having started for Gugaard, the mental pain inevitably resulting from falling short of that intention would far exceed the amount of physical inconvenience arising from walking ten miles farther: for such is the distance I had yet to make, according to the information I received from the inhabitants of Flathyl.

It appears that I had gone quite away from the proper track, and got on to another which runs nearly parallel to it at a distance of five or six miles farther south. It may be that I lost it at an early part of the journey, where, according to my map, it passes between the Ule Vand and the Staa Vand, and then continues on the north side of the chain of lakes. Certainly I saw no path corresponding to the broad line marked upon the map.

I reached Gugaard at about nine o'clock in the morning, after a walk of above fifty miles, including my deviations from the proper track; and this over ground that can scarcely be measured by miles, the greater part of the way having been over bogs and moraines, up and down mountains, &c. There is an immense number of small lakes on the fjeld, especially towards the latter part of this walk.

I found quite a fertile country at the journey's end, and a considerable number of farms. I stopped at one belonging to a man whom I overtook on the way. My host was a bachelor for the time and alone in the house; his wife and family being at the saeter He cooked me some coffee and gave me fladbröd and cheese, of which I made a hearty meal.

I have found that the coffee is always good in Norway, even at the poorest places; and this, I think, is partly attributable to the mode of preparation, and partly to the fact that the stock of coffee berries at a farm is laid in only at long intervals, and thus it often happens that they have been kept for a long time. It is a fact worth knowing that the quality of coffee is much improved by keeping the berries for

a length of time in the raw state : it has even been
asserted that the commonest coffees may thus be
induced to acquire the aroma and flavour of the
best Mocha. A ripening action takes place, which
develops an increased quantity of the volatile aro-
matic oil, on which the flavour of the coffee mainly
depends. Moreover, the Norwegian farmers always
roast the coffee as required, and grind and infuse
it while still hot. The apparatus commonly used
for roasting it is a sort of covered shovel, or
tray, made of sheet-iron and riveted to an iron
handle. The tray is put into the fire and the
berries shaken about in it. When such a special
apparatus is not possessed, a frying-pan is used,
which answers the purpose equally well. My host
used one on the present occasion, and then turned
the hot berries into a wooden mortar and ground
them with a wooden pestle. This is the usual method
of coffee grinding ; and the wooden mortar and pestle
appear to be kept exclusively for the purpose. The
Norwegian farmers roast their coffee much more than
our coffee dealers do : they make it nearly black ;
and I think this is an advantage when the coffee is
immediately consumed. It is not likely that our
dealers who sell coffee ready roasted will over-roast
the berries, as they lose weight in roasting, and the
amount of loss is proportionate to the extent of the
roasting : when roasted only to a reddish brown they
lose 15 per cent.; to a dark brown 25 per cent.

As the best means of preventing drunkenness is by
supplying an agreeable substitute for intoxicating
drinks, any improvement of the poor man's coffee is

of great social importance; I therefore suggest to the benevolent ladies who so nobly exercise the attributes of woman by visiting with kind intent the dwellings of the poor, that they might do great service by teaching them how to roast, and grind, and make coffee; and, where it is practicable, by presenting the poor man's wife with an apparatus for the purpose. It appears to me that the iron tray and the wooden pestle and mortar answer their purposes admirably; and the two might be profitably manufactured and sold for one shilling, if a quantity were in demand. From what I have seen, the newly roasted coffee may be pounded as quickly and effectually with the wooden pestle and mortar, as it can be ground in a small coffee mill; such a pestle and mortar, kept exclusively for this purpose, would be a valuable addition to the furniture of a cottage. One of these, with a roaster, a pound or two of coffee berries, and a lesson in the use of them, would be a suitable marriage present to the bride of an agricultural labourer; for by their judicious use she might win her husband from the beer-shop, and thus avert the domestic miseries so commonly associated with it.

The wooden walls and ceiling of the room in which I had this meal were curiously decorated; being painted all over with figures of ovals within ovals, considerably eccentric, reminding me of diagrams of the microscopic structure of starch granules.

After a few hours' sleep, and a repetition of the meal just described, I started at two in the afternoon and walked on by a good road to Nordgaard.

On the way I was hailed by a man on the other side of a hedge, to know if I had seen two horses on the fjeld. On finding me to be an Englishman he spoke to me in good English, and told me that long ago he emigrated to America and lived there for sixteen years; but the desire to see his "Gammle Norge" again had brought him back, and finding his daughter married, with a farm and family about her, he was persuaded to remain and end his days there. I asked him which he liked the best, America or Norway? He preferred America. Why then did he not return? He tried to explain; and, after some help in wording and shaping the expression, told me that he liked America, but did not love it; and that he loved Norway, but did not like it; and as loving was stronger than liking, he resolved to die at home.

CHAPTER XV.

The silver brooches, &c., of the peasantry of the Tellemark — A
commercial suggestion — Painted chambers — The Tellemark
as regarded by Norwegians — The Totak Vand — Horse-racing
— The "houseman," or farm labourer of Norway, and his relations to the "bonder," or peasant proprietor — Social equality
of farmer and labourer — The merry-makings of Yule time —
The poor relations of our Norman aristocracy and the royal
families of Europe — Carved cottages — A region of soft bogs —
How to escape smothering in a bog — Presence of mind attain-
able as an art — The "eng," or detached hayfarm — A mud
poultice.

1856.—I ARRIVED early at Nordgaard, which is a rude
farm-station at the road side. All the men here wear
fine silver buttons on their wonderfully short jackets,
the largest obtainable number of similar buttons on
their waistcoats, large silver links at the neck and
wrist-bands of their shirts, and silver brooches on the
shirt-front. The brooches are of the pattern known
by our goldsmiths as the "Maid of Norway" brooch,
and are all of native manufacture. The one worn by
the son of the host cost two dollars at Vinje (a few
miles south of this), where it was made: it was of
silver gilt, of rather elaborate pattern and fine workmanship. I think it might be a good speculation to
purchase some of these for the English market, they
would probably command a ready sale and good
prices as genuine Norwegian brooches; the patterns
and workmanship are so quaint and peculiar that

they could not easily be imitated by any of our short mechanical processes of stamping, &c., and if they were made in England by the same processes of simple hand-labour as in Norway they would cost a great deal more, on account of the higher cost of such labour.

Note, 1876.—(Norwegian jewellery of this and other kinds is now rather commonly offered for sale in London shops, and appears to have become to some extent fashionable. The metallic girdles, which have been so largely worn by ladies of late, are mostly of Norwegian pattern or style. These of course are of Birmingham manufacture, with the exception of a few silver girdles that are imported from Norway, and sold at high prices.)

1856.—I slept in a painted chamber again, but the pattern was more elaborate than the starch-granule decorations of my last night's lodging-place. There were processions of red, green, and yellow cavaliers along some of the beams, and similarly coloured ladies on horseback bearing flower-pots on others. The apostles were distributed on other parts of the walls, the vacant spaces being decorated with paintings of independent flower-pots. There were no real growing flowers, and the floor was wretchedly dirty; the bed, as usual, of straw.

I was now in the famous district of the Tellemark, a district that even the Norwegians regard as romantic.

The peasants of the Tellemark are celebrated as

the most picturesque people in Norway, on account
of their jewellery, their general costume, their
strongly-marked features, their poverty, dirtiness,
and sporting tendencies.   The Tellemark is the
wildest, most barren and dreary of the inhabited
regions of Norway; the district and its inhabitants
bearing a similar relation to the rest of Norway that
the wilds and people of Connemara do to the rest of
Great Britain and Ireland.   A native Norwegian
reared upon fladbröd, and accustomed from his
infancy to rancid smöer, considers it an exploit, a
great effort of hardihood and endurance, to make a
carriole journey through the Tellemark; the idea
of voluntarily doing it alone, and on foot, or without
any commercial inducement, never suggested itself
to any but a mad Englishman.

August 18*th.*—The Totak Vand is my next destination, but the high road makes a considerable bend
following the river to Vinje; to avoid this and to
make my walk more interesting, I determine to leave
the road again and steer across the mountains
towards Kosthveit.   No track is marked on the
map, but on crossing a bridge I find one that ascends
to a high ridge that lies in the required direction.
On the way up I feast luxuriously on wild strawberries, the finest and most abundant I have yet
seen in Norway.   The summit of the ridge commands
a fine view of a long valley and many lakes.   After
this I continue on the high ground of a mossy fjeld
where bogs prevail—very soft bogs—and small
stagnant pools, formed by recent thawing of the
winter snow of which some vestiges were still

visible. This style of country continues to the Totak Vand, which is a lake of considerable dimensions, some fifteen miles long, and from one to six miles wide. With much difficulty I obtained a boat. Being quite beyond the region of regulated tariffs or posting, or any kind of travelling, I had to hire a boat used by the farmer for his personal transport only. He was evidently doubtful whether I was asking him to row me across as a gratuitous favour, or whether such a rough-looking fellow as myself could be induced to pay a trifle. After a preliminary scrutiny, he accordingly asked me how much I would pay him. I offered him a mark, $10\frac{3}{4}d$. (the distance is about four or five English miles), which he accepted eagerly and with evident astonishment at my reckless prodigality.

The scenery on this lake is not remarkable. There are several farms dotted about the slope of the mountain forming the shore on which I landed. It is marked Gaardsfjord on the map. I tried at several houses, and found them all uninhabited and locked up; but there were people working in some of the fields, and they directed me to the best farm-house of the district. I arrived there just as the housemen were returning; and on asking them whether I could have a bed, they told me that the "huusbond" (which, literally translated, means *house-master*, and from which, of course, our word husband is derived) was not yet returned. I waited accordingly; and in the meantime these housemen, or farm labourers, amused themselves with horse-racing of a remarkable break-neck, steeple-chase character. They seized the bare-backed horses by the mane, and throwing themselves upon them commenced beating, and kicking, and howling at the beasts; which, evidently accustomed to the sport, and taking as much interest in it as their riders, started off at a scrambling, furious gallop over the cultivated patches, the bare rock, loose stones and boggy hollows of the mountain side, up hills or down hills of any inclination, apparently intent upon breaking their own knees and their riders' skulls at every step; but they did neither while I was looking on.

The relation of these *housemen*, or farm labourers, in Norway, to the *bonder*, or freehold peasant farmer, is peculiar and interesting. They hold cottages and patches of land, generally sufficient to support two cows and some sheep, and to grow the rye, barley, or oats required for the consumption of the family. These sub-farms, as they may be called, are usually situated on the skirts of the bonder's farm, and are held under him at a fixed rent for a term of two lives—that of the houseman and his widow. The houseman is under an obligation of furnishing a certain number of days' work on the bonder's farm at a fixed rate of wages: usually about 3*d*. or 4*d*. per day, with food. The houseman can give up his land and remove, on giving six months' notice, and in such case he is entitled to the value of house, buildings, &c., he has erected at his own expense; but the landlord cannot remove him, or his widow, so long as the stipulated services are rendered and the rent paid. The unmarried sons and daughters of the housemen are usually employed as day labourers, on the main farm or that of their parents. The eldest son of a houseman commonly succeeds his father by customary inheritance, which in some districts is so usual as to amount to a sort of tenant-right. A labourer is not considered in a condition to marry respectably until he has obtained a house-man's situation and allotment; and the pastor of the parish commonly refuses to marry a couple not thus provided. As the supply of labour is fully up to the demand, and a vacancy for a houseman but seldom occurs, a considerable check is thus put upon early marriages; but at the same time a great amount of illegitimacy is also consequent. By Norwegian law, illegitimate children become legitimate by the subsequent marriage of their parents.

The farms of the bonders seldom change hands · they pass from father to son through many generations, and are usually not more than large enough to provide for the wants of the family. It is but rarely that one can distinguish the bonder from his houseman by any difference in dress or manner. They usually take their meals together, and live on terms of apparent equality. The exceptions that I have seen to this were chiefly in the large farms of the Guldbrandsdal, and in the neighbourhood of Trondhjem, where there are thirty or forty labourers on one farm, and who are called to their meals by the tolling of a bell, hung for the purpose in a little belfry on the roof of the main building.

In the winter time a greater degree of separation and inequality doubtless exists; for that is the great junketing period in Norway, especially in the extreme

north, where Yule time is a long term of continual
darkness. Then the farmers pay long visits to their
neighbours, half-a-dozen families stopping at one
farm; and the host and his family, joining the
guests, start in procession over the snow to the house
of one of his visitors, then to another, and so on till
the round is completed and each has been a host
and guest to all in turn. Dancing is the favourite
amusement at these gatherings, and the polka, or
" polsk," as they call it, the favourite dance. It was
one of the common dances of Norway long before its
introduction into England. I have heard some very
animated accounts of these merry-makings, the
remembrance of which evidently lasts through the
summer; and if I may judge by the blushes and
laughter that have replied to my inquiries, there
is quite as much love-making at these " Yulekiks "
as at the saeters in summer time.

I have already alluded to the length of time that
some of these bonder estates continue in one family.
Mr. Laing quotes some interesting instances of this.
Hrolf Blakar, of Blakar, in Lom parish, " preserves
a headpiece or helmet complete, with an opening
only for the eyes, and parts of a coat of mail, a long
sword, and other articles of his ancestors; and a
writing of King Hakon Magnussen the younger, who
lodged a night in Blakar Gaard, in the fourteenth
year of his reign, anno 1364." *

In many instances the title-deeds by which the
existing families hold their estates are written in a
dead language, the old Norsk, or Icelandic.

* Laing's ' Residence in Norway,' p. 260.

Many of the relations of Rolf Ganger, the conqueror of Normandy, and the ancestor of our Norman line of kings, are still represented by their descendants, who are peasant proprietors in Norway and Iceland. If the royal families of Europe, and our aristocratic families whose ancestors "came over with the Conqueror," could trace their lineage far enough, they would find the farms of their ancestors among the "gaards" of Norway, with nearly the same boundaries as they had a thousand years ago; and in many instances the present bonder would be the direct descendant of the elder son of the common ancestor, while the prince or nobleman has descended from a younger son: for then, as now, when the farms were too small for subdivision, the elder sons inherited them intact, while the younger went to seek their fortunes on the seas and in distant lands. Then they manned the vessels of the terrible sea-kings, and settled on the shores of England, Scotland, France, Spain, Portugal, and even of the Mediterranean; besides colonizing Greenland and the shores of the unknown Western world, which they called Vinland. Now they help to man the ships of the British and American navy and merchant service, and are among the most successful agricultural emigrants to that New World which their ancestors discovered.

The proud beauty I met walking through the valley of the Otta in the parish of Lom, and so near to the farm of Blakar where the king slept, may be as nearly related to some of our proudest Norman families as her Norman features and bearing indicate;

but hers would be far purer Norman blood than theirs, just as her face and figure were finer, and more typical of that style of beauty, than any I have seen among our nobility.

After waiting and watching the horse-racing for above half an hour, the bonder, or possible cousin of half-a-dozen kings, approached. He was informed of my requirements, bade me welcome, supplied me with fladbröd and a bowl of butter, and then joined the group who were dipping their spoons into a pile of Roman cement dabbed down upon a board. On only one occasion have I been asked to partake of this composition, though I have usually found that it is the chief article of food. I suspect that fladbröd and smöer is considered more of a delicacy; especially as I have sometimes seen the bonder and his wife sitting apart and partaking of these.

While wandering about in search of a lodging I saw several very remarkably carved cottages, some of them most elaborate. They are all of a top-heavy design, but vary considerably in detail: they are very old, and not used as residences, but for the storing of hay: the hay is put in at the door of the upper story, and taken out from the lower. Most of the houses hereabouts have some kind of carving about them, but those devoted to human residence have the smallest amount of such outside decoration.

I slept in a comfortable straw bed in the state apartment upstairs, the panels of which were decorated with paintings of cities in gaudy colours.

August 19th.—My next destination is across a roadless country to the Mjos Vand, and from thence to

Holvik, situated at the easternmost end of this lake, and at the mouth of the valley through which flows the river that connects the two lakes of the Mjös Vand and the Tin Sjöen.

The Mjös Vand has a forked shape, and Holvik is at the extremity of the farthest prong; the track marked on the map sweeps round the nearest, but I was told that by going to a place called Synderland, I might cross this part of the lake in a boat, and save some miles thereby. I made for it accordingly, steering by compass over many miles of most detestable bog, alarmingly soft at some parts, and ankle-deep at the best. My boots had stout cloth tops firmly laced up the middle; any sort of shoe would have been inevitably left behind, and even a tight-fitting Wellington boot might have been drawn off, for at every step a great muscular effort was required to drag the foot out of its black muddy peat encasement. I sank knee-deep several times, and a shuddering cold sweat oozed out of every pore on each occasion. Nothing is more horrible to my imagination than the idea of being smothered in a bog; it is a nasty, dirty, disgusting, undignified, and Quilpish death: a quicksand must be bad enough, but that is more cleanly. I had rather be masticated alive, feet first, by any imaginable slow-feeding wild beast, than be smothered in a bog. I am not quite certain whether there do exist any bogs soft and deep enough for a man to sink into and be buried perpendicularly; but if such things are possible, they surely may be found in this district. I saw several patches with a smooth watery surface and a decided pool-like character. They had been pools of water, since filled up with moss, and have well-defined boundaries; so that I could stand upon the brink, and probe them with my walking-stick, which failed to find the bottom. I considered what would be the best to do, in case of stepping unexpectedly into such a gulf, and determined that the best course would be to throw myself backwards immediately, then turn over, and scramble in the direction from whence I came. In the first place, there would be less danger of sinking when lying at one's length than when standing upright; for a certain weight, say 150 lbs., all concentrated on a small surface like that covered by the feet, would have far more penetrating power than the same weight spread over a large surface such as that of a perpendicular section of the body : thus, one might roll safely over a bog upon which it would be impossible to walk. The horrible helplessness of sticking in a bog arises from the effort required to pull the leg out of the close-filling hole, in the total absence of any fulcrum upon which to rest one foot, while pulling up the other. · The object of falling backwards rather than forwards would be, of course, to make way towards the ground of known solidity : that which had been just walked over and thereby proved : while to go forward would probably be progression from bad to worse.

It is always desirable when placed in any position of *possible* danger to suppose the occurrence of the danger, and carefully consider the steps to be taken in such an event; and if the risk is considerable, every step in this predetermined effort for escape

should, as far as practicable, be continually re-
hearsed. By such means, presence of mind may be
acquired as an art. If passengers of an emigrant,
or any other ship on a long voyage, were put
through a course of daily drill, by which, on the
signal of danger being given, each should mechanically run to his proper place, in readiness to take
his turn in getting into the boat pre-assigned to
him, the terrible confusion, the overcrowding and
sinking of the first boat, and most of the fatal
results of blind terror, so apt to prevail on such
occasions, might be prevented; for though there
are but very few who are capable in the moment
of extreme peril of thinking calmly upon what is
best to be done, most people are capable of doing
what is best if they know what that is, more
especially if they have had some practice in the
doing of it, and have confidence in the co-operation
of those around them. This is the basis of military
efficiency.

On arriving at Synderland, I found several
houses, but no inhabitants; they were all absent
at the saeters, or "*engs.*" These latter are distant
pasturages, usually on high, flat ground: small
table-lands. They differ from the saeters, inasmuch
as the grass is mowed and made into hay at the
engs, while the saeter pasturages are rocky regions,
where mowing with a scythe or sickle would be
impossible; and therefore the grass is cut by the
teeth of the cows and goats, and harvested in the
form of cheese. Mr. Laing very ingeniously sup-
poses that the name of England is derived from

these, as the old sea-kings who visited our shores used
the land they appropriated as " engs," or detached
supplementary farms; and thus it was their land of
engs, or England. I passed over several engs on my
way this morning: they are oases of thin brown grass,
amidst the desert of bog; the grass itself growing on
a boggy foundation. The top of this grass is mowed
with a small sickle-like scythe, and stored in wooden
houses, built for the purpose on the spot. These are
easily mistaken for human residences, some being as
large as the farmhouses, and even better looking outside. The people live a gipsy sort of life during this
harvest, as the engs in some districts are many miles
from the farms. I saw some picturesque groups
taking their meal of cement, round fires surmounted
by wooden tripods; a great black cauldron, suitable
for a Macbeth stage property, hanging by a stout
black chain from the tripod. At night the har-
vesters on the eng all tumble pell-mell into the hay-
barns to sleep.

As I depended upon finding a ferry at Synderland, its uninhabited condition was rather awkward.
Finding nobody to help me, I endeavoured to help
myself, by coasting along the lake in search of a
boat. At last I found one; but it was on the opposite side, and the lake being above a mile wide, I
called in vain for some one to bring it over. After
much hesitation as to whether I should swim across
or walk round, I determined upon the latter, and
proceeded accordingly for several miles over vil-
lanous ground, consisting of soft bogs, variegated
with boulders. Being unable to reach Holvik till

the next morning, and by no means willing to attempt such bogs at night, I stopped at a place called Bospen, situated upon the slope of a hill rising from the boggy, trackless wilderness through which I had been struggling all day long.

The effect upon the feet of such a day's bog-walking is rather curious. The mud finds its way into the boots in spite of every kind of lacing; it surrounds the foot, and forms a kind of mud poultice which softens and whitens the skin, and produces a numbness or partial insensibility, such as an ordinary bread poultice would, if applied for a similar length of time.

CHAPTER XVI.

1856.—THE farm at which I stopped was a miserable place; the common room and kitchen being very small and low, and curiously dirty, the windows nearly all broken and pasted with paper. It was crowded with men and women, all of them nearly as dirty as the floor. I entered the room in semi-darkness, and gradually became conscious of the existence of two luminous bodies, shining in a gloomy recess close by me; and, on growing accustomed to the darkness, I perceived, first that they were two human eyes, then that they belonged to a woman, and finally, that the woman was young and of remarkable appearance. The eyes before referred to were pale blue, and the largest human eyes I had ever seen; the woman's nose was short and wide, with great distended nostrils, and yet not ugly; her hair salmon-coloured, and very thick and long: a heap of it was gathered on the top

T 2

of her forehead, and in it was stuck a large round
silver brooch. The brooch in her hair was partly
occupied in securing a kerchief of many colours,
which covered the top of her head and hung loosely
backward and on each side. Another brooch of
similar dimensions shielded her breast. Her whole
aspect was remarkably bold and almost ferocious;
somewhat boy-like and decidedly handsome in its
way. The brooch and high bunch of hair above her
forehead added greatly to the effect. Her portrait
would make a good picture of one of the old Scan
dinavian goddesses; but as I do not remember the
name of any one equally suitable, I shall call her
"Juno," on account of her ox-like eyes. Another
girl—possibly her sister, though quite unlike her in
expression, being very meek, gentle, and rather
pretty—sat at the fireside: she may be called
"Vesta." I fell into a romantic state of mind: the
darkness concealing the dirt upon their faces, I
imagined them both very beautiful, and built up
rustic love stories, of which they were the heroines;
until Vesta, reaching from one of the beams overhead
a short pipe, lighted it, as I supposed, for her father;
but, to my horror, and the total destruction of all
the little novels, she commenced smoking it herself
and then handed it to Juno, who sucked in turn and
handed it back again. They spat noisily into the
fire, and altogether behaved in the most unromantic
manner imaginable, for two girls of about fifteen and
eighteen years of age. After long and patient
waiting, I asked Juno whether I could be provided
with any supper. She answered abruptly, "No;"

but an old man, who, being the dirtiest of all, was, I suppose, the master, brought me some fladbröd and drab-coloured smöer.

There were two very dirty beds in the room; and these were evidently all that existed upon the establishment, although eighteen persons besides myself were crowded in this small low kitchen. The bonder asked whether I would sleep in the hay; to which inquiry I joyfully answered "Yes;" for having already felt a procession of fleas moving up my legs, I had gloomy forebodings of the animated condition of the clay-coloured bedding.

It was now quite dark, and the man conducted me across a field to the door of a large building. I entered it, and scrambling over a great depth of hay, commenced arranging some sort of bed, when I was startled by a loud laugh of decidedly soprano pitch, then by a voice and another voice answering it. The laughter and voices were those of Juno and Vesta in alarming proximity to me: presently I heard other voices, and then I found that I was one of a large company of bedfellows of both sexes, all sleeping together in the hay. It was a cloudy night and very dark, so that I can testify nothing regarding the arrangements for separating the sexes. For above an hour there was a continual talking, with occasional squeaking, followed by much laughter; then the number of talkers gradually diminished till only a couple or so remained, and finally nothing but snoring was to be heard. During all this time I was endeavouring to make myself comfortable, and was much surprised at the complete failure of all

my efforts, for after my experiences of rough lodging
and nights out of doors, I expected to find a bed on
the new-mown hay quite a luxury: but I found it
most miserable.

Some people can sleep anywhere provided they
are warm, and on anything provided it is soft; for
my own part I can endure exposure, cold, and a hard
resting place, but to be half buried in odorous
material and perpetually tickled with straws,
irritates me beyond endurance. In order to understand what it is to sleep in such a place, it must be
remembered that the hay in this boggy country is by
no means composed exclusively of grass: about half
of it consists of dried leaves and stalks of various
wild plants, including a great proportion of thistles;
moreover it is not carefully stacked and pressed
down, but pitched anyhow into these receptacles, and
falls on the floor and rises to the ceiling in a state of
promiscuous entanglement: it was about 10 feet
deep, and very loose, in the region of my night's
burial place. To tell how the stalks and blades and
thistle-leaves got down my neck, and up my sleeves.
and ferreted all over me, would require a whole
chapter. Nor were these representatives of the
vegetable kingdom my only tormentors, for the
entomology of all Scandinavia seemed to be illustrated by the animated specimens that crawled all
over me. Among these the ants predominated. I
have a great respect for these little animals: their
social institutions, their industry and public spirit,
always awaken in my mind feelings of the deepest
interest; but in spite of all this they tickled most

horribly, for their very active legs are extremely thin, cased in a shell of metallic hardness, and their toe-claws wondrously sharp.

There is an important acid, called formic acid, from *formica*, the Latin name for ants; the old chemists obtained it by bruising unhappy ants in a mortar, and distilling their remains. When ants are irritated they eject this acid, and so do the leaves of the stinging-nettle; from which it may also be obtained by distillation. Chloroform receives its name from having the same composition as formic acid, but with chlorine substituting the oxygen. It is supposed by some that the perspiration of ants consists of this acid, and thus their reputed aversion to walk over chalk has been explained; the theory being that the formic acid causes the chalk to effervesce, and suffocates the ant with the evolved carbonic acid. These facts and speculations surround the ant with an additional interest to the chemist in his laboratory, but by no means increase its desirableness as a bedfellow under circumstances calculated to irritate the worthy little animal. That they were seriously irritated in this haybarn there can be no doubt; they had been gathered with the hay, and carried far from their native communities, and were wandering fretfully among the labyrinth of dried vegetation in search of some solid ground by which they might reach their homes. My body was such a landing place, and once reached, their enterprising disposition led them to explore the island by crawling under my clothes and all about my skin. If I had ever doubted the theory of their irritant acid per-

spiration, this night's experience must have converted
me, for on no other supposition can I account for
their special powers of torture.   The intense pain
produced when a small fly, or especially a winged
ant, is drowning in the lubricating moisture of one's
eye is probably due to this acid, which is nearly allied
to cantharadine, the active principle of blisters.

Besides these, there were many other creatures
with many legs wandering with like uneasiness in
search of their lost homes, their eggs, and maggot-
babes ; and as I fell into short beginnings of feverish
slumbers every blade of grass seemed to be a centi-
pede or a wriggling worm, the dried leaves became
crawling beetles, and every bit of stick or twig
assumed the changing form of some intolerable
creeping beast.

I might have borne all this much better had I
adopted the night dress (that of Paradise) before
alluded to (page 226), which seems to be usually
worn when sleeping thus ; for the irritation was all
exaggerated by the vegetable fragments and the
industrious animals being confined between the
clothes and the skin.   But there were many difficulties in the way of adopting this costume : first of all
it was doubtful whether I should ever find my clothes
again if I once parted with them ; then there was the
uncertainty as to whether any sort of fence existed
between me and the proprietors of the female voices:
the possibility of coming in positive contact with
Juno and Vesta in the course of my blind struggles
with the hay, or of sleeping till daylight, and then
having to hunt for my clothes in their presence, were

fearful subjects of apprehension to a man whose leading characteristic is extreme modesty.

Besides all this, I was not aware, and am not now, whether the custom of sleeping in the hay in Adam's costume is extended to these communities of sleepers, as the sleeper whom I startled on my way to Lunden was apparently solitary. I might have ascertained this had my powers of endurance been greater, but I was forced to yield before daylight. I scrambled towards the hole by which I entered, took off my clothes in the adjoining field, and shook away the inner lining of tormentors.

On returning, I found that the bonder had risen, and general activity was commencing; and I was much surprised at finding him busy in preparing for me a breakfast of trout and coffee, and showing a degree of attention which contrasted strongly with the apathy of the night before, when it seemed doubtful whether I should get any food at all. This change was probably produced by my showing some money and offering payment after supper; though he refused it, and told me to pay next morning. He, his housemen, and Juno and Vesta, had all evidently thought me a houseless wanderer who had come to beg for food and shelter; the idea of a tourist being of course utterly unknown to them, as no one within the memory of man had ever travelled for amusement thereabouts, so far away from the regions of roads or any sort of highway. When, after breakfast, I paid the farmer 20 skillings (about 9d.), he looked at the money with astonishment, exclaimed that it was " enogh," with a pronunciation that would pass

for good lowland Scotch; he then shook hands in
token of thanks, and insisted on walking with me to
the top of the neighbouring hill to point out the way.
At Gaardsfjord, where I stopped the previous night,
I gave the host one mark, which he returned to me,
saying it was *"for meget,"* too much, and I had much
difficulty in inducing him to accept it.

August 20th.—The hill that I ascended with mine
host is the first of a series, and my route for several
miles was an almost continuous ascent—a welcome
change after the previous bogs. The highest point
attained commands a fine panorama of an immense
extent of country, consisting for the most part of
rolling hills, with boggy and pool-filled hollows and
flats between. This seems to be the prevailing
character of the Tellemark country, and may have
considerable influence in producing some of the
peculiarities of the people. I have no doubt that
most of these boggy regions might easily be drained,
and thereby converted into fertile plains. The drainage of a flat, boggy country nearly on the sea-level
is a very difficult problem; but an elevated plain
may frequently be well drained by cutting a single
trench. All that is required is to find the lowest
part of the boundary of the elevated marshy land
which is situated near to a descending valley, and
then to cut a deep channel, establishing a communication between the marsh and the valley; this would
drain most of the land lying above the level of the
bottom of the cutting. I am satisfied that vast areas
hereabouts might be thus reclaimed at a very small
expense.

On descending, I came upon a repetition of bogs and small lakes, which continued, with occasional alternations of low ridges, to the Mjös Vand. After about an hour's walk to the eastward, along the steep and rugged banks of the lake, I reached its easternmost extremity, from which the river forming the Rjukan Foss issues. This lake is very shallow and has apparently a rich alluvial bottom. Some thousands of acres of land might be gained by simply lowering the bed of the river Maan, forming its outlet. This might be very easily done, as the river makes some rapid descents very near to the lake, which is of great extent, and its level limits the natural drainage of a vast amount of surrounding country. The simple lowering of this lake would alone drain many of the surrounding bogs; but if, in addition to the lowering of the Mjös Vand, the principal channels of communication between it and these boggy regions were cut deeper, a vast region, now a noxious, boggy waste, might be rendered as valuable as any of the existing land at this latitude and elevation: moreover, the climate would be greatly improved by the reclamation of so much bog and so great a surface of stagnant pools.

On reaching the head of the river, I found no track down the valley, as I expected, and no bridge or any other visible means of crossing to the opposite side, on which a track is marked on the map. I scrambled onward through bushes, and over rocks, till I came to a perplexing obstacle—the edge of a small precipice, a perpendicular wall of rock about 15 feet high; rather too deep to jump or drop down, and not suffi-

cient to turn one back without severe humiliation.
I walked along it for some distance; and finding
that it grew worse as I went farther, I returned to
the most promising point, and stood for some time
in doubt whether to hang as far down as possible,
and then drop, or to make a long journey round—
until at last, in a moment of courageous determina-
tion, I pitched my knapsack down, so as to be
compelled to follow. There is a steep slope, covered
with bushy plants, at the foot of the rock-wall, and
the fate of my knapsack was far from encouraging,
for it rolled, and bounded, and bumped over and
over a terrible distance down this slope; and when I
dropped I followed its example to a small extent,
but with no other damage than torn clothes and
some scratches.

After scrambling on still farther, I came opposite
a saeter situated on a slope on the other side of the
river; and at the foot of the slope was something
that appeared like a boat. I shouted loudly and
long, and was just about giving up hopes of a ferry,
when an old man, bent nearly double, emerged from
the saeter and moved slowly down the hill; he then
drew the boat to the bank and spent a considerable time in baling water from it. At last he stepped
into it and rowed across; first pulling with the oars,
and then, while the boat moved on by the impulse
thus given, baling out water—then another pull, and
more bowls of water over the side,—and so on until
he reached the shore with the boat nearly filled.
The boat was a curiosity, being made simply of two
squared pieces of the stump of a tree, forming the

stem and stern; to these ends some deal boards were nailed, and thus the bottom and sides were formed; it was a sort of rude packing-case with thick ends, and no top; and some lumps of stone were placed in the bottom for ballast. The old man got out, and we hauled the box ashore, to let the water run out of its sides; then I threw out two big stones that ballasted one end, and took their place, baling out the water as the old man rowed. When I remarked that the boat would not last much longer, he smiled; said that it would last as long as he should himself, and patting its side, told me that he made it fifteen years ago: he seemed to have a strong affection for it, and I could not help fancying that he intended it to be his coffin.

After crossing, I walked up to the saeter, answered a great many questions from the curious inhabitants, and then followed a track which ascends to a great height above the river and commands some fine views. Many tourists visit the renowned Rjukan Foss, but they come from the other side, and very few ascend to this part of the valley. After passing another saeter, where I was supplied with milk in a kind of trough shaped like a London butcher's tray, and demanding much skilful management to drink out of the corner without overwhelming oneself, I arrived at the farm of Westfjordalen, which was the residence of Marie, the heroine of the *Marie Stige*. This farm is situated on the side of a mountain, which blocks up the valley.

The ordinary track by which the lower part of the valley may be reached, ascends about 1000 feet over the ridge of this mountain, and then, of course, a corresponding descent has to be made. But the river! How does that find its way down the valley? There is a deep cleft, a great chasm, nearly 2000 feet in depth. Ages had passed away, and nobody had dreamed of any other way to reach the lower valley than that over the mountain; but Marie, whose lover lived below, had heard of his rival's plot to waylay him as he came by the track over the ridge to visit her, so she tried the dreadful precipice, and found that by clinging with fingers and toes to the little ledges of the rock, she could pass in a direct line along the face of it. Thus she warned her lover of his danger, and enabled him to meet her secretly and safely, by traversing the giddy path she had discovered; and the lovers evaded—as lovers always do—both the cruel father and his accomplice, the wealthy rival. By this path they met as usual, until at last detected; and then Ejstein Halfoordsen, the lover, was prevailed upon to fly, in order to escape new plots against his life. In the course of years the father died, the rival ceased to persecute, and Ejstein returned with fame and wealth. He came by the shortest way; Marie saw him coming, and called his name aloud; he raised his arms and waved his hands as a signal of recognition, and by doing so was overbalanced and fell. She watched his falling body till it disappeared in the foam of the Rjukan Foss; when the dark veil of madness fell over her mind, and fulfilled its beneficent intent by shutting out a knowledge too horrible for endurance.

A little girl from the farm guided me to the edge of the precipice, from which a distant view of the fall is obtained. From this point it is much like the Vöring Foss, but better seen. My guide then showed me the beginning of the track leading to the Marie Stige, telling me that she was forbidden from going to the Marie Stige itself. I gave her 4 skillings, which she protested was too much, at the same time offering to return two, and it was with great difficulty that I induced her to keep the whole, amounting to rather less than 2d.

I then proceeded along what I supposed to be the Marie Stige, a ledge of rock trodden with footsteps, varying from 6 inches to a foot in width, with a sloping wall of rock above and the chasm below; this continued until I came to a part where there are two tracks, one apparently leading over the hill, the other directly to the perpendicular wall of the precipice, which is seen a little farther on rising to a fearful height overhead, and proceeding downwards to the gulf below with an unbroken smoothness that looks utterly hopeless: but I determined to go on as long as there was any vestige of a track. Following thus the marks of footsteps, I came out at last, not upon the edge, but upon the face of the precipice which is formed by the splitting down of the barrier mountain before referred to; it was a giddy path, but I kept along it, placing my feet upon the worn ledges and clinging to other ledges above, until I came to a tree which grew upon a ledge similar to those I had stepped upon, but much wider, and which seemed to be the end of the track

I was following. Some initials cut upon the tree, as triumphant indications of the carver's exploit in reaching it, rather confirmed the notion that I had only followed a track leading to this as a station for viewing the waterfall and the whole of the great chasm, which are well displayed from this point.

Concluding that such was the case, and that the other ascending track leads to the Marie Stige, I was about to return, when I saw far away below me, standing on a large table of rock, five student-looking young men, with a peasant, who appeared to be their guide; they hailed me and I returned their salutation, but could not hear what they said. Then the peasant took off his shoes, left them, and presently reappeared moving along the face of the precipice like a fly on a wall. His means of adhesion were totally unintelligible from the distance, but as he approached I perceived that he was clinging by fingers and toes to narrow ledges of rock from 1 to 4 or 5 inches wide. At last he reached me, and asked me whether I would accompany him back, which I consented to do; though it appeared rather a dangerous exploit: I found, however, that it was much easier than it appeared to be from the distance. The rock has a perpendicular lamination (and doubtless a corresponding cleavage, to which the formation of the chasm is due); the abrupt terminations of these laminæ form ledges, which though very narrow are perfectly firm and safe, affording a reliable foothold without the slightest tendency to slipperiness; besides these, there is an abundance of similar ledges affording firm finger-hold, which, though but an inch wide, give a most comfortable assurance of safety to the climber, who, bending the hands claw-fashion, clings to them with the finger-ends. I would rather, under such circumstances, have a firm two-inch foot ledge, and one inch of such finger-hold, than an eighteen-inch pathway with nothing for the hands. At about half way I stopped to contemplate the scene, which is magnificent, and its grandeur is heightened by the peculiar position from which it is seen.

Imagine yourself "holding by your eyelids," as the sailors have it, in the manner just described, to the face of a precipice which rises overhead some 500 or 600 feet, the upper part being, in fact, quite out of sight; then, with great care, and some fear and trembling, you turn yourself round, gradually placing your heels on the former position of your toes, removing your hands one at a time from their clutching-places, and finding a lower ledge upon which to rest the wrist-end or heel of the hand. Having anchored yourself thus, and keeping your back quite flat against the rock (as any leaning forward would be fatal), you look in the direction of the upper part of the valley, and see far below and far away, a dark chasm partly hidden by branches of trees. Through this the river flows, and as it comes nearer reaches a wider opening of the gorge, advancing towards the edge of a precipice, over which it rolls towards a gully of its own cutting, and then pitches down an unknown depth: for the mass of falling water plunges into a white cloud that hides the bottom of the dark abyss, and rises up high into the sunshine. This is the perpètual spray, the reeking, or "*rjukan*," from which the name of the fall is derived. You may, however, estimate the depth, for looking straight down the gray wall to which you are clinging, you see that it terminates in dark, quiet water. This is the same that a few minutes since was thundering and tearing down so furiously, and partly rising again to form the ever-hanging, though ever-falling, cloud of waterdrops.

Note, 1876.—(According to the recent measurements of Vibe the height of this fall is 780 Norsk feet, about 800 feet English. The part of the wall upon which I halted is quite as much above the top of the fall as the height of the fall itself, and therefore the depth of precipice below must have been about 1600 feet. The wall is not absolutely perpendicular, but within a few degrees of it.)

1856.—On reaching the end of the Marie Stige and landing on the platform of rock upon which the five tourists stood, I was congratulated on my escape, but at first did not understand the meaning of these earnest congratulations. One of the tourists, an Anglo - Portuguese - South - American merchant, explained in English that, seeing me halting in that terrible situation (by the tree before mentioned), they concluded that I had got so far and was unable to advance or retreat, and were under the impression that the accident of their arrival with the guide had been the means of saving my life. They were rather disappointed when I told them that I was in no danger, and proposed to recross with them. The Portuguese exclaimed that he would not do so for a vast amount; and all the rest concurred. I can easily understand that, viewed from this position, where the ledges are quite invisible, and both the height above and depth below fairly seen, it must be somewhat thrilling to witness the passing of the Marie Stige—far more so than to do it.

This platform of rock affords by far the best view of the fall, and those who come from below have no occasion to cross the Marie Stige, except for its own sake. The quantity of falling water is much greater than at the Vöring Foss, but the height does not appear to me so great. Much of the effect of the quantity of water is lost, on account of the narrowness of the chasm down which it falls.

After lingering till the sun had set, I walked on, in company with the Portuguese and his four Norwegian companions, to the farm below, where they remained. This farm is said to have been the residence of Marie's lover, and many tourists who walk up the rugged way from it to the platform of rock from which the best view of the fall is obtained, imagine that they have thereby crossed the Marie Stige. I walked on by moonlight through a fine valley, passing many cascades, until I reached Dale, at a late hour. This is a good station, and a regular halting place for visitors to the Rjukan Foss.

Note, 1876.—The Krokau farm, which is very near to the Rjukandfoss, is now the property of the Tourists' Club, and is rented by Miss Ingebord

Engell, who, as I am told, provides good quarters and excellent food for tourists.

I have not met with anybody who has repeated my walk between Röldal and this point, and I suspect that very few have done it. The Norwegians themselves, and the English sportsmen and tourists best acquainted with Norway, regard this walk as an exploit of unusual hardihood. I do not think it probable that I shall repeat it myself in the same manner, though many tourists will hereafter pass over much of the same ground under very different circumstances, as an excellent post-road affording direct communication between Bergen and Christiania by way of the Hardanger Fjord to Odde, and the Hardanger Fjeld, over which I walked between Odde and Röldal, and thence over the Haukelid Fjeld by a course nearly parallel with my walk, is now in course of construction, and nearly completed.

Government stations will be appointed on the road, so that the tourist who desires to see genuine Tellemark peasant life will require to deviate from this road by similar paths to those I have described. He need not fear that the *whole district* will be modernized; the influence of this strip of road will not extend very far on either side of it.

Tourists who are satisfied with a moderate glimpse of the Tellemark may obtain it in the course of a trip from Christiania to the Rjukandfoss (see next chapter) by deviating a little from the now well-beaten route which is curiously changed since I was there, for it has become a railway, steampacket and post-road excursion, not merely for foreign visitors, but also as a favourite Saturday and Monday trip of the citizens of Christiania. During the summer, the Tourist Club Hotel at Krokau is usually crowded on Saturday nights.

CHAPTER XVII.

The Tin Sjöen — Tellemark costume — A sociable squirrel — Pine forests — Dirt, rags, and finery — A few facts indicating that tourists with weak stomachs should not visit the Tellemark Solid chairs — Breakfast with the bonder — An investigation of the contents of my knapsack — Sudden change in the social aspect of the country — Wine-shops, commerce, and mining Kongsberg — A public-house and Sunday amusement — The long town of Drammen — My reception by the hotel keepers of Drammen — Home-like scenery and its associations — Gaiety of Christiania — Family affinity between ourselves and the Norwegians and Danes — Back to London.

August 21*st*, 1856.—WALKED down the valley to Mael, on the Lake of Tin Sjöen, then took a boat to Haakenaes, where there is a good station, and from thence by another boat I proceeded to Graver, 10 miles farther down the lake. The boatmen were two fine-looking fellows, tall, and powerfully built, with the large and strongly marked features that characterize the peasants of the Tellemark. Their short jackets and waistcoats were as usual thickly covered with silver buttons, and at the knees of their knee-breeches there were as many more buttons as could be placed there. The lake is rather a fine one, bounded by high wooded hills and fertile little bays, with farms upon them in every bend of the shore. Wild waterfowl abound here, and we were much amused with a sociable squirrel that followed the boat for a long distance, as we rowed close to the rocky shore.

On landing at Graver I inquired for the track leading to Kongsberg, by Bolkesjö; a well-defined path was shown to me, and I was recommended to stop at the farm of Lier, which, according to my informant, would afford the most comfortable quarters in the district. There is much fertile country, and some tolerably good farms in the neighbourhood of Graver. (*Note*, 1876.—A steampacket the 'Rjukan' now plies daily on the Tin Sjo during the summer.)

The first part of my walk was amidst the rich scenery of fertile winding valleys, and then through silent forests of tall pines, with stems so large, so high and straight and uniformly tapering, that Milton's lines,—

> " His spear, to equal which the tallest pine
> Hewn on Norwegian hills to be the mast
> Of some high admiral, were but a wand,"

haunted me continually as I walked along. After eight or ten miles of such forests, the track passes over some curious glacier ground,—great plains of smooth, flag-like rock, with very slight inclination and remarkably deep groovings. Finally, I reached Lier, which is situated on the flank of a curiously shaped mountain, overlooking a melancholy lake. I should never have found it, had I not overtaken three dirty men who were going out a-fishing, and with whom I walked for about an hour. They pointed out the farm, which was not visible from the track, and is situated in a region so hopelessly rocky that I could scarcely believe any agriculture possible: I should not have thought of looking for a house thereabouts. On reaching it, I found, as usual, that there was nobody at home, but saw some people in the distance, and therefore went in at the open door, and sat down till they came.

The housemen and women came first, then the master; all of them incredibly dirty, and profusely decorated with silver brooches and other silver and gilded silver trinkets. The master, as usual in the Tellemark, was the dirtiest, and wore the greatest amount of jewellery. On his shirt-front were three huge circular brooches that touched each other for want of space between them; the neck was fastened by silver shirt-links with chains hanging from them. There were three rows of silver buttons on his immeasurably short waistcoat, and three rows more on the sides of each knee, and all were brightly polished; but his stockings were full of holes, and the garments upon which the silver was displayed were miserably ragged. It appears here to be the general custom to wash and shave once a week, so that the bristles and the dirt accumulate on their faces simultaneously, and are both pared off with a razor on Sunday mornings: it now being Friday evening, and hot weather, these decorations had nearly reached their weekly maximum.

My supper consisted of dirty fladbröd, good butter, and sour milk; this last the master brought me in a bowl, quite filled: he held the bowl with one hand, and his thumb was immersed in the sour milk, which exercised its solvent powers upon the film of dirt that overlaid his skin, so that by the time he placed the bowl before me his immersed thumb was surrounded by an aura, or dark halo of dirt particles, suspended in the beverage. By skilful management, drinking from the opposite side of the bowl, and avoiding any agitation of its contents, I contrived to drink some of the milk without reaching the portion thus beclouded.

The room had the usual dirty floor and pasted paper windows; half-a-dozen people were eating cement, but there was no Juno or Vesta here. Besides the kitchen, or common room, there was a little second room, in which I slept in a very dirty bed, and breathed a cheesy atmosphere, produced by two very large tubs filled with stale milk in a state of putrescent, caseous fermentation, and covered with a thick mouldy film, from which arose an intensely sour odour of rotten cheese. In this room were two specimens of a curious chair, such as is occasionally met with in those parts of Norway where the largest pine trees abound. They are made by simply cutting a log about 3 feet long from the thickest part of a large pine trunk; one side of one half of this log is adzed out to form a seat, the other side being left in the rough for the back, which is curved inside, and thus a solid seat, a block with a back, is formed.

August 22nd.—On rising I found that the housemen had all departed and were working in the fields, but the bonder and his wife were waiting at home to take breakfast with me. This was quite a state repast, consisting of coffee and rye-bread and butter. The loaf was new, better than usual, and had apparently been prepared on purpose, or was possibly part of the family provision for Sunday.

After breakfast, my hat and stick were carefully

examined, and such longing glances were cast upon
the outside of my knapsack that I felt morally compelled to exhibit its contents, which afforded an
immense amount of delight. Small as it was, mine
host and his wife evidently regarded it as a museum
of wonders : the scarlet flannel shirt was an object
of special admiration; the softness of the material,
the brilliancy of the colour, the buttons and stitch-
ing, were all commented upon with the utmost
enthusiasm, and they evidently considered me guilty
of a great waste of splendour in wearing so brilliant
a garment inside. Had it belonged to the bonder,
he would certainly have worn it as an overcoat, and
have covered it with all the silver brooches and
buttons in his possession. If I had possessed another
besides that on my back, I should have made him a
present of it, and waited over Sunday to witness the
result.

As a protection against the weather, and immersion
in rivers, &c., I made up the contents of my knapsack into small parcels rolled in oiled silk, each
secured by an indiarubber ring. These rings interested the investigators immensely, and when I
stretched one of them to its utmost and passed it
over my head, the bonder threw up his hands,
exclaiming, "O min god fader!" "O min god fader!"
and repeated the exclamation every time I showed
him a new application of their wondrously expansive
powers. When, at the conclusion of the show, I
gave him two of these rings, he rushed off to show
them to his housemen, and he evidently valued them
above the artificial flies and fish-hooks.

Walked on to Bolkesjö, where I am regaled with an absolute dinner. The cleanliness of the station plainly indicates that I am now emerging from the Tellemark. The beams of the room are elaborately decorated with scroll carvings and Latin inscriptions in relief; the letters very large, and painted alternately red and yellow on a green ground. I intended to take a carriole to the next station, in order to have some experience of this mode of travelling before leaving Norway; but I was told that they could not fetch a horse in less than three or four hours, and therefore I travelled by my usual means of conveyance, along a good road and through a well-peopled country. I was much struck with the change in the appearance of the people and the condition of the houses that was evident immediately upon passing the boundary of the Tellemark. At Moen, I found a small but comfortable station, and enjoyed the luxury of sleeping in a clean uninhabited bed.

August 23rd.—On approaching Kongsberg this morning, I was rather surprised at passing some wine-shops; the first I had seen in Norway. In order to ascertain what sort of wine is popular here, I called for a glass at one of the shops, and was supplied with some cherry wine, strongly flavoured with the prussic acid from the kernels. The charge was 2 skillings per glass.

Kongsberg is a considerable town, with indications of commerce that are quite novel, after Norwegian country life; for besides its mining industry, there is much trading in timber, as the logs and rafts in

the river testify. Being Sunday, I could not visit
the great silver mine; and having only just time
enough to reach Christiania by the starting of the
packet, was unable to afford the two days' delay that
such a visit would cost; therefore I pushed on to the
next station, intending to take a carriole there, but
found there was none: nor was there any food, but
there was an abundance of ale. It was, in fact, remarkably like an English beer-shop, and the people
about were beer-shop customers such as mining districts usually supply.

At Hougsund, which is rather more than half-way
to Drammen, there is a very large station; quite a
public-house, with a skittle-ground and tea-gardens
attached, where a game nearly the same as American
bowls was being vigorously played by artizans in
their Sunday clothes. There were other games, such
as throwing a suspended ring upon a hook, &c., and
there were many players, but I observed no indications of gambling; and though most of the players
and the loungers, who were very numerous, were
drinking ale, there was no drunkenness. This is
evidently a favourite place of Sunday resort for the
artizans of the vicinity. The reader must remember
that I have now left behind the wild district of
Tellemark, the region of bog and mountain and thinly
scattered farms, and that I am now in the midst of
a dense population and much business. Most of
the company consisted of working men in their
Sunday clothes, in which guise they looked singularly
like Scotchmen under similar circumstances. Like
Scotchmen on Sunday, they dress all in black; like

Scotch artizans on Sunday, they seemed oppressed with a consciousness of being in full dress, and move about in a bashful, uneasy manner ; and like Scotch-men, they can evidently take a great deal of ale without inconvenience ; but they are unlike Scotch-men *in Scotland* on Sunday, for they conduct them-selves as consistent Christians, following the example of Christ in making the Sabbath a wholesome and cheerful holiday. They are Lutherans, and are mindful of the words of the great reformer when he told them to " keep the Sabbath holy for its use to body and soul ; but if anywhere the day is made holy for the mere day's sake, if anywhere anyone sets up its observance upon a *Jewish* foundation, then I order you to work on it, to ride on it, to dance on it, to feast on it, to do anything that shall remove this encroachment on the Christian spirit and liberty."

These Norwegian workmen while they scrupulously abstain from following their daily labour, make the Sunday a bright and cheerful holiday—going to church in the morning, taking country walks in the afternoon, and singing and dancing in the evening.

I had a dinner of broth and mutton, the broth prepared with barley precisely after the manner of Scotch broth, and then walked on to Drammen, meeting many people on the way, some on foot, other in carrioles and gigs, many fishing on the banks of the river, and several carrying guns ; these, and the continual banging that I heard in the fields around, showed that shooting is a favourite sport in this neighbourhood. Among other provisions for amusement were some " öl vogus," or ale waggons, carts built for the purpose of carrying bottles of ale, and retailing them on the wayside. The two that I passed were besieged by customers, and corkscrews were in great demand. There are several terraces in this valley of the river Drammen, but they are not so high above the level of the river as those of the northern valleys.

Drammen is a very long town, longer even than the "lang toun o'Kirkaldy." It has some fifteen thousand inhabitants; is four or five miles long and nothing broad, being simply a row of houses on each side of a wide river. There are many handsome villas in the neighbourhood belonging to the rich timber merchants; they are built of wood, brightly painted, and have handsome gardens around them. There is no national costume in Drammen: round hats and ample skirts prevail among the women, and black dress-coats and Panama hats are most common among the men. I heard many pianos and a good deal of singing in the houses, and passed some public rooms where there were many dancers. It was about sunset when I reached the commencement of Drammen, and quite dark by the time I had walked partly through it.

I was dismissed very cavalierly from the first hotel at which I applied. It was the chief hotel of the place, and possessed a waiter, who, with the natural instinct of his species, looked up and down me, estimated the value of my clothes, and then showed me the door. It is true that my boots were reduced to the last extremities of barely adhering to my feet; my trousers, which originally were of shepherd's plaid, had acquired a uniform tint, similar to that which distinguishes the garments of brick-makers and navvies; my coat of the same material, was in a similar condition, but not so decidedly bricky. Besides this, there were many mendings of my own, the stitches of which were large enough to be distinctly visible to the naked eye, and the colour of the thread was not exactly the same as the material it held together; my last clean collar was consumed, and my complexion was many shades darker and redder than that of a civilized Caucasian; still, I did not anticipate so unceremonious an expulsion, and might have been indignant had not my sense of the ludicrous prevailed.

Finding no other hotel or inn in the neighbour-hood, I made inquiry of a passer-by, who proved to be a shoemaker, and a very civil fellow. He took me to the nearest inn, where, in order to conciliate the authorities, I ordered a bottle of ale before commencing my chief negotiations; but it was of no avail, my boots and trousers, wild beard and complexion, were too much for them, and I was politely told that the house was full. The shoemaker then conducted me to another house of apparently still smaller pretensions, where another bottle of ale and another application led to a like result. We then crossed the bridge—which, according to the shoemaker's belief, is the longest and finest bridge in the world—and boldly entered the second grand hotel of Drammen. I called for a bottle of ale and asked for the master: the latter came bearing the former; he spoke English fluently, and said at once that he perceived that I was a tourist who had been roughing it up the country. I told him how I had been turned away from other hotels as a rogue and vagabond; he laughed, and assured me that he, who was a man of the world and accustomed to Englishmen, could distinguish an English gentleman at a glance, whatever might be the state of his clothes; whereupon I called for another bottle of ale, and we all three hobnobbed together, then had more ale and an hour's gossip. The shoemaker would not stop for supper, and was only prevented by physical force from paying for all the ale, though he had already paid for one of the previous bottles.

August 24th.—After much walking I finally emerged from the long street into the country, which is very fertile and well cultivated. At the Gulbeck station I hired a carriole and horse to the next station, a distance of 1⅜ Norsk miles, about 10 English statute miles; the charge for which was 2 marks 16 skillings, or about 2s. in English money. The principal difficulty I encountered was in the disposal of my legs, which have to be somehow arranged between the front of the vehicle and the tail of the horse, either dangling or resting on the shafts. The chief excitement of carriole travelling is the running down the hills, which Norwegian ponies perform in a manner peculiar to themselves: the steeper the hill, the greater the speed; the rougher the road and the larger the loose blocks of stones upon it, the greater is the sense of security enjoyed by the horse, and the more frolicsome are his movements. As there are no other springs than the elasticity of the shafts, the tourist mav or may not, according to taste, participate in the animal's enthusiasm.

The scenery is very beautiful all the way between Drammen and Christiania. It has a smiling, home-like English character. The wild mountains and the dreary fjelds, the snow-peaks and glaciers, bogs, boulders, torrents, and cascades, the vanishing foot-tracks, and barriers of gray precipice, all seemed now to belong to a distant land and a past age of dreamy remembrance; while this common highway passing between rich fields, skirting small lakes with water-lilies on their surface, and crossing tranquil rivers that have bending willows overhanging from their grassy banks, was like the way home from some friend's house in the country, and set me longing for my books, my easy chair, some music, a clean collar, and civilization. These feelings were heightened as I approached Christiania, and passed numerous villas of considerable beauty; at one of the finest of these was a garden party, with the customary display of gaily-dressed and, therefore, happy ladies, escorted by smiling martyrs of the other sex in tight, varnished boots and lavender trousers; these, all visible from the road, were promenading on a terrace that over-looked an Italian garden with flower vases, statues, and fountains, and all was enlivened by the music of an excellent band.

Christiania appeared extravagantly gay and Paris-like: there were pleasure-boats sailing on the fjord in the neighbourhood of Oscar's Hall, the king's summer palace on the waterside; the Klinkenberg

seemed filled with visitors; there was a grand
concert in another place, the "Lust-salle;" the
Walhalla theatre was open; there had been a performance there last night (Sunday); and everybody seemed to be brilliantly dressed and keeping
holiday. Whether this was attributable to the contrast with the Tellemark, or due to the fact that this
is the gay season at Christiania, and the festival of
Saint Monday, which is kept to some extent by the
artizans of Norway, I cannot positively say; perhaps
all combined to give the city the altered aspect it
presented to me.

I was greeted with a hearty welcome by mine
host of the Hôtel du Nord, who knew exactly where
I had been, how I had travelled, and almost everything concerning me. It appears that the station
keepers have to make some sort of periodical report,
of which the newspaper editors of Christiania avail
themselves to chronicle the movements of the more
illustrious tourists, and my want of rank was fully
compensated by the eccentricity of my mode of
travelling.

On the next morning I left Christiania, and, sailing
down the fjord by a steampacket that called at
many stations on the way, arrived at the open sea,
and bade farewell to Norway. Then passing through
the Kattegat and Great Belt by the flat sandy shores
of Denmark, I landed at Kiel, where I was surprised
at finding that everybody spoke German, and that
the Danish tongue was almost unknown. I felt
positively annoyed with this, in spite of a great
respect for Germany and its people, for my short

stay of a little over two months had created a sort
of Scandinavian enthusiasm, an earnest wish to
witness the consummation of a great Scandinavian
confederation, of Norway, Denmark, and Sweden,
and the formation thereby of a powerful barrier
against Russian encroachment on the one hand,
and Austrian Court influences on the other. Such a
confederation, united by a strong sense of common
nationality and common language, if in firm
alliance with Britain, would have great influence on
Europe; and an influence exercised by a people of
so solid, calm, and pacific a character would greatly
aid the spread of sound constitutional liberty and
the general progress of mankind.

I feel strongly tempted to dwell upon this and
kindred subjects in order to show how Englishmen
are bound by a sort of national filial tie to Norway
and Denmark, for undoubtedly the best blood of
Britain has been derived from the shores of Scandinavia. No observant tourist can visit Norway (and
the same applies to Denmark) without having continually forced upon his attention the moral and
physical family likeness between these northern
people and ourselves; for all our special English
characteristics are even more visible in Norway than
in England: all those peculiarities of physiognomy,
of manner and character, by which an Englishman
is distinguished from a Frenchman, and even from a
German, are seen to be purely Scandinavian peculiarities. I often thought, when in the most wild
and primitive parts of Norway, that they now represent, in everything but costume and the presence

of guns and a few other modern inventions, very
nearly the state of Old England in the days of
Alfred; and that a practical knowledge of the
physical and social condition of Norway at the
present time must be of great value to the student
of English history and the progress of English
civilization. But another volume would be needed
if I were to attempt a dissertation on this interesting
subject.

Note, 1876.—(When writing the above more than
eighteen years ago, I was strongly tempted to
express my firm opinion on the desirability of an
union between the royal families of Great Britain
and Scandinavia, but abstained from such expression,
feeling that it would be a personal impertinence on
the part of a private subject like myself to make
such a suggestion. With such decided feelings on
this subject, I need scarcely tell my readers how
heartily I participated in the national rejoicings
that hailed the marriage of our genial and hearty
British Prince with the elegant and accomplished
daughter of Denmark; and although it is not the
fashion now-a-days to suppose that royal alliances
have much political effect, I do hope and believe
that this will have considerable influence in the
direction above indicated.)

Having left Norway far behind; its mountains,
fjelds, and valleys, lakes and fjords, its glaciers and
waterfalls, its kind honest people and their fladbröd
having all sunk far below the northern horizon—I

must now bid the reader farewell; leaving him to picture for himself the rest of the journey from Kiel, by the railway that passes through the cornfields and butter-yielding flats of Holstein to busy Hamburg, and then by sea to the giddying roar and whirl and rattle of still busier London.

APPENDIX.

EXPENSES of travelling, board, lodging, &c., from the time of leaving Hull to the return to London—two months and eleven days.

	£	s.	d.
Passage money (second class) from Hull to Christiania	3	10	0
Food and steward	0	10	0
Breakfast at Christiansand	0	2	0
	£4	2	0

	D.	M.	S.*
Admission to Klinkenberg	0	0	6
Seat in theatre at ditto	0	1	0
Orange at ditto	0	0	12
Map and vocabulary	0	5	0
Bill at Hôtel du Nord	0	16	0
Rail to Eidsvold (third class)	0	2	18
Supper, bed, and breakfast at Eidsvold	0	2	2
Fare by steamer on the Miosen Lake	0	3	0
Dinner on ditto 18 sk.; ale, 10 sk.	0	1	4
Supper, bed, and breakfast at Hammer's Hotel, Lillehammer	0	2	12
Dinner at Mosshuus			
Supper, bed, and breakfast at Holmen			
Steamer to Elfstadt			
Dinner at Hundorp			
Supper, bed, and breakfast at Vik			
Ditto at Laurgaard			
Ditto at Dombaas			
Dinner, bed, and breakfast at Jerkin			
Dinner at Drivstuen			
Supper, bed, and breakfast at Rise			
Dinner at Stuen			
Supper, bed, and breakfast at Bjerkager ..			
Dinner at Hov			
Bed and breakfast at Soknaes			

* Specie-dollars, marks, and skillings. A specie-dollar is equal to about 4s. 6d. English, a mark to about 10¾d., and a skilling rather less than one halfpenny. 24 skillings make 1 mark; 5 marks, 1 specie-dollar.

	D.	M.	S.
Dinner at Leer	0	0	12
Supper, bed, and breakfast at Oust	0	1	12
Belle Vue Hotel, Trondhjem :—			
Dinner and coffee	0	2	12
One bottle of ale	0	0	10
Supper	0	1	
Half-bottle Sauterne	0	1	
Servants	0	0	
Passage from Trondhjem to Hammerfest	15	1	
Provisions on board	7	2	2
Landing and embarking	0	0	1
Breakfast at Hammerfest	0	1	
Dinner and wine at ditto	0	3	
Landing and embarking at Tromsó	0	0	1
Ale and breakfast at baker's shop at ditto	0	0	1
Passage from Hammerfest to Trondhjem	15	1	
Provisions on board	5	1	
Landing	0	0	
Bill at Belle Vue, Trondhjem	1	3	
Ferry, 2 sk. ; dinner, 8 sk.	0	0	1
Supper, bed, and breakfast at Bye	0	1	
Two bowls milk at Fandrem	0	0	
Supper and bed at Langsaet	0	1	12
Breakfast at Garberg	0	0	7
Supper, bed, and breakfast at Quam	0	0	5
Dinner at Honstad	0	0	12
Boat and men	0	3	8
Tilsegelse	0	0	4
Supper, bed, and breakfast at Baekkan	0	2	0
Boat and tilsegelse	0	1	4
Milk	0	0	2
Supper, bed, and breakfast at Lonsaet	0	1	12
Boat and tilsegelse	0	0	6
Boat, man, and boy	0	0	0
Dinner, 8 sk.; milk, 2 sk.	0	0	0
Boat and men	0	1	4
Boat to Veblungsnaes	0	2	0
Dinner at ditto	0	0	8
Supper, bed, and breakfast at Oimein	0	1	0
Ditto ditto at Molmen	0	1	12
Ditto ditto at Hoset	0	1	0
Bed and breakfast at Skeaker	0	2	0
Supper, bed, and breakfast at Mork	0	1	12
Ditto ditto at Mork Saeter	0	1	0
Ditto ditto at Mjelvior	0	1	0
Bill at Ronnei (two days)	2	0	0
Dinner at Sogndalsfjoeren	0	1	2
Boatmen and tilsegelse	0	2	10
Supper, bed, and breakfast at Lunden	0	0	16
Men and boat to Gudvangen	1	2	3
Dinner at Gudvangen	0	1	0

	D.	M.	S.
Bill at Vossevangen	1	1	20
Boat	0		2
Boat to Vik	0		0
Boat across lake to Saebo and back	0		8
Guide to Vöring Foss	0		6
Milk	0		6
Bill at Vik	0		0
Boat to Utne	0		0
Dinner at ditto	0		0
Supper, bed, and breakfast at Lofthuus	0		12
Boat to Odde	0		0
Supper, bed, and breakfast at ditto ..	0		0
Dinner at ditto	0		0
Mending boots ..	0		16
Supper, bed, and breakfast at Hildal	0		0
Man with wooden shoes ..	0		6
Supper, bed, breakfast, and ham and fladbrod, for journey, at Roldal	0	1	12
Milk at saeters			
Supper, bed, and breakfast at Nordgaard ..			1
Milk			
Supper, bed, and breakfast at Gaardsfjord			
Milk			
Supper, bed, and breakfast at Bospen			2
Milk, 4 sk.; * ferry, 4 sk.			
Guide to the Marie Stige			
Ditto across ditto			
Supper, bed, and breakfast at Dale			
Boat to Hildal			12
Ditto to Graver			0
Supper, bed, and breakfast at Lier			1
Dinner at Bolkesjo			
Supper, bed, and breakfast at Moen			
Dinner and ale at Hougsund			
Ale			1
Supper, bed, and breakfast at Drammen			
Carriole			
Hôtel du Nord, Christiania		4	
Steam to Kiel		0	
Provisions on board		3	
	86	1	11

The frequent repetition of milk hereabouts is explained by the fact that, milk being the most nutritious food obtainable, I dined on bowls of milk whenever I could get them. Fresh milk is abundant enough on the fjelds during the summer, as the cows are all at the saeters, but none is to be obtained at the farms below. In the above account each 2 skillings represent one bowl of milk, containing nearly a quart.

	£	s.	d.
86 specie-dollars, 1 mark, 11 skillings, equal to	19	7	4
Add expenses from Hull to Christiania	4	2	0
Ditto fiom Kiel to London	2	0	0
Total expenses ..	£25	9	4

By examination of the above account, it will be seen that the whole expenses for board and lodging for the ten weeks amounted to rather less than 9*l*.

Note, 1876.—As may be expected, the development of tourist traffic in Norway has been accompanied by some increase in the general expenses of travelling, but I think I may venture to say that, on the whole, this is not greater than the improvement in the accommodation that is now afforded to the tourist.

Some of the heaviest items of the foregoing are considerably reduced since 1856. This is the case with the first, viz., the second-class fare from Hull to Christiania, which is now 2*l*. 13*s*. 4*d*., instead of 3*l*. 10*s*.; the first-class fare is now reduced to 4*l*. From London direct to Christiania the fares are, first class, 4*l*. 4*s*.; second, 2*l*. 13*s*. 4*d*. Return tickets from Hull, first class, 6*l*.; second class, 4*l*. From London, 6*l*. 6*s*. and 4*l*. Provisions from Hull, first class, 1*l*.; second class, 12*s*. 6*d*. From London, first class, 1*l*. 5*s*. The vessels, the table, and the general accommodation are now incomparably superior to those of 1856. The items for boating on the fjords, which amount to a considerable proportion of the 19*l*. 7*s*. 4*d*., are nearly all reducible now that steampackets are so abundant. The fares vary from 1*d*. to 1½*d*. per English mile for first class, and from rather less than three-farthings to not quite one penny for second class, the difference depending on the distance, the rate per mile diminishing as the distance increases.

This is about one-third of the cost of boating, and the

saving of time, of course, diminishes the other expenses of getting over a given distance.

The fares by coasting steamers remain the same for single journeys, viz. :—12 *skillings* per Norsk mile for first class, 8 *skillings* for second, 4 *skillings* for 3rd : a Norsk mile being rather more than 7 English miles.

A considerable reduction is now made on return tickets. I suspect that it was the same in 1856, and that the steward of the *Constitutione* took advantage of my ignorance, and made me pay full fare both ways. During my last visit no such extortion was attempted. On the contrary, I was scrupulously informed of the advantage obtainable by taking return tickets in all those journeys where a return was probable.

Married people are counted as one and a half on the coasting packets, and considerable reductions are made on *bonâ fide* family tickets, i. e. for father, mother, sons, and daughters, but not for parties of friends.

As regards hotel expenses, those in the large towns where there are hotels, properly speaking, remain about the same as in 1856, while the accommodation has improved.

The increase of expense is at the country stations. Supper, bed, and breakfast for $2\frac{1}{4}d.$ is an experience not likely to be repeated. Pedestrians must now expect to pay at least double as much as I did, on all the posting roads, and those who travel by carriole may multiply my station expenses by three or four. My total expenses for ten weeks, board and lodging, amounted to less than 9*l.*; or deducting the town hotel bills, and the cost of provisions on board the packets, which remain unaltered, my country station expenses averaged scarcely more than 10*s.* per week. If this be doubled, or even quadrupled, the amount is by no means serious.

Thus, in spite of the fact that Norway has become almost "fashionable," a reasonable Englishman is, even now, more likely to be oppressed by a sense of obligation to his simple-minded entertainers at the country stations, who give him so much for so little, than to complain of any approximation to overcharge. This is especially the case in reference to the charges for posting, which are unreasonably low and demand revision, seeing that the price of horses, of fodder, and of labour, have risen so much since the legal tariff was originally framed. I shall have more to say on this subject, when describing the smoother or more luxurious aspect of Norwegian travel in 'Through Norway with Ladies.' In the meantime I cannot refrain from expressing my extreme gratification in finding that English tourists have not yet succeeded in corrupting the primitive honesty and simplicity of the Norwegian bonder, and an earnest hope that they never will. The refreshing sense of moral security, the ever-present consciousness of being surrounded by men and women whom one can firmly trust and sincerely respect, however unpolished they may be, is the primary and inestimable charm of Norwegian travel.

APPENDIX II.

FOR the benefit of tourists visiting Norway this season, I append the following information respecting the Norwegian steampackets for the summer of 1876, as officially announced in the 'Norges Kommunikationer,' of 24th May, 1876

1st. Between London and Christiania, *via* Christiansand, the *Albion*, every alternate Thursday evening.

2nd. Between Hull and Christiania, *viâ* Christiansand, the *Angelo* and *Hero*, every Friday evening. (The *Angelo* is the best boat on the service.)

3rd. Between Hull and Bergen, the *Argo* (stopping at Stavanger), every alternate Thursday.

4th. Between Hull and Trondhjem, the *Tasso* every alternate Thursday. All of these are "Wilson liners," and full particulars concerning them may be obtained by application to Messrs. Wilson & Co., shippers, Hull.

5th. Occasional steamers run between Leith and Christiania, between Newcastle-on-Tyne and Christiania and Bergen, &c., and there are regular packets between London and Gottenburg, and between Hull and Gottenburg, from whence Christiania may easily be reached by rail or steampacket. As the particulars concerning these are given in Bradshaw, I will not occupy more space with them, but proceed to the purely Norwegian traffic.

The vessels steaming round the Norwegian coast are the following :

1st. The Bergen and Nordenfjelde Steampacket Company's packets, making the long route from Hamburg round the North Cape to Vadsö. These run weekly from 8th April to the end of August, starting every Saturday from Hamburg, reaching Christiansand on Monday, then proceeding westwards (not to Christiania), stopping at many intermediate stations, and reaching Stavanger on Tuesday;

then to intermediate stations and Bergen, from which, after a day's halt, they start again on Friday, and by Aalesund, &c., reach Molde on Saturday; then by Christiansand, &c., to Trondhjem, where a long halt is made, and the journey resumed on Wednesday; then, after calling at twenty-five minor stations, a halt is made at Bodó. Start from Bodó on Friday, and call at fourteen stations before reaching Tromsö on Saturday night. Halt again and start on Sunday night, calling at six intermediate stations, and reach Hammerfest in time to halt there for some hours, and go on again on Monday. Then round the North Cape to Vardó and Vadsö, which with twenty intermediate stations, occupies two days more. A halt of one day is made at Vadso, and then the packet returns on Thursday; leaves Hammerfest on Sunday, Tromsö on Monday (midday), Bodó on Wednesday, Trondhjem on Saturday, Aalesund on Sunday, Bergen on Wednesday, Christiansand on Friday, and reaches Hamburg on Saturday—about five weeks altogether.

These vessels do not cross to the Lofodens, but communicate with the service of inter-Lofoden packets (see pp. 101–2), which they meet at Bodó on Fridays. These small packets, after completing their round of the Lofoden stations, return to Bodö on the following Thursday; but tourists who wish to go on farther northwards may generally meet one of the northward packets before returning to Bodo.

2nd. Another line of packets belonging to the same Company, run from Christiania round the coast to Tromso and then return, calling at twenty-nine intermediate stations. These leave Christiania every Thursday *at midday*; Christiansand on Friday, Stavanger on Saturday, Bergen on Sunday, 11 P.M.; Christiansand, Thursday; Trondhjem on Friday, Brono on Saturday, Bodó on Sunday; reaching Tromso on Monday night or Tuesday morning, and returning on Wednesday. These cross to the Lofodens and call at a few stations there.

In addition to these there are two newly added packets on this route, the *John Schoning* and the *Jonas Lie*, which go from Christiania to Vardo. They also cross to the Lofodens, and call at a larger number of Lofoden stations. Their route is similar (though not exactly the same) to that of the old *Constitutione*, and I recommend tourists who can catch them to select these if not hurried, and wish to see the Lofodens on their way to the North Cape. They are not so regular as the others. They start from Christiania on the 7th and 16th June, 2nd, 14th, and 28th July; Bergen, 11th and 21st June, 6th and 19th July, and 2nd August; Trondhjem, 13th and 24th June, 9th and 22nd July, and 5th August. I have no later information.

These do not appear to belong to the Bergen and Nordenfjelde Company, and I am not aware whether the return tickets of that Company are available by them. Return tickets issued by either of this Company's boats are available on all others on the same route.

Generally speaking, when not otherwise stated, the starting time is midnight, but the meaning of this requires explanation. What we call the midnight of Wednesday, the Norwegians call morning of Thursday. Therefore, when a boat is to start on Thursday, read 12 midnight on Wednesday, and same for other days. Inattention to this may cause serious disappointment.

Besides these, the *Michael Krohn* and *President Christie* sail at intervals between Bergen and Vadso, by nearly the same course, and call at nearly the same stations as the long route steamers between Hamburg and Vadsö. Only the May sailings are at present announced, but further information is obtainable from G. A. Gundersen, Krohnexpeditören, Bergen.

Between Christiania and Trondhjem there is another weekly service by the three packets, *Bravo*, *Bjorgvin*, and *Fiskeren*. One or the other of these leaves Christiania every Saturday at noon, Christiansand at 2 A.M. on

Mondays, Stavanger at 6 A.M. on Tuesdays, Bergen at 1 A.M. on Thursdays, Molde at 6 A.M. on Fridays, Christiansand at 3 P.M. on Fridays, and arriving at Trondhjem at about midnight on Fridays. They start from Trondhjem to return on Tuesdays, 6 P.M.; Christiansand, 8 A.M.; Bergen, 5 P.M. on Fridays; Christiansand, 1 P.M. on Sundays, and reach Christiania about 10 A.M. on Mondays.

The above information, coupled with the programme on page 118, will doubtless be very valuable to English tourists, who wish to catch the midnight sun, and cannot leave England early in the season. They must allow three clear days between Hull and Christiania, or two days between Hull and Christiansand; about four days for land journey from Christiania to Trondhjem. Two and a half days Hull to Stavanger, or three days Hull to Bergen. The *Tasso*, direct from Hull to Trondhjem, starts on Thursdays, 8th and 22nd June; 6th and 20th July; 3rd, 17th, and 31st August. About four days should be allowed for this trip.

Besides these the *Motala* and *Nyland* sail alternately between Christiania and Bergen, one or other leaving Christiania every Friday at 10.30 P.M., Christiansand every Sunday at 5 A.M., reaching Bergen on the day following, and returning from Bergen every Thursday at 11 A.M., from Christiansand on Saturday at 3 A.M., reaching Christiania on Saturday evening.

English passengers travelling by the Hull and Christiania packets may meet these at Christiansand, and proceed by them to Bergen.

There is another service between Christiania and Bergen, the *Kong Sverre* and *Stavanger*, which leave Christiania every Monday at 10.30 P.M., Christiansand every Wednesday at 5 A.M., and reach Bergen at about midday on Thursday. They return from Bergen on Mondays at 11 A.M., Christiansand at 3 A.M. on Wednesday, and reach Christiania at about midnight on Wednesday.

Both of these services include about twenty intermediate stations.

Between Hamburg and Christiania the *Sauct Olav* and *Gauger Rolf* run weekly, from Hamburg every Saturday, and from Christiania every Saturday at 3 P.M., arriving at their respective destinations on Tuesday night or Wednesday morning.

This is a fortnightly packet between Christiania and Havre, 2nd and 16th June; from Havre, 27th May, and 10th June from Christiania, and onward from these dates during the season.

All these coasting packets are usually punctual in *starting* from the principal stations where they make a halt, but not so to their time of arrival.

The packets in the Christiania Fjord are too numerous to specify in detail. They run daily to the various stations between Christiania and Frederiksvaern, some of them going round to Christiansand, others proceeding on to Gothenburg and Copenhagen, &c.

These, and the multitude of small packets now running on the Hardanger Fjord, the Sogne Fjord, Nord Fjord, and all the other important fjords and lakes of Norway, will chiefly concern the tourist *after he has reached Norway;* where he will best obtain on the spot the information he requires. Or he may study these details on his way across in the 'Norges Kommunikationer,' a copy of which he will usually find on board of Messrs. Wilson's packets, or which he may obtain from Messrs. Wilson at Hull, or from Mr. Bennett of Christiania. This is a Norwegian paper, but nevertheless he will be able to read it, provided he follows the rules I have given page 143, and diligently uses a Danish dictionary, or better still by using Mr. Bennett's special vocabulary, which he issues as a key to this 'Kommunikationer,' which contains the time tables of all the Norwegian railways, as well as those of the steam-packets.

CPSIA information can be obtained at www.ICGtesting.com
Printed in the USA
BVOW05s1734271115

428474BV00052B/513/P